Praise for *Enemies of the People*

"Marton's story is one of bravery, suffering, survival and vindication. She tells it in straightforward, lucid prose . . . and with her emotions well under control. This is not a woe-is-me memoir of the sort so much in fashion these days, but a carefully reported, almost clinical account of what it is like to live in a totalitarian state and how hard it is to escape from it. . . . It's a terrific story, and Marton tells it very well."
—Jonathan Yardley, *The Washington Post*

"Suspenseful. . . . Marton's family portrait reconstructs the absurdism of a world where 'everybody in your circle, whether your parents trusted or did not trust them, was informing on them.'"
—*The New Yorker*

"A must-read for anyone born after the Berlin Wall fell and maybe for a lot who weren't paying attention before that. . . . An Orwellian primer of totalitarian barbarity; don't miss it."
—John J. Monaghan, Jr., *Providence Journal-Bulletin*

"Not to be missed."
—*Good Housekeeping*

"A poignant and beautifully written biography of her parents that doubles as a memoir."
—Betty Gordon, *The Atlanta Journal-Constitution*

"Kati Marton's gripping account of personal triumph over daunting odds is a compelling reminder of the evil and destructive force of totalitarianism."
—James Hoge, *Foreign Affairs*

"A remarkable tale of human courage and a love letter to her father, a man she came to know in large measure through the historical record of a terrible time."

—Frank T. Csongos, *The Washington Times*

"Reading this book makes one deeply appreciate the lifelong benefits of growing up in a democracy."

—Bill Marimow, *The Philadelphia Inquirer*

"Marton . . . turns her investigative skills to her own family history. The result is a real-life thriller . . ."

—Billy Heller, *New York Post*

"Kati Marton's *Enemies of the People* is a revelation. It is a tender yet unsparing portrait of her glamorous and complicated parents locked in the hell of a totalitarian state, and their escape from Hungary to America. . . . Marton masterfully details the betrayals of those closest to her family and the uncommon courage it took her parents to survive."

—Marie Brenner, *The Daily Beast*

"Effectively renders an enormously unsettled, painful time of shifting allegiances and political treachery. . . . A dark, compelling narrative of secrecy and betrayal."

—*Kirkus Reviews*

"Kati Marton has written a candid and courageous book about a chapter in her parents' lives that most daughters would have preferred to leave unexamined."

—Louis Begley

ENEMIES OF

(NY-July 26)ARRESTED IN HUNGARY--Hungarian Interior Ministry announced
today over Budapest radio the arrest of Endre Marton, left, and his
wife, right, on charges of espionage for U.S. intelligence and been
today over Budapest radio the arrest of Endre Marton, left, and his
wife, right, on charges of espionage for U.S. intelligence and been
the right, on charges of espionage for U.S. intelligence and been
wife, right, on charges of espionage for U.S. intelligence and been
corresponded for U.S. press from 1947 until his Feb.
Both are correspondents for U.S. press from 1947 until
correspondents from his cases abruptly. Both he and his wife,
correspondence from his cases are Hungarian nationals.(AP
when command for the United press, are Hungarian nationals.(AP
Wirephoto)SEE WIRE STORY)(sll)71442fa1a) 1955

THE PEOPLE

My Family's Journey to America

KATI MARTON

SIMON & SCHUSTER PAPERBACKS
New York • London • Toronto • Sydney

SIMON & SCHUSTER PAPERBACKS
1230 Avenue of the Americas
New York, NY 10020

First Simon & Schuster trade paperback edition October 2010

SIMON & SCHUSTER PAPERBACKS and colophon are
registered trademarks of Simon & Schuster, Inc.

For information about special discounts for bulk purchases,
please contact Simon & Schuster Special Sales at
1-866-506-1949 or business@simonandschuster.com.

The Simon & Schuster Speakers Bureau can bring authors
to your live event. For more information or to book an event,
contact the Simon & Schuster Speakers Bureau at
1-866-248-3049 or visit our website at www.simonspeakers.com.

Designed by Dana Sloan

Manufactured in the United States of America

10 9 8 7 6 5 4 3 2 1

The Library of Congress has cataloged the hardcover edition as follows:

Marton, Kati.
   Enemies of the people : my family's journey to America / Kati Marton.
—1st Simon & Schuster hardcover ed.
      p.   cm.
   Includes bibliographical references and index.
   1. Marton, Kati—Childhood and youth.   2. Marton, Endre, 1910–
2005.   3. Marton, Ilona, d. 2004.   4. Budapest (Hungary)—Biography.
5. Journalists—Hungary—Budapest—Biography.   6. Political prisoners—
Hungary—Biography.   7. Hungary. Allamvedelmi Hatosag.
8. Hungary—History—1945–1989.   9. World War, 1939–1945—Hungary—
Budapest.   10. Hungarian Americans—Biography.   I. Title.
DB992.M37 2009
   305.9'069140922439—dc22   2009014480
ISBN 978-1-4165-8612-8
ISBN 978-1-4165-8613-5 (pbk)
ISBN 978-1-4165-8619-7 (ebook)

For Mama and Papa—
who led us on our journey.
And for Richard.

CONTENTS

Introduction ∞ 1

CHAPTER 1   War to Cold War ∞ 7

CHAPTER 2   A Happy Childhood ∞ 31

CHAPTER 3   Mama and Papa ∞ 43

CHAPTER 4   The Americans ∞ 51

CHAPTER 5   Sin Upon Sin ∞ 61

CHAPTER 6   Reprieve ∞ 73

CHAPTER 7   The End of Childhood ∞ 85

CHAPTER 8   The Prisoner ∞ 89

CHAPTER 9   The Three of Us ∞ 103

CHAPTER 10   A Terrible Summer ∞ 117

CHAPTER 11   My Father Is Broken ∞ 133

CHAPTER 12   Our New Family ∞ 145

CHAPTER 13   My Parents' Trial ∞ 153

CHAPTER 14   From the Other Side of the World ∞ 165

CHAPTER 15   Reunited ∞ 173

CONTENTS

CHAPTER 16   Revolution ∽ 187

CHAPTER 17   America ∽ 209

CHAPTER 18   "Flower" ∽ 221

CHAPTER 19   To Budapest and Back ∽ 231

CHAPTER 20   Another Surprise ∽ 245

              Epilogue ∽ 251

              Acknowledgments ∽ 259

              Index ∽ 263

ENEMIES OF THE PEOPLE

INTRODUCTION

A photograph of me at age two or three,
which I found in the secret police files.

"I<small>T WOULD BE</small> better if you came alone this time," Dr. Katalin Kutrucz, the head of the Hungarian Secret Police Archives, suggested on the phone. The last time we met I had been accompanied by a friend, a lawyer who knew his way around the Archives. Then, Dr. Kutrucz had been all business: crisp, impersonal, bureaucratic. An old-style apparatchik, I had assumed, simply allowing me to see—as was my right under the laws of post-Communist Hungary—the secret police files on my parents. Now her voice sounded different—more human, more compassionate. Her new tone made me anxious.

1

Just a short while earlier, one of Hungary's most respected writers had been given his father's files—and discovered a history of breathtaking intrigue and betrayal even of his family. The foremost historian of the AVO, the Hungarian secret police, had warned me that I was "opening a Pandora's box," when I first applied for access to the files. But I wanted to know the truth about my parents, about what had really happened in Budapest, in those distant Cold War days, when my sister and I were children. My parents had glossed over large portions of our history—even though my father was a celebrated journalist of his era, who won awards and recognition for his coverage of the 1956 Hungarian Revolution. "You are an American," Papa would say, "you cannot ever understand what it was like under the Fascists and the Communists."

That night I slept fitfully. What did I fear most? I suppose evidence of some act of compromise or betrayal that would shatter forever my image of my parents. The risk was real. From Günter Grass to Milan Kundera, secret police files from the Gestapo to the KGB continue to disgorge the debris of half a century of such betrayals. I understand why so many people do not want to learn about the past; let sleeping dogs lie, they say to me. But I want the truth, even if it is painful.

Eyes burning from a sleepless night spent wondering about the archivist's changed tone, I climb the grand staircase of an Italian Renaissance palazzo, the birthplace, in 1946, of the AVO. The building had been the scene of some of the terror state's worst crimes. By 1950, the palazzo couldn't contain the work of thousands of uniformed and nonuniformed agents and their vast network of informers whose job it was to infiltrate every corner of their fellow citizens' lives. So the AVO requisitioned other choice bits of real estate on and around the elegant Andrassy Boulevard, which had been renamed Stalin Boulevard. Today, the building flies the European Union's blue and gold banner and shares the block with two health spas.

Dr. Katalin Kutrucz, a short, high-strung, bustling woman in a synthetic pants suit and wearing sort of open-toed Dr. Scholl's shoes with socks, ushers me into an oval-shaped room with high ceiling and intricate molding—a room that seems suitable for an intimate musical evening. She plunks down next to me at a faux wood table. Blinking fast, she says, "It turns out that yours is one of our bigger files." Should I feel proud? I am terrified and eager to plunge into a growing mountain of manila files that clerks in white coats are wheeling in on shopping carts and unloading. Dr. Kutrucz does not smile, but the fact that she calls me Katika, the Hungarian diminutive of my name, only increases my agitation.

All my life, my parents' defiance of the Communists, their stubborn courage as the last independent journalists behind the Iron Curtain until their arrest, trial, and conviction as CIA spies, has been at the core of our family identity. On February 25, 1955, at two in the morning, following a game of bridge at the home of the United States military attaché, my father was abducted by six agents of the secret police. His arrest was front-page news in *The New York Times.* Four months later, they came for my mother. The following January, almost a year later, *The New York Times,* in another front-page story, reported that "Endre Marton, a correspondent for the Associated Press in communist ruled Hungary, has been sentenced to six years in prison on a charge of espionage. His wife, Ilona, who worked for United Press was sentenced to three years . . . The Martons have two young daughters, Kati and Juli." Accompanying the article was a photograph of a handsome, elegant couple and their smiling little girls, a happy family, self-contained and seemingly indestructible, on our last Christmas together in Hungary, before everything changed. Thus did I make my debut in the press, although I did not see the story until decades later.

My parents were forward-looking people. They looked back only selectively. When, toward the end of his life, my father was given Hungary's highest civilian award from the foreign minister of a free and democratic Hungary, he did not come to New York to receive it in person, leaving it to me to accept for him. That evening, the foreign minister surprised me with a large manila envelope containing AVO

3

material on Papa. My father never opened that file; he was done with all that. To him, history—at least his history—was a burden. For me, it was the beginning of my search.

It has been said that childhood is a foreign land. This is especially so if the child is uprooted early from that small universe where all is familiar, and transplanted to a country where no one knows how to pronounce her name. After my parents both died—my mother in 2004 and my father the following year—I became obsessed with learning everything I could about what precisely had happened to them and to my sister and me in the land where everything began. No subsequent chapter in my life had matched those Budapest years for intensity and the power of family love. My parents and sister and I formed a tight unit partly because the world outside was hostile. Once safe in America, each of us would pursue our own lives, and our family ties inevitably loosened. We had successfully made the crossing. Strangely, I still longed for a time that had been dangerous and painful for all of us—yet had bound us together. I missed the closeness of our lives in Budapest.

A child growing up in a State built on terror learns early that she, and even her parents, is nothing compared to the power of that State. However accomplished or witty or glamorous the parents—and mine were all of those things—they were playthings in the hands of the State. In such a place a child has no rights, not even the right to her parents. So when they were taken from me—and this is how it seemed to a child, they were *taken from me*—a separation marked me, not just them, and forever. I wanted to open the files in order to put that trauma to rest.

There was something else that puzzled me as the files disgorged secrets. Why did my parents take such risks? During the Cold War, most Hungarians would cross a street rather than risk being seen greeting an American. But my parents' best friends were American diplomats and journalists. What every grown-up I knew whispered, my parents spoke out loud. At a time when there were roughly two thousand private cars in all of Hungary, our family drove a white Studebaker convertible! We might as well have ridden a rocket.

So, when some years later I, too, received the same award from the Hungarian government as my father, I returned to Budapest, to this stately house of horrors, and filled out all the requisite forms. For several months I waited in New York to be summoned by the head of these archives, Katalin Kutrucz.

PERIODICALLY MOISTENING her finger, Katalin, as I am now encouraged to call her, flips through the hundreds of pages of our family file. She is familiar with their contents. As the pages fly by, names from my childhood unspool. Even more names are inside quotation marks, code names for informers. Reading my thoughts, Katalin says, "Everybody in your circle, whether your parents trusted or did not trust them, was informing on them. That was just the way it was." She shrugs. Flipping through a series of reports under code name "Gaspar," I am struck by the frequency of my name and my sister, Julia's. I do not want to risk losing these pages amid the thousands, so I place a hand on hers. "Please." She pauses for a moment. "These are all yours. You can take them and do what you like with them." As if to say, "We are a different country now!" But I can't wait. Who is this energetic informer "Gaspar" and why her constant reference to two little girls? "Well," Katalin answers, pursing her lips, "I am not allowed to inform you of such things, the actual names of agents. But I will tell you this: the code usually has some connection to the real name." Gaspar. Of course. Gabrielle. Our French nanny! A zealous agent, to judge by her contribution to the file. Along with anger I feel some vindication. I never liked her, and it was mutual. I can still hear the clop, clop, of her high heels every morning as she reached for the venetian blinds directly over my head, raising them with maximum clatter, while calling out in her shrill high-pitched voice, *"Levez-vous, mes enfants!"* No wonder she was always in a hurry. She had more important business.

Out of another file falls artwork by my sister and me: a house with a smoking chimney, and birds the size of people strolling in the foreground, and another with a long row of snails climbing a hill, with the inscription, "Mamikanak," "To Mommy." Another stick figure drawing is inscribed with handwriting I recognize as my grandmother's. "Kati did this and she isn't even in school yet!" And, more chillingly, shots of my parents, clearly caught unawares on a street, by a telephoto lens. I am struck that, even though oblivious to the camera's intrusive eye, my father is ramrod straight, his face composed, his expression inscrutable. A man who, having barely survived the Nazis, was caught again on the losing side, wearing protective armor against the outside world. But no armor could protect him from a State that collected his children's artwork.

But now my guide is speeding forward. A new file with the letter "B" in bold on the cover. I know by now that "B" stands for *Beszervezes,* "agent recruitment" for the secret police. "Izorche" is the code name on this one. "That, I can tell you, was your father's code name." My mouth is too dry to speak. How dare she imply such a thing! So this was the reason for the compassion that was absent at our first meeting and her warning to come alone. The date on the last report in my father's recruitment file is 1967. This is impossible—by 1967 we were living in America. We were safe. Or so I have always assumed.

But I don't want to argue with her that this is ludicrous—two people who resisted the all-powerful AVO in its own territory? How could they imagine my parents would be *Beszervezes* material, once they were safely in the United States?

Closing the last file, she turns to me. "These are all yours," she says, with the practiced sympathy of a doctor breaking bad news. "But do not judge *them,*" she warns, "judge the system." She retrieves a photograph that dropped out of the files. A curly-haired child, three or four, wearing a bib with butterflies and cherries on it, and holding a spoon. A chubby, earnest, unsmiling child whom I recognize as my younger self. I recall the historian's warning, "You are opening a Pandora's box."

Chapter 1

WAR TO COLD WAR

My parents, Ilona and Endre Marton, at Versailles, on their
final trip abroad before the Communists stopped issuing
passports in 1948.

C HILDREN CANNOT FULLY know their parents. As the colossal
figures of our childhoods diminish into often irritating presences during our adolescence and early adulthood, our parents emerge eventually as mortals. But the AVO files changed that normal progression in
an unexpected way after my parents died. The thousands of pages of
my parents' surveillance, arrest, and interrogation, supplemented by

7

interviews with their surviving friends from that period, reveal my parents to have been more complicated than I realized.

How ironic: to owe to one of the most brutal twentieth-century institutions, the Hungarian secret police, a priceless window into my parents. I am not saying that I am grateful to the secret police for stripping my father to his emotional bone and revealing intimate secrets about my mother. But the files have preserved them in a vivid, living way that no memories, perhaps not even a diary, could have done.

I remember Papa as a debonair, pipe-smoking figure who seemed to glide above and between worlds with such ease. In fact, at times he was a desperate man. This seemingly detached figure was in reality nothing of the sort. ("Things just sort of happened to me: people, jobs, opportunities, all came to me. I never really had to struggle in life," he liked to say.) Feigned passivity was part of his psychic survival mechanism. Act as if you aren't desperate, and maybe you won't be.

My father was born in the waning days of the Austro-Hungarian Empire, when Franz Joseph, with his ruddy cheeks and enormous whiskers, was still the reassuring patriarch. My grandparents had prospered during Budapest's Golden Age, a brief time of liberal values and relative tolerance, during the last three decades of the nineteenth century, when Jews were given full rights—at least on paper. My grandparents did not hide their Jewish roots (though, like many, they Magyarized their Germanic-sounding name early in the twentieth century, feeling that Hungarians should have Hungarian-sounding names) but they were not deeply religious. At ease in European capitals, spas, and ski resorts, they loved best their city on the Danube. Wealth, status, and security had come to them with Budapest's own flowering. Their Budapest, the Austro-Hungarian Empire's second city after Vienna, had the air of Paris under the Second Empire—and shared its grandiose aspirations. For my parents and grandparents, Venice—and its grand hotels—was Western civilization's crowning glory. Austro-Hungarian troops had recently occupied an Ottoman province called Bosnia, without too much struggle. But a shot fired on a street of its capital, Sarajevo, was about to change the course of history, and my own family's saga.

Raised as a nineteenth-century man in the twentieth century, my father was a figure from Thomas Mann's *Buddenbrooks*. But World War I had already smashed that cozy world and its rituals. By the time my father reached adulthood, the strongman regime of Admiral Nicholas Horthy was shrinking opportunities for even the most assimilated Jews. Papa was unprepared for the Age of Fanatical Utopias.

"His appearance, manners, character as well as his far-flung interests," my father's old friend and fencing partner from those days, Ferenc Zold, recalled sixty years later, "earned him the respect of those he came in contact with. At the fencing club we called him 'My Lord,' because he was such a passionate Anglophile. But your father's Anglophilia was an idealized version of something that no longer existed. Everyone accepted this about him—and forgave him for it. In everything he pursued, his study of languages, his doctoral work, his fencing, he pushed himself to excel. He was liked because he was always ready to help. I remember, we would ask him to translate our love letters to girls we met on the European fencing circuit. He could do that in three languages. But your father was very discreet about his own love affairs."

I realize now how filled with contradictions he was. Proud to the point of arrogance. A devoted if undemonstrative husband and father. Scorned by elements in his own country as a result of his Jewish origins, but a fervent Hungarian patriot, Papa insisted that even Shakespeare was better in the Hungarian translation. Called up for military service at eighteen, this athletic young man, a prizewinning fencer, was found "unfit" because of his Jewish roots. My father had drive, discipline, intelligence, and good looks. Appearance was very important during a period when, if you looked a certain way, you might survive. Naturally gallant, he was determined to make a strong impression with his diligence and quick mind, in fencing competitions and at Alpine skiing events. For such a proud man to be shunned by his own society must have created a lot of suppressed rage. I have still not fully untangled my father's complicated feelings about the Jewish legacy that he reluctantly inherited. But even more, I wonder about Papa's occasional reckless bravado, which sometimes put his family in danger—as the AVO files show.

Fencing—an aristocratic sport, with its historic roots in dueling and gallantry—was one outlet for my father. When he won the Budapest high school fencing championship, his photograph was displayed in the lobby of his gymnasium. Later, in university, his swordsmanship had other uses. "Once a year," he told his children years later, "for a few days there were anti-Semitic demonstrations at the university. I would drag frightened Jewish girls and boys into my office [he was a Ph.D. candidate] when they were chased by the mob, and challenged the leader to a duel. Of course," he recalled with a smile, "I won."

That pride, his lifelong shield, prevented my father from admitting something that the AVO files make clear: anti-Semitism shaped Papa's life choices. Despite a stellar academic record, he was turned down for law school, as a result of Hungary's infamous *numerus clausus* quota on Jewish students. He married my mother, of Jewish background like himself, for love, certainly, but there had been others he could not marry. Late in life he finally explained to his children why he wore a signet ring bearing the family crest of an Austrian countess. "Because I had to swear to wear it when I finally persuaded her to go back to her native Vienna, as marriage was impossible. Hitler was already ruling Germany."

My parents survived the final year of World War II, with Adolf Eichmann racing to round up Hungarian Jews, because they were defiant and resourceful and lucky. Under the Hungarian Fascists, those qualities could make a difference. Oddly, whenever my father talked about those years, it was with a strange nostalgia for the era "before the catastrophe"—the catastrophe being the Communists, against whom personal initiative was useless.

It used to annoy my mother that he had so many fond memories of the 1930s, before she entered his life. It bothered me as well, once I began to study this period, the backdrop of my father's "golden" youth. Blinding himself to unpleasant truths was yet another one of Papa's survival mechanisms. He blinded himself to what was happening to Vienna, after Hitler's Anschluss in 1938. He managed to exorcise his memories of how his friends, cultured Viennese Jews, were hunted like animals and shop windows on Kärntnerstrasse were tarred with the words "Jewish shop." A few days after this, Hungary's own regent, Admiral Horthy, proclaimed to the world that his country had invented Fascism, having passed the first modern anti-Jewish law in 1920. "We must have humane, decent, anti-Jewish laws," the Horthyites argued, "then the Hitlerites won't bother us." In fact, each time a "decent" Jewish law was passed, Jewish students at my mother's and father's universities were beaten up. As Hungary was soon surrounded on three sides by Hitler's empire, the Age of Dueling was replaced by the Age of the Jackboot.

My father's literary heroes were Lancelot, Robin Hood, and the Scarlet Pimpernel. He adored Gary Cooper and emulated the fluid elegance of Fred Astaire. The man my father most revered was his geography professor, Count Pal Teleki, who became Horthy's prime minister in 1940. *Sub pondera crescit palma,* the palm grows under pressure, the first Latin phrase I learned from my father, recalled one of Teleki's admonishments to him. Teleki was another "decent" anti-Semite, who thought Hitler would leave Hungary alone if it dealt with its Jewish "problem" its own way. When Horthy gave Hitler permission to march through Hungary to attack Hungary's ally, Yugoslavia, in 1941, without consulting Teleki, the prime minister wrote his boss an eloquent letter of protest and shot himself—an honorable but useless gesture. Still, my father always spoke of Teleki with respect and even affection.

In the last months of the war, the local Hungarian version of the Nazis, the Arrow Cross, rounded up Jews and marched them to firing squads by the Danube, often working with Hitler's envoy in Budapest, Adolf Eichmann. My parents survived. The secret police files reveal that they did so by moving constantly among their Christian friends' homes and never wearing the yellow star (a crime punishable by death). They had fake IDs.

But my parents almost never discussed all that. Nor did they tell their children the truth about themselves—or Mama's own parents—my maternal grandparents. As we grew up safe in America, almost regular American teenagers in Bethesda, Maryland, my sister, my brother, and I were told that Mama's parents had died during the air attacks on Budapest, near the end of the war. To this day, I have never seen a photograph of them—a fact I find distressing. I am a careful keeper of family albums. At the slightest hint from a friend, I am always ready to produce an album and say, "Here, this is what my parents, my children, or my husband looked like at that time." This obsession runs in the family. When we finally left Hungary, we took little but our clothes and a "sentimental" suitcase of photo albums. Now I read in the files that among my father's fears when he was in prison was that, along with all our other possessions, the AVO had taken the irreplaceable photographs of my sister and me, which he had left on his desk. Yet there is an unfillable hole in our family albums—the missing grandparents.

In fact, the story my parents told us about Mama's parents was wholly fake, something I discovered years later, on my first trip back to Budapest since we had fled the Communists after the 1956 Revolution. In 1980, I was writing a biography of Raoul Wallenberg, the heroic Swede who had saved thousands of Hungarian Jews before disappearing into the Soviet Gulag. During the course of an interview in Budapest with a woman saved by Wallenberg, she said, quite casually, "Of course, Wallenberg arrived too late to save your grandparents from the gas chambers." That was not only the first time I heard what had actually happened to my maternal grandparents, Anna and Adolf Neumann, it was the first time I realized that we were of Jewish background. When I called Papa from Budapest with news of my "discovery," he was cold. His secret had been revealed to his daughter, and he had lost control of his own narrative for the first time. It put a strain on our relationship for the next twenty-five years.

For my mother, too, these topics were off limits. If I raised them, her eyes would fill with tears, which would silence me. Perhaps her own guilt at having survived, and for not being able to save her own parents, partly explains her lifelong dependence on sleeping pills. Did the absence of a death certificate or any record of her parents' actual murder in Auschwitz help her erase their memory? She never returned to Miskolc, her dingy, industrial birthplace in eastern Hungary, where my grandparents lived until they were sent to the death camp. I did make the trek to that unpleasant city in 2003, with my husband, and found a large synagogue, now in disrepair but intact, where my grandparents had worshipped—and from which they had begun their journey to Auschwitz. On a wall plaque, in the courtyard, among a list of Eichmann's victims, were inscribed their names, Neumann, Anna and Adolf.

My discovery of our Jewish roots when I was already thirty opened a sad rift between my parents and me. I pressed for details of our history, but they considered such exploration "an American luxury." "You will never understand what it was like for us," he repeated. "It is simply beyond your comprehension. We were not Jewish. We were Hungarian. Absolutely and totally assimilated." I refrained from saying the obvious: Hitler and his Hungarian allies did not share that feeling. But the topic was closed as far as my parents were concerned. My stubborn insistence on knowing more—even without their help—frayed our old trust. Only during his last year, when, after my mother's death, my father moved in with my husband and me and his memory was failing, did I feel that we closed the breach.

My own reaction to the discovery of our Jewish heritage was relief. A void was filled. I had sensed a missing piece: the absence of photographs or mementos from my mother's side of the family. Somehow, the discovery—even the tragedy of my grandparents' murder by the Nazis—made me feel more grounded in history, more substantial than the refugee whose history began upon arrival to the New World. Painful as it was, I was finally in possession of the truth. As to our Jewish heritage, I was fine with it, and even proud of it. It made sense that a middle-class family of Budapest professionals who placed a premium on education would be Jewish. But by then I was a fortunate child of the New World. My parents were bruised survivors of both the Holocaust and the Cold War.

Why didn't Papa tell us more about his remarkable courage in those dark days? The AVO files tell me that he not only evaded the Gestapo and the Arrow Cross, he played an active role in the small anti-Nazi resistance movement. He volunteered to escort French officers, secretly in Hungary, on a hazardous mission to Slovakia, to help organize an armed anti-Nazi uprising there. One day, according to the files, a well-known figure in the resistance was observed leaving my parents' hiding place in Buda, forcing my parents to flee, just one step ahead of the Gestapo. My father a war hero? I knew none of this from my parents. They never spoke of such things.

The file also lists the jobs my parents—two Ph.D.'s between them— were fired from as a result of their "bloodlines." More than five decades later, I still feel outrage at this quintessential twentieth-century moment. But it is not just a historical fact for me: these are my *parents*. My outrage is fresh as I read the AVO files, since my parents talked neither about their persecution nor their courage. It used to frustrate and annoy me that they kept us away from our own history. Now truth emerges in the bureaucratic prose of the Communist secret police who are compiling a family history for their own purpose, so different from mine. They are looking for exploitable weaknesses in my parents, I am looking for truth.

Theirs was a wartime romance. My parents met over a bridge game, under the rain of Allied bombs, at the home of my future godfather, Bela Hallosy. My flirtatious, reckless-in-love mother had met her match at bridge, and in life. My father, an economist, my mother, a historian, both unemployed as a result of the latest anti-Jewish law, were both reduced to giving English lessons to make ends meet. They were very different: she emotional and melodramatic, he tightly wound, disciplined, snobbish. They both loved books and ideas. But their stylistic differences were deep. What kept them together? I sometimes used to wonder. Now, thanks to the AVO, I better understand their bond; it was forged in their shared defiance of the Gestapo, the Arrow Cross, the Communists, and the AVO. I cannot imagine either of them surviving without the other.

They did not like to acknowledge suffering. Suffering entailed a loss of dignity. When I was pressing him for details of what it was like during the final, nightmarish year of the war, under the Arrow Cross, my father told me he once wrote a letter resigning from his anti-Semitic fencing club, a preemptive strike against expulsion. "My coach simply filed the letter away," my father told me, "and allowed me to fence until the final months of the war, when the Arrow Cross made it impossible." He made it sound like a triumph. Or the time he encountered a former fencing partner wearing an Arrow Cross uniform and, after locking eyes for a beat, continued without stopping. The time my father outmaneuvered a drunken Russian "liberator" who wanted my mother. These were among the few episodes they recounted to us. But they never spoke of the routine terror under which they lived.

This brings me to an essential mystery of my childhood: having barely survived the Nazis, my parents should have kept their heads down. Yet, when the Communists took over Hungary, my parents brazenly and openly aligned themselves with the new Enemy: the Americans. How could they have taken such risks? Having outwitted the Gestapo and the Arrow Cross, were they swollen with a sense of immortality? Or did they just want to enjoy life again? They were still in their thirties, full of unspent vitality, and suddenly sought after by American and British diplomats and journalists, who had come to witness the Sovietization of this unfortunate corner of Central

Europe. Their English was good and their manners and bridge game even better. Having such "powerful" friends may have given my parents a sense of invulnerability. After the stigma of being Jews in an anti-Semitic society, what a balm that must have been.

There is a look of sheer exhilaration, mixed with relief, on my parents' faces in the photographs just after the war. Budapest was joyful at having survived the brutal fifty-one-day siege that ended with the surrender of the Germans to the Russians. But the beautiful city was reduced to rubble-filled lots, my family's own house on the Hill of Roses occupied by Soviet officers. The skyline above the Danube was unrecognizable—Castle Hill, where the Germans made their last stand, was a lunar landscape. The once graceful bridges were collapsed in the river.

But beneath the smashed landscape, life surged. The wreckage left by Allied, Soviet, and German bombs was cleared much faster than anyone expected. Men in business suits and ladies in fur coats—including my parents—volunteered for clean-up duty, a few days a month, sweeping, laying brick into walls. Gundel's, the famed restaurant in the City Park (which the Wehrmacht had lately used as stables), was packed again with diners miraculously wearing copies of the latest European styles. At the Café New York, they hauled the red plush banquettes out of the cellar. On the same dance floor where my parents had courted while Adolf Eichmann, a few blocks away, finalized his plans, they danced once again to my mother's favorite Cole Porter tune, "Night and Day." They had faith in the future. In a supreme act of optimism, and almost unique among their friends, they planned to have children.

For a while after the war, they traveled again to the European capitals and summered in the surviving grand hotels on Hungary's Lake Balaton—before they were nationalized and transformed into "sanatoria" for the Communist Party elite. The first time the occupying Red Army took note of my father was in 1946, when Papa, working for a Hungarian newspaper, reported the ultimatum of General Vladimir Sviridov, the Soviet chair of the Allied Control Commission, the body that ruled Hungary in the war's immediate, chaotic aftermath. Sviridov ordered Hungarian authorities to dissolve youth organizations, including the Boy Scouts, and ban anti-Soviet politicians from public office. In his report, Papa pointed out that this was the first time a foreign power had overtly interfered in Hungarian affairs since the end of the German occupation. This report led the AVO to open my father's file. Two decades of near total surveillance of my parents followed.

Let me tell you about the AVO. I cannot recall a time in my life when those three letters—standing for State Security Agency—did not arouse a strong reaction in me. I never heard that acronym uttered in a neutral voice. My parents made the word sound like a blend of loathing, fear, and contempt, which hung in the air whenever the subject arose. Children like to think of their parents as powerful, able to protect them from any threat. When I heard the word "AVO," I knew it stood for a force beyond my parents' power. I was terrified.

Certain key dates, years, and names were as deeply engraved on my memory as the birthdays of family members. When did I learn that 1946 was a decisive year for the Soviets and their Hungarian allies? (Another word returns from the deepest recesses of childhood: "Moscovite," the word spoken by my parents with special contempt, in reference to those Hungarian Communists who returned to Budapest with the Red Army. The foremost and most loathed Moscovite was Matyas Rakosi, a future prime minister.)

Having failed to win the first postwar election, the Communists moved fast before another election would have put Hungary into the European family of democracies. The main instrument of Sovietization was the AVO, which reported directly to Stalin's secret services—the NKVD and the KGB. Set up in September 1946 (in the same elegant Renaissance palazzo where I would read my parents' files), it had seventeen divisions, each with a special function. Everybody knew that the Red Army stood squarely behind the AVO, which was in effect a Soviet party within the Hungarian Communist Party. Its chief characteristic, I would learn growing up, was a brutality against which ordinary political and diplomatic actions were useless. Division One was supposed to infiltrate and control Hungarian political life, through a vast network of informers, usually recruited through intimidation. Typically, targets would be snatched from their beds late at night, and released on condition that they would become informers. This included, as I now learn, most of my family's immediate circle. In the case of more dedicated agents such as our nanny, they were well paid for their work.

By 1946 my father was on the Soviet radar. Did my parents know this? To an astonishing degree, they defied the new order of the day. They dressed too well. Their friends were Westerners. Maybe a certain fatalism had crept into their lives: if you could survive Hitler and Eichmann, you could survive anything. In 1948, after a trip to London with the Hungarian fencing team, they paraded their love of all things British. (In the photographs they look like advertisements for Burberry's.) And my mother had been calling my father Andrew since their first meeting.

Upon arrival in Budapest, more and more British and American journalists made a point of checking in with the Martons. A young *Time* magazine reporter named Simon Bourgin, a lanky native of Ely, Arizona, arrived in Budapest on assignment after the war. My parents showed him around the city. "Budapest still had an aura," Bourgin remembered in 2008. "Before it was wiped out, it made the city the most exciting patch in Europe. It was a society frozen in the old ways. The beautiful women, the tailors who would whip up suits they had seen in the West, and have them ready in a day or so. It was like Hong Kong today, but with charm and wit. The Bristol had been bombed but was still there by the Danube. It was the journalists' headquarters, and had an eerie charm. The old furniture was still in the lobby, and the people at the desk had manners. Like the city, it kept its style for quite a while.

"Your mother and father were indispensable," Bourgin said. "They gave us leads that we didn't have. They were models of what journalists should be under difficult circumstances. They were bright, and had charm and such professional integrity. We had this intimate bond. We really cared about them. We knew they were on thin ice. But they just kept on reporting."

Another figure in my early childhood, who reappeared when we settled in Washington, was a somewhat mysterious figure—neither journalist nor quite a diplomat. This was James McCargar, a nattily dressed man, always in a tailored blue blazer, tall and impressive. To my child's eye, he was very *American*. McCargar did not have the casual airs of the reporters who streamed through our home. I know now that McCargar was a CIA officer under diplomatic cover, trying to recruit Hungarians for a highly clandestine operation called the Pond. By 1947, he had spirited seventy-five Hungarian anti-Communist politicians out of Hungary to the West. McCargar was the real deal: a dashing secret agent, a James Bond, whose relationship to my parents was not clear. (The CIA has refused to release information to me about my parents, McCargar, or anything else.)

Here is how McCargar recalled the city he first glimpsed in 1946. "The vitality of the Hungarians was nowhere more evident in the summer of 1946, when I arrived, than in the comparison between Vienna and Budapest. In Vienna, prostrate under four occupation armies, life just barely dragged along. . . . In Budapest, which had suffered a degree of destruction comparable only to the major German cities and which lay at the not so tender mercies of the Red Army, there was whipped cream for the numerous daily coffees—and milk for the babies, reconstruction went on energetically . . . the theater flourished wherever a stage could be found, and the nightclubs were legendary."*

According to the AVO, at a lunch McCargar hosted at his Buda-

---

* Christopher Felix, *A Short Course in the Secret War* (New York: Dutton, 1963), p. 163

pest residence in 1947, he and my father got into a heated argument. McCargar had offended my father by commenting on how easily Hungarians accommodated themselves to foreign occupations, German or Soviet. The American ended up apologizing to my father. Much later, McCargar, retired from the CIA and still a friend of my parents, was a helpful source for me in my research on intelligence matters. I was shocked when I called his old Washington number in the spring of 2008, and his French wife, Monique, answered. Her voice breaking, she told me Jim had died very recently. "He spoke of you near the end," she said, "with a very special affection." Another link gone.

BY 1949, Matyas Rakosi, having outmaneuvered the opposition parties with what he called "salami" tactics, had become Hungary's undisputed ruler. It was now literally a crime to publicly admire the West. Outspoken critics of the Communist Party were branded Fascists, and systematically disappeared, tortured, and sometimes killed. If my parents' Jewish roots had made them targets of the old order, it was their "bourgeois" background and their affection for all things Western that endangered them in the new. Every single AVO document relating to them begins with the words, "of high bourgeois background." My mother had a brief window between the Nazis and the Communists when she was employable, but by 1948, she had been dismissed from her job in the Ministry of Education, placed on the B list as "politically undesirable." A year later, the Communists closed the independent, politically moderate newspaper my father managed, *Kis Ujsag*. He, too, was out of work.

With ever fewer options, but with good English language skills (as well as fluent German and French), my father was hired as Budapest correspondent for the British *Daily Telegraph* newspaper. But in 1948, when he visited London during that fencing trip—their last abroad for a decade—he found that there were no "suitable" jobs in London for a Hungarian who did not relish driving a taxi.

The AVO files contain things that surprise me. At times there is a desperation that my parents always concealed from their children. To my astonishment, AVO records that in 1948, my parents applied for emigration to New Zealand. The image of my parents, *Mitteleuropean* to their fingertips, lovers of the café culture—that mix of irreverent humor and high-level gossip that was Budapest's oxygen, with their passion for bridge and the opera—contemplating a life in the placid setting of Wellington, New Zealand! This attempt to emigrate to New Zealand was yet another chapter edited out of the family saga, along with my maternal grandparents' deaths in Auschwitz, my father's role in the anti-Nazi resistance, and my parents' own Jewish roots.

As New Zealand evaporated as an option (as a result of the sudden departure from Budapest of the British consul, who had been supporting this plan), a Pulitzer Prize–winning reporter from Yuma, Arizona, arrived in Budapest. Daniel De Luce, the Associated Press's star European correspondent, proposed a dangerous solution to my parents. Stay here, he urged, where the news may be grim, but it is plentiful. The show trials, the closing of churches, the savage liquidation of all opposition parties, and the deportation to brutal internment camps of members of the old "bourgeoisie": a great story! The pay was commensurate with the hardship involved. So my father signed on as a stringer with the Associated Press, the world's leading press agency.

My father liked working side by side with the low-key American. He later said De Luce taught him to be an "American newspaperman" (that is always how he referred to himself, and with so much pride). I assume he felt that working for one of the world's most powerful news organizations might offer him some protection. After all, his other options were running out. And there was something else, a more human motive for signing up with "the Enemy" at a time when merely receiving letters from America could get you fired from your job. "What a glamorous life these men and women seemed to live, in comparison with our monotonous, gray existence," my mother observed in her unpublished memoir, which she wrote in the late 1950s and entrusted to me sometime in the 1970s. At that time, I'm ashamed to say, I wasn't much interested in our history. "What unheard-of luxuries, nylons, lipstick, foods available to Hungarians only on the black market, were their staples. And most of all, their lives were rich with books and newspapers and the exchange of free thoughts and ideas. Life in a Communist country is an intellectually empty life and we suffered the constant pangs of intellectual starvation."

In early 1948, De Luce's report on the brutal Sovietization of Hungary was front-page news around the world. In Hungary, it hit a nerve. The American reporter received a personal call from the man who made all Hungarians tremble: Rakosi. One more piece like that, the Communist Party chief warned De Luce, and you will be evicted from Hungary. De Luce replied that he could not work under such threats. He only knew one way of reporting. He wasn't going to wait to be booted out, he told my parents. He was leaving. At De Luce's recommendation, my father succeeded him—a huge, life-changing event for Papa.

Being a fully accredited, full-time AP correspondent had a nice sound. Soon, my father persuaded my mother to accept a similar post from the rival United Press, or UP (later UPI). "We had often lain awake at night worrying," my mother wrote, "what would become of our two little girls in the event we were imprisoned. Their welfare was still our first consideration. But it was clear to us that our precarious position would not be worsened by my following [my husband's] footsteps. All our experience had shown that when the Communists imprisoned a man for activities on behalf of a foreign service, the wife was also imprisoned, no matter how far removed she was from sharing or even understanding her husband's activities." So, she became my father's "rival" as United Press's Budapest correspondent. (In actual fact, though my mother was a sharp observer and a witty commentator on events, she was no writer. Unbeknownst to the wire services, my father was filing for both AP and UP.)

Side by side, my parents covered the gruesome show trials of 1949. These travesties of justice, which Arthur Koestler immortalized in

Darkness at Noon, featured a prominent public figure in the dock, tortured into pleading guilty to a long list of "crimes against the State and the People." My parents soon made names for themselves as the last permanently accredited independent press behind the Iron Curtain. "You were off to a flying start on the Rajk trial,"* came a telegram from his AP bosses on October 1, 1949. My father proudly wrote back, "It is hell to see that the competition each have two, Reuters even had three men in the court room and I am alone . . . but I saved us a lot of money, and was a few seconds ahead of the others with Rajk's death sentence."

More than speed, my father's reporting was informed by his own background, and a bred-in-the-bone sense of history missing among American journalists. He desperately wanted to rouse America to the fact that its wartime ally was as dangerous as the one the Soviets had helped to defeat. He thought he could do that by simply reporting the facts of daily life in Hungary.

Every one of the hundreds of stories my parents reported for the benefit of readers from New York to San Francisco was translated, examined, and kept in the growing AVO files. By 1950, the AVO already had 1,600 pages in the Marton file.

For a while, by keeping news of Hungary on America's front pages, my parents subverted the Soviets' attempt at flying under the West's radar. Their reports were straight and unembellished, but the accumulation of facts was damning. They were locals, they could not be expelled, and they seemed too high-profile to be easily "disappeared." So the AVO bided its time, cast an ever wider net of informants reporting on my parents' every movement, what they ordered at which

---

* The 1949 show trial of Foreign Minister Laszlo Rajk, accused of trumped-up charges of being an "agent" of Yugoslav premier Tito, with whom Soviet dictator Joseph Stalin had just fallen out. Rajk, under the most brutal treatment and with a promise of a safe haven for himself, his wife, and newborn son, "confessed" to treason. Instead of amnesty, Rajk was led straight to the gallows, his wife arrested, his son placed in an orphanage under an assumed name. That son, Laszlo Rajk, Jr., is today a distinguished Hungarian architect and a very close friend of mine.

restaurants (waiters formed an important part of the AVO's network) or purchased at our neighborhood grocery. Every envelope the mailman delivered to our home had been steamed open.

The AVO observed my parents' growing international reputation as fearless reporters. In their file, from an unspecified American newspaper dated February 10, 1949, is the following news clip: "Associated Press Gets Complete Coverage of [Jozsef Cardinal] Mindszenty Trial—In Face of Ban on Correspondents." "The Budapest regime is refusing to grant visas to AP correspondents based on the fact that AP already had a resident, Endre Marton. The Hungarians previously expelled an American stationed in Budapest by the AP [Daniel De Luce]. Marton is an experienced reporter and editor. Associated Press executives are confident that he presented a factual report of what went on in the courtroom. This confidence is based not only upon reliance on Marton but also upon comparison of his stories with those received from other western reporters. Correspondents in Hungary of whatever nationality are subject to action by the government if they offend the regime. Hungarian nationals face imprisonment. The usual action taken in the case of Americans who displease the authorities is to expel them."

My parents continued to brief "visiting firemen." Our apartment was the first stop for newly arrived Western correspondents. I remember my paternal grandmother bustling over elaborate dinners (my mother preferred chatting with her colleagues to cooking) for these extremely tall (so they seemed to my toddler self), very *relaxed* men in their loafers and rumpled clothes. In contrast to my father's formal comportment and speech, these men draped their arms over chairs, leaned way back, and slouched. Secure and at their ease, nobody was threatening them with anything worse than a career-boosting expulsion.

In September 1950, the AVO abducted my father's former secretary from her workplace and drove her to a "safe house." Years later, Melinda (Marika) Hallosy recalled the place as "rather homey," with lace doilies on end tables, bric-a-brac, and photographs of someone's family. But she can still summon the terror that shot through her as she was ordered to sit down in a cozy armchair, while the agent made coffee. Somewhat disabled from childhood polio (she walked with the help of a cane), Marika was more vulnerable than most. Her fiancé was Bela Hallosy, one of my father's oldest friends, a well-placed member of an old Hungarian family, who, as a non-Jew, had helped and sheltered my parents from the Nazis. Even though wheelchair-bound, Bela had been active in the anti-Nazi underground, and the postwar publisher of a moderate newspaper the Communists had just recently banned. He was also my godfather.

Now the agents threatened that if Marika didn't report everything discussed at their weekly bridge game with my parents, they would overcome their "scruples" and arrest Bela. Of course she was ordered to tell no one any of this. This vow she broke the minute she got home.

When my parents arrived for their weekly game of bridge at Bela's, he related to them Marika's situation. "Well," my father answered, "we'll make it easy on you. We will just stop coming." The AVO are not that stupid, Bela replied. They will know immediately that Marika tipped you off, which would be very dangerous for her. "All right, then," my father agreed. "We will keep coming and I will bring a report of our week's activities for Marika to submit." And so, each week, before they dealt the cards, my father presented his typed report on himself and my mother to Marika, who copied it in her hand, then burned the original. (I marvel at how busy my father must have been, keeping the AVO, AP, and UP all supplied with reports.) Marika also recalls that my gallant father reimbursed her for her weekly round-trip cab fare to her AVO "safe house." The AVO would only cover public transportation.

As they included us in so many other adult events, my parents sometimes took us children with them for their weekly bridge games. It wasn't only that they loved our company. It was also the fact that among their circle of friends, and even their siblings, they were unique in having children. It had taken a tremendous leap of faith to start a family in the ravaged, demoralized, largely destroyed city of Budapest. My godfather was an amateur photographer who, with no children of his own, loved taking our photographs.

From the AVO files tumbles one of Bela's shots. It is a serious little girl with her legs awkwardly crossed, standing in the doorway of his balcony on the Hill of Roses. The straw boater I am wearing was my first nonbabyish headgear, and I was very proud of it. Imagine the Hungarian secret police keeping such personal mementos, only to have them fall into my hands a half-century later.

My parents and godparents played this game with the AVO for two years. Shortly after they finally arrested my father, the AVO came for Marika. My father had boasted of his little joke to a cell mate, who immediately reported it. As punishment, they kept Marika locked up for 108 days. "But I owe my marriage to the AVO," she says now with a smile. "Bela thought they'd stop harassing me if he married me."

On September 18, 1950, the AVO formally decided that my parents were, in classic Communist jargon, "the sworn enemies of our People's Democracy and faithful adherents of the American way of life and, though they pursue their professional work openly, their reporting is mocking and hostile to our national interest." The internal memorandum—which, of course, was unknown to my parents, and which I discovered in 2008—then went on to an astonishing conclusion: "We are working on the Martons' recruitment, especially since they are in constant contact with the American embassy." Andras Budai, the AVO officer who filed this report, plaintively noted, "Until now, we haven't had luck recruiting their domestic employees, who, after a very brief time, are relieved of their jobs." Armed now with Marika Hallosy, who they thought was a high-quality informer, the AVO hoped to finally turn my parents into Communist agents—bizarre though this may seem.

The Cold War was getting colder. On July 3, 1951, the U.S. mission in Hungary was officially accused of "taking part . . . in a conspiracy to overthrow the Hungarian People's Republic . . . [and] establishing close ties with Arrow Cross and Horthyist elements hostile to the

People with the goal of organizing and encouraging them for espionage and aiming at the annihilation of land reform." The rant goes on in a vein that would be comical, if its intent had not been dead serious: "These Arrow Cross generals, bloodthirsty ghetto commanders, inhumane murderers . . . who seven years ago served the Hitler regime, are now appearing as the champions of democracy on the 'Voice of America,' howling and agitating in the name of liberty and progress against everything created by the liberated Hungarian People."

In a subsequent "diplomatic" note to the legation, dated July 31, 1951, the People's Republic "demands that the government of the United States close the library, and cease showing movies and playing [American] music by the United States Information Service which has proved to be a front for espionage and subversive activities."

When my father's AP colleague Richard O'Regan visited Budapest in 1953 to cover the World Peace Council, an international Communist propaganda effort, he filed a story that shattered America's final illusion about a system that had imprisoned its entire population. For my parents—desperate to get out—the story was personal. Under the headline "How Does the Iron Curtain Look? What Chance Has a Refugee to Escape?" O'Regan writes from Vienna:

Death waits today at almost every crack and chink in the long, desolate Iron Curtain through which thousands used to slip to freedom in the West. Barely a few dozen refugees a month now manage to squeeze through the ghost villages, the treacherous minefields and the barbed wire entanglements that stretch 2,500 miles from the Baltic to the Black Sea. Their escape requires great courage, careful planning and much luck. . . . You may run into trouble as soon as you leave your hometown. On country highways, security police and militia throw up constant roadblocks. You must have a permit, real or forged, to be traveling away from your job. If you get through the roadblocks and the nightly checks on hotels and inns you finally reach the "restricted zone." This is a desolate area of almost empty villages and towns, running the whole vast length of the Iron Curtain. . . . You cannot

enter without a special permit, a special identity card. . . . As you approach
the actual frontier, it becomes more dangerous. You're likely to step into a
minefield. Watchtowers begin to appear. Border guards are hidden in the
tops of trees. The nearer you get to the frontier, the closer the watchtowers.
Fierce dogs are likely to find you. If you try to run, border guards have
orders to shoot to kill.

Though my father did not write this piece, the AVO blamed him
for yet another "slander."

The government's frustration with my parents was growing. "It
is suspicious that every time an English or American correspondent
comes to Budapest," an undated Foreign Ministry memo reads,

the Martons know about it, though the Ministry does not inform them. Af-
ter the correspondents arrive [the Martons] handle them and go everywhere
with them in a way that sometimes the Ministry can't contact the foreigners
because they say that the Martons will do everything for them and organize
programs for them. We've seen cases where the Martons have purposely
tried to prevent the Ministry, though the Ministry's function is to deal with
foreign journalists. It is probable that they use these occasions to spread in-
formation harmful to the country. It is necessary to mention a particular case:
Edward Korry (United Press, Vienna) got a visa for the World Peace Coun-
cil. The Ministry prepared a separate program for the foreign correspondents,
Korry was taken care of by the Martons and did not wish to participate in
any official programs and did not even visit the World Council conference
and after three days he left the country. After returning to Vienna, he wrote
the most hostile, slanderous articles about the situation in Hungary: the
economic crisis, the misery of many classes, and the persecution of the Jews. It
is probable that Korry got the information for his articles from the Martons,
having been in contact with no one else during his trip to Hungary.

My father's coverage of Hungary, read as a whole, gives a reasonably wide-ranging picture of political suppression, often with a subtle

touch. From sports, to theater life, to the difficulty of booking a room at a hotel on Lake Balaton if you are not among the Party elite, he covered every detail of life in our forgotten corner of Europe from 1947 until 1955. Never inflammatory, he used irony and humor to convey the often absurd excesses of the People's Republic. Of the German-Hungarian Friendship Treaty, for example, he wrote: "A Hungarian Rip Van Winkle who fell asleep in 1945 and woke up around the last days of October 1952 had reason to rub his eyes. To see articles headlined 'Eternal Friendship Between the Hungarian and German Peoples' only seven years after World War II is really amazing."

Inside his reports lay a personal background few Americans possessed. He used it to illuminate the hypocrisy of the Communists. "It is hardly necessary to explain Rip Van Winkle's surprise. Hungary had been a satellite of the Hitler-Mussolini axis, was de facto occupied by German troops . . . and the end of World War II really meant liberation from the horrors of Nazi cruelty. . . . Differences between prewar and postwar Germany and between the western and eastern parts of Germany were duly explained to Hungarians by their newspapers during and after Mr. Rakosi's Berlin visit."

My father was relentless in exposing Rakosi's autocratic rule. On September 8, 1950, he reported the expulsion of more than eleven thousand priests and nuns from their thousand-year-old monasteries and cloisters. That same year he wrote with irony of Rakosi's latest edict, "The most exciting part of his speech was undeniably when [Rakosi] disclosed the 'conspiracy' of Social Democrats. It was a thrilling story indeed. . . . The fact that he did not mention anybody by name, makes no difference: there cannot be any doubt in this respect. On the other hand it seems safe to say that it means that these figures will not be tried in open court, consequently the people have to be content with what [Rakosi] finds appropriate to disclose.

"And so the curtain fell after the last act of a tragedy: a major political party, the only representative of industrial workers for decades disappeared in the trapdoor of Hungary's political stage."

On the extraordinary performance of the Hungarian team at the 1952 Helsinki Olympics my father wrote with undisguised derision, "All 16 Hungarian gold medal winners considered it their first duty to send a telegram to the Vice Premier and undisputed boss of this country . . . expressing their gratitude. 'Dear Comrade Rakosi! I report happily that I succeeded in winning the 16th gold medal for our country. My gratitude to the Hungarian workers, to the Party and to You, ardently beloved Comrade Rakosi.'"

In a September 2, 1953, article entitled "Obituary," my father summarized the end of the free press in Hungary. Did his American readers have any idea what risks their Budapest correspondent courted to bring them such news? Though he neither dramatized nor embellished their reports (irony was his chief weapon), the straight story was bad enough. And, increasingly, Endre and Ilona Marton were the only ones reporting it. In 1948, sixty-five foreign correspondents were accredited in Hungary. As a result of arrest, escape, and intimidation, three remained by 1953. Two of them were Endre and Ilona Marton—and the third was informing on them to the AVO.

Chapter 2

A HAPPY CHILDHOOD

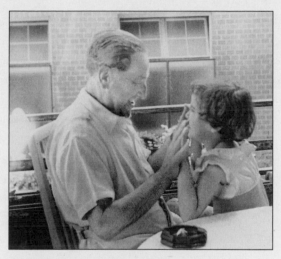

I loved my Nagypapa—my grandfather—with whom I
practiced my first English phrase, "Attycake, pattycake, baker's
man," on our Budapest balcony. (Behind us are the opaque
windows installed by U.S. diplomat Sidney Lafoon to block
communication between our two houses.)

MEMORY IS FAMOUSLY deceptive. Many of my early childhood
recollections probably come from my parents' recounting of them,
conflated with my own memories. But even with so many grim
events swirling around us, I recall my early childhood as happy. Inside
our apartment, my parents had created a separate Western universe.
The four of us formed a tight unit. The sense that the world outside our
apartment was not a friendly place strengthened our bond, as did the

fact that Mama and Papa worked from home, phoning in their stories to AP and UP news desks in Vienna, London, and, very occasionally, to that place whose name was imbued with magical properties, New York.

It was obvious even to a child that our family lived by different rules than everybody else. We acted as if having British and American journalists and diplomats visiting our home and inviting us to theirs, having a cook and a French nanny and going to Mass on Sundays, were not dangerous, provocative acts in the eyes of the all-seeing authorities of the People's Republic of Hungary. If my parents seemed so confident, surely we were safe.

My paternal grandparents' house on the Hill of Roses had been requisitioned by the Soviets after the war. Their younger son, my Uncle Feri, had already emigrated to Australia; my grandparents awaited permission to join him in Melbourne. While they waited, they moved in with us. I adored my grandfather, my "Nagypapa," with whom I remember playing endless games of "attycake, pattycake, baker's man" on our apartment's sunny balcony. Both of us were eager to pick up some English words (though I wonder now at the utility of that rhyme in the new life he was preparing for in Australia). The first English word my parents taught me (that is, I thought it was a single word) was "Holdon!" Anybody calling for my mother or father in a foreign language was told to "Holdon!" My grandfather sounded exactly like the elderly gentleman practicing "Vitch vatch," in *Casablanca*. I can still feel the scratchy gray fabric of Nagypapa's suit, and see his polka-dot bow tie, as I sit on his lap, wearing my bright yellow American sunsuit with white rickrack trim. With those four grown-ups, my parents and grandparents, and my sister, Juli, all sharing a small space, I felt safe.

Sometime during the summer of 1954, our grandparents' emigration permits miraculously materialized. I had always assumed that this unusual benevolence on the part of the regime was a result of my grandparents' age and hopelessly bourgeois ways. They were expendable. Now, having read our AVO file, I see it was a cruel calculation in preparation for my parents' arrest. My sister and I were the strongest weapon in the State's arsenal against my parents. To break my mother and father, their children had to be left entirely at the mercy of strangers.

But in August 1954, when my parents and sister and I saw my grandparents off at the train station, we were oblivious to the coming danger. On that smoky, cavernous platform, I waved goodbye to my beloved Nagypapa, and watched my grandparents' Vienna-bound train slowly disappear in the distance. What I most remember is seeing my father cry for the first time in my life. Children have no notion of "never," but my father knew we would never see his father again. Erno Marton, grandson of an Austro-Hungarian rabbi, who had made a good life for himself and his family in pre-Communist, pre-Fascist Budapest, would die at age ninety-one in Melbourne, Australia, in 1973. He was the sweetest, most tender man I ever knew.

I thought Mama and Papa were the most glamorous parents in the world, and knew they were the envy of all my friends. The aura of danger no doubt had something to do with that. All the other grown-ups seemed so *timid*. My parents did not whisper like my friends' parents did, especially when speaking of *certain subjects*. My father still had all his suits custom-tailored by Gerhardt on Budapest's Vaci Utca, from soft tweeds and gabardines and even seersucker shipped or smuggled in by British diplomats and American journalists. His —and our— shoes were handmade by a famous shoemaker named Cauper, from leather brought in the same way. My mother still used her prewar milliner, Sari Friedmann (code name "Bubi" in the AVO files, unclear whether suspect or informer). Mama had the Budapest woman's flair for transforming any ensemble into a fashion statement. She moved in a cloud of Arpège, and I loved to watch her flash her ruby red nails as she dealt cards with the virtuosity of a Monte Carlo croupier.

My sister and I were at the center of our parents' universe. My mother, effusive and charming in French and English, and wickedly funny in her native Hungarian, loved to bring visiting foreigners into our bedroom to hear us say our prayers, *"En Istenem, Jo Istenem . . . ,"* taught to us by the fanatical Catholic nun who lived downstairs and—

after her religious order was disbanded by the Communists—was employed as nanny to two of our playmates, Peter and Balint. Her name was Sister Marta, though we were told to call her Aunt Marta, Marta Neni, for the State frowned on her retrograde Catholicism and priests and nuns were prohibited from wearing their cassocks and habits outside church. I admired Marta Neni's radiant and very personal affection for Jesus, whom she spoke of as if he were her friend. Once, I saw her ask a neighborhood boy whose parents were aggressive nonbelievers to hold the cross she hid most of the time under her cardigan. *"Szeretlek Jezuska,"* she whispered urgently in the boy's ear. "I love you, Jesus." With Aunt Marta's eyes burning into his, the boy repeated his love of Jesus. I was drawn to her stark simplicity, in such contrast to my mother's stylishness. Once, when she and her charges, Peter and Balint, slept over (one of us had chicken pox, and our parents decided we should all have it at the same time), I was determined to discover what she wore in bed (a special nun's nightie? I wondered), for she always waited until the light was out to undress. When everyone in the room was asleep, I whispered to her, "Marta Neni, do you sleep in a nightgown?" She told me to be quiet and go to sleep. But I kept nagging her, uselessly, until I, too, dropped off. She was as obstinate as I was, but had more stamina.

I loved holding Marta Neni's cool, dry hand as we walked to Mass at the Varosmajor Church at the bottom of the hill. We lined up Saturday afternoons before the confessional booths, and I usually took the longest. Stepping out of the church into the biting cold as dusk was falling on the little park with its giant, bare trees and gravel paths, I would pick up chestnuts, polish them on my sleeve, and feel, briefly, pure. Did I wonder why our parents never attended Mass with us, yet seemed so eager that we go? I don't think the reason occurred to me until years later. (Utterly secular themselves, they were permanently marked by Hungary's anti-Semitism and wanted their children to be Christians, however much the State persecuted the Church. A bizarre and bewildering calculation on my parents' part.)

Csaba Utca, a leafy corner atop one of Buda's hills, was all I knew of the world. We could hear the soft hum of the streetcars and buses in nearby Szena Ter, renamed Moscow Square, though nobody called it that. We were a safe distance from the business side of the city in Pest, which we visited only to go to the doctor, the opera, or to Gerbeaud, a *Mitteleuropean* survivor of the old days. Most of the other old cafés had closed, or turned into stand-up coffee bars where people hurriedly knocked back little cups of espresso. Loitering was not encouraged. Travel was out of the question. The word "passport" when uttered by an adult always had a nostalgic tone, usually followed by a string of memories of Paris, London, Vienna, and Venice, polished stories, preserved like jewels by the grown-ups. To us children, those were just names in a book; our four-story apartment house on the Buda hill was a happy and sufficient world. In the winter, wearing our tiny protective goggles, all of us would lie on our bathroom floor under the sunlamp; in those days people thought that a healthy thing to do. When our friend Peter or his brother, Balint, or the boys upstairs, Sandor and Bandi, were done with their potty duty, the whole house could hear, *"Ich bin schon fertig!"* "I am ready," as they had been taught to discreetly announce in German, a phrase that still brings back a rush of memories. Our parents were all members of the officially despised bourgeoisie, so we shared a common enemy.

That was my world: atop that Buda hill, with summer trips to magic Lake Balaton. I remember counting the long row of cypresses receding behind us as we approached the lake of my childhood. On our drive back, my parents and sister and I would break into the song *"Ahol a sarga villamosok jarnak, ott van Budapest"* ("Where the yellow trams run . . . that's where you'll find Budapest") as we rounded the bend of the country road and the dim lights of the capital came into view.

A child accepts his world, and adjusts to it. I did not think it odd that when the front doorbell of Peter and Balint's apartment rang, one of the grown-ups would cover up the altar built into a wall with a picture of a Chinese fan. Nor did we need our parents to tell us that the Kalmars, who lived across the hall, were not "our sort." We knew they were "important" Communists. We children gleaned this from their dress, body language, and stiffness in our company. Some time later—I believe during the 1956 Revolution—we learned he was an AVO officer. I also had more concrete proof. The Kalmars had three kids, and the six of us "bourgeois" progeny were naturally wary of them. But I had a little girl's crush on the older daughter, Zsuzsi, with her long, glossy black braids and serious, purposeful air. She struck me as somebody who could teach me things about the world my mother—seemingly from another planet—could not. Somehow I ingratiated myself into their apartment. A large portrait of Stalin lighting his pipe was the only artwork I recall. It was the first such portrait I had ever seen in a private home, so I imagined the Kalmars to have been close personal friends of the Great Father—who usually gazed at me from high above the blackboard, the post office, and on May Day parades. I did not tell my parents about my visit, as I hoped to be asked back. I even secretly admired Zsuzsi's mother, Mrs. Kalmar, who wore a sort of Communist equivalent of a nun's habit: gray, shapeless, and unembellished. There was something appealing about her plain, soft features, with never a spot of makeup. This struck me as more appropriate for the times than my mother's red lips and matching nails.

I remember going back to our place after visiting the Kalmars, and suddenly feeling that everything in our apartment was old, musty, and embarrassingly out of step with the New Hungary: my grandparents' faded Persian carpets, the dark oil landscapes, and the portrait of the Madonna (by a member of da Vinci's school, I was always told, but who was da Vinci?). And all those old, cracked, leather-bound books! Seemingly thousands of books, many with broken bindings, which had miraculously survived the siege of Budapest, by authors and in languages nobody read anymore: Thomas Mann, Rudyard Kipling, Charles Dickens, Sinclair Lewis. I felt their inappropriateness in the country we young pioneers were building. (I was now a "kisdobos," or "Little Drummer," and once a week wore a blue neckerchief.) And then I felt disloyal to my parents for these feelings.

Children were an essential part of the new states the Soviet Empire was planting "from Stettin in the Baltic to Trieste in the Adriatic," as Winston Churchill warned in his "Iron Curtain" speech in 1946. With new standards and values, they started indoctrinating children very young. Socialist teachers were trained in academies throughout the Eastern Bloc. They were called "People's Teachers," and their job was to inculcate Socialist values from our first day in nursery school. As a result, I sometimes felt squeezed between the twin poles of my existence: school and home.

Once a week we marched around the schoolyard singing praises to Comrade Rakosi and those distant gods known only from giant photographs: Stalin and Lenin, Marx and Engels. I secretly enjoyed those rousing tunes, savored momentarily being just like everybody else. (Though, as yet another form of parental protest, my sister and I wore our black patent leather Mary Janes, which screamed America, to these events.) "Cheerful Pioneer like a Squirrel" was one of my favorites. Another song, "Tremble Counts, Barons and Bourgeoisie, It's the Hour of the Proletariat!" was a little too close to home.

Budapest in those days was not a place of color or beauty. Only red broke the gray wash. Red stars or red flags fluttered atop all big buildings and schools, the red banner was more present than the Hungarian tricolor. Even the flower bed in front of the Chain Bridge was planted with red flowers in the shape of a hammer and sickle. Every child knew that the blazing red geraniums in the window box of 60 Andrassy Ut—renamed Stalin Ut—were watered by the AVO, to make their headquarters, formerly those of the Arrow Cross, look friendly. En route to Gundel's restaurant in the City Park, we hurried past the hated building. As the AVO and its window boxes spread to encompass virtually a whole block, it became harder not to look up.

Most buildings in the city were still pockmarked from shrapnel and many still missed windows and parts of roofs from the Allies' bombs of a decade before. There was a dingy feel to everything: buildings and people, making do with prewar remnants endlessly altered, or this year's State Store model overcoat. Even the apples in bins in front of the cooperative store at the bottom of our hill looked beat-up and bruised. I fantasized about someday living in a house with a smooth, unscarred facade, like the American diplomatic residences.

WE WERE politicized children. It wasn't that we were more serious than American or other little kids around the world. We just knew that the Communist Party and its chiefs in both Budapest and Moscow impacted on our personal lives. We knew this from our parents, our teachers, and the iconography that surrounded us. Above all, we were familiar with Rakosi, Hungary's much feared Stalinist leader. He lived not far from us on another Buda hill and occasionally we caught a glimpse of his motorcade of long, sleek, curtained Zil limousines snaking down toward Pest. Rakosi seemed a much closer threat than the others. There was no limit to the cult of Himself, imposed by this fat, bald, neckless little man whose head sat directly on his shoulders. One of our nursery school songs was an ode to this odious thug, "We Thank You, Comrade Rakosi!"

Tito, Cardinal Mindszenty, and Laszlo Rajk were other names familiar to me. Sometimes I was confused by the two versions of each of these names: one inside our apartment, the other, outside. (My parents covered the show trials of the last two—Mindszenty and Rajk—both convicted of faked charges of espionage, the cardinal given a life sentence, Rajk, the foreign minister, sent to the gallows.) There were other names I knew better than to drop outside our home: Christian Ravndal, the American ambassador, and a whole string of American and British diplomats who formed my parents' social circle: the Abbotts, the Rogerses, the Downses, the Simpsons, and many others.

Once in a while, I forgot the unspoken rules governing our split lives. When all of us in my nursery school were asked to bring our favorite toy to class, I chose a little wind-up monkey who beat on a tiny drum as he twirled around. All the children dropped to the floor to marvel at this breathtaking bit of (obviously) Western technology. I was summoned to the principal's office for a child's version of the feared AVO interrogation. Where did you get that toy, she asked, looking at me as if I had been caught trading nuclear secrets with the Enemy. I knew better than to reveal that it was a Christmas present from my "Aunt Ruth," Ruth Tryon, press attaché at the American legation, pronounced persona non grata and given twenty-four hours to pack up and leave Hungary shortly after presenting me with the magic monkey. With a child's self-centeredness, I connected those two events.

Most Hungarians feared and avoided my parents. Since Rakosi had virtually declared war on all things American, even a small child could sense that the Martons had become radioactive. It seems odd now, but politics seeped into everything in those days. Somehow, I understood that Zsuzsi Kalmar could not reciprocate my visit to her home for fear of being contaminated by us. And that when she finally did come over, she was there for some other purpose than to play with me. Childhood in such a state is not a protected zone.

I suppose my sister and I were too young to be considered really dangerous, but in our striped T-shirts and argyle knee socks, American diplomatic kids' castoffs, we were walking billboards for the Enemy everybody was supposed to despise. It was a funny feeling for a child who wanted above all to be liked by all the other children. Riding around in our white Studebaker convertible, while people the color of slush waited for creaky buses spewing black smoke, my sister and I felt like princesses.

I knew from the songs we sang at school and from billboards ("Buy Peace Bonds and Give an Answer to the American Imperialists!" urged a popular one) that my mother and father consorted with Criminal Imperialists. While in school we memorized clever rhymes about Dwight Eisenhower's big fat head being filled with oxygen that could explode at any instant, my parents drove their big American car to the American legation each Tuesday morning. My mother called the car my father's "little vanity." But now I wonder, how did he even have the nerve to buy such a flashy piece of American technology from the departing American diplomat, George M. Abbott? We used to visit Mr. Abbott, a weathered, lean, slightly hunched man who proudly showed us how he turned the backyard of his diplomatic residence into a small farm, planting tomatoes and zucchini in his flower beds. I thought my elegant father, with his beautiful, manicured hands and his driving gloves, looked much better behind the wheel of that sleek machine than Mr. Abbott. But why be that deliberately provocative? According to the files, as reported by informer "Andrassi," a Foreign Ministry spokesman chided my father, "Well, you'll be that much easier to follow, driving around in that car!" To which my father replied, "They can follow me around all they want! I have nothing to hide." My father sometimes left us in the back seat of the Studebaker while doing his errands, and gawkers would immediately gather, small children pressing their noses against the window to inspect this marvel. I felt a mix of pride and embarrassment.

The plus side of our internal exile was that we did almost everything as a family. My parents didn't believe in doing "childish" things, like trips to the zoo or amusement parks. Instead, they took us with them to the Turkish baths, which, even in the stripped-down 1950s, imbued the city with a certain hedonistic quality. I learned to swim hanging from a long fishing pole in the steamy Lukacs baths, where the remnant of Budapest's intellectual elite circled around me with measured breaststrokes, never breaking their conversation. And to the opera! Our ravishing Aunt Magda was married to an opera conductor, my Uncle Laci, so the opera was practically our day care center. By age six I could (quietly) sing along with the major arias.

My sister and I were often part of the adult world that gathered around the tiny, wobbly marble tables at Gerbeaud. I was, of course, oblivious while spooning the whipped-cream-topped chocolate mound (called an "Indianer," it was my favorite and may explain my frequent trips to Pesti Pista, the family dentist, whose name never ceased to amuse me, and whose office was conveniently close to the Gerbeaud) that half the Nenis and Bacsis, "aunties" and "uncles," chatting with my parents were going to report their every witty remark to the AVO. In fact, records now reveal that not even our dentist with the amusing name was spared from the AVO's visits.

I remember my father as reserved, somewhat distant. I do not remember ever sitting on his lap or even holding his hand. (It occurs to me that his nearly two years in jail might have had something to do with that later remoteness.) His occasional eruptions of temper were all the more frightening as they were thunderclaps without warning. Once when I—the mischievous one he called, mysteriously, "Dennis the Menace"—was teasing my sister, while my mother napped, and woke her up, my father chased me around the apartment so he could administer his famous soccer kick to my bottom. Had I known then the pressures my parents were living under, I would have been quiet as a mouse during adult naptime. But thanks to the AVO's surveillance record, I now know he was both devoted and affectionate.

Surveillance record, August 27, 1954:

10:05 A.M. [Marton] in a gray and black striped suit [I remember that favorite seersucker suit of his] and his two little girls left their home and got into car (license plate CA894) drove to Alkotas Utca 1, where we photographed him stepping out of the car. He then went into a stationery store with the little girls. Inside, he bought them school supplies. Ten minutes later, the little girls carrying their school supplies, Marton left the store.

11:43 Marton drove to Gerbeaud and, after finding a table, ordered ice cream. The three consumed the above while chatting.

12:20 P.M. Holding his children's hands, Marton walked back to his car. They drove to Vaci Ut 7 and entered a toy shop.

12:30 Holding his daughters' hands, Marton left the shop. One of the little girls carried a package wrapped in pink paper.

13:20 Marton and his little girls drove to the Duna Hotel, where they occupied a table in the garden. We continued surveillance while they ate their lunch.

To the AVO I owe a long-ago late-summer day, washed away by dramatic events to come. It is now restored to me.

Chapter 3

MAMA AND PAPA

Papa the AP correspondent teaching Mama of UP the fundamentals
of foreign corresponding: how to get an international operator on
the line to London or New York.

THEY LIVED and worked "as if . . ." As if driving to Freedom Square,
parking in front of the lemon yellow building flying the Stars-and-
Stripes, and entering that other world, which filled most Hungarians
with a strange combination of dread and longing, were normal. As if
reporting consistently bad news from behind the Iron Curtain were
part of their job as reporters.

The Tuesday "press conference" at the legation (in Hungary the
United States deliberately did not call their diplomatic mission a full-

43

fledged embassy) was part of their routine, even when the only Western press left were Endre and Ilona Marton. And, most remarkably, they seemed not to crack under the daily pressure of the telltale click at the beginning of every phone conversation, or the sight of obviously steamed-open letters in their mailbox. Yet the files reveal an even greater scrutiny than they imagined. Someone was watching them, or listening to them, during most of their waking hours. Of their private lives, there remained virtually nothing.

I remember teary, pale-faced country girls confessing to my parents that the condition of cleaning our apartment or cooking for us was that they inform on us. There was an Eta from Transylvania who chose to return home after a few months with us. Eta was followed by Terez, who also opted for her village over stressful life with us. My parents tried their best to reassure them, and dissuade those who wanted to scurry back to their village to stay. One cleaning lady asked my artistically challenged mother to help her draw a floor plan of our apartment with little sketches of every piece of furniture, for the AVO's benefit. Another was ordered to collect the envelopes of our incoming mail. That exercise seems like an extraordinary waste of time, since all our mail had gone through the censors anyway. My father often drafted their AVO reports for them. "It's the ones who don't tell you they are informing," he said, "that you have to worry about."

There was one who stuck with us like glue. I have already mentioned her, but I failed to fully describe her. Yet she is indelibly etched in my mind. Gabrielle Guillemet, from Chinon, France. With a chalk-white complexion framed by a helmet of hair the color of pitch, she was hired by my parents not only to look after my sister and me but also to teach us French. I cannot recall a time when Madame wasn't around. Why did my parents think this irritable, black-clad presence with her clip-clopping high heels was an appropriate choice for the role of nanny? I still don't know. The options were limited, I suppose, and my parents were determined that we should learn French.

Madame (whose title we turned into a verb that my sister and I still use, as in "to Madame," or to boss around) fulfilled that part of her assignment. I could have told them she wasn't suited to look after small children! But I had no credibility, as Madame was particularly strict with me, the troublemaker. My parents, though suspicious, underestimated Madame's dedication to her real masters. The AVO files show an industrious spy whose real job, under her code name, "Gaspar," was to provide detailed accounts of the most minute details of our family life for the years she lived with us.

I sometimes thought my parents were so caught up in the drama of their own lives that they barely differentiated between my sister and me. Our names always came out as a single word: "Juli-Kati." But the AVO reports tell me that my father was aware of certain differences between his daughters. In his cell, where his every confidence was betrayed by agent/cell mates, he expressed particular concern for "his younger child's emotional state, as a result of separation from her parents." In fact, my sister and I were and have remained very different people who, once outside our home, went our separate ways. She was always eager to "do" things, while I was a daydreamer, very happy to line up my dolls and read to them, faking it well before I could actually read. But I was also frustrated at being prohibited from having real fights with Juli. She had been grievously ill with tetanus, from a dose of toxic vaccine. In my view, she was given a pass by our parents after that. My father simply could not bear conflict in the house, and would burst into our room with a look so fierce we called an immediate cease-fire.

Much as the AVO was itching to get their hands on my parents, and made regular requests for permission to arrest these two "spy suspects," something or someone was protecting them. Having read the files and spoken with historians of AVO, I have come to the conclusion that my parents' unique access made them too valuable to lightly squander by routine jailing. The prisons were full. The AVO had plenty of other souls to torture. Rakosi was biding his time. No one in Budapest was as trusted and *liked* by the Americans, British, and French as Endre and Ilona Marton. Surely they would eventually lead Rakosi to something big. Meanwhile, they were as free as two exotic birds in a well-appointed cage: under total surveillance, their every move dogged, every conversation recorded, in the hope of learning more about the Americans. But their cage was getting smaller.

On January 14, 1953, the counselor of the legation, George Abbott, wrote a memorandum addressed to Secretary of State John Foster Dulles. Marked "Secret," it was only declassified (as a result of my Freedom of Information Act request) on June 5, 2008. Reading its thoughtful and insightful description of my parents so many years later is profoundly moving. "Marton is the only important [correspondent]," Abbott wrote.

On the last two Tuesdays [press conference days] Marton came to the Legation alone, laughing wryly at the thought of being accompanied only by a ghostly company of former colleagues. While aware of the risk involved in visiting the "Enemy" Legation, Marton professes to believe that this is not much greater than it has been for the past two years, so he plans to continue coming. The Legation, while aware that his visits might be concocted into a "provocation" by the regime, plans to continue seeing him unless new factors affect the problem, meanwhile observing its usual caution in all dealings with Hungarian citizens. . . .

"Press conference" has become an innocent euphemism for our meetings with western correspondents, in the sense that almost no news can be made available by the Legation. The occasions now are actually informal social visits, and are more useful to the Legation than to the correspondents, since they offer opportunities to discuss and compare interpretations of local events and trends, and to acquire intelligent backgrounding from a Hungarian viewpoint.

Several factors help to explain the Martons' continued willingness to visit this Legation. First, while the Legation has suffered much abuse and harassment, it is still freely entered by a trickle of courageous Hungar-

ian visitors . . . Second, the Martons have been coming here regularly on Tuesdays for over two years, also visiting the British Minister at least monthly, and have been regular patrons of the frequent American and British Legation movies which are open to the Western diplomatic community. . . . Furthermore, the Martons are well connected in cultural, academic, and sport (fencing) circles in Budapest and they are generally prudent in their personal conduct and in avoiding cause for charges of meddling or undue curiosity ("espionage").

In the last month, Marton has betrayed a new awareness of the curiosity (to say the least) which his position must evoke in the Hungarian Foreign Office. . . . He has shown considerable courage in his selection of stories and in interpretive possibilities. Inevitably, now he will have to use greater caution.

Marton's situation obviously is a delicate one, which may turn desperate at any time. He and his wife have increasingly had trouble hiding the strain under which they live and work. There is every reason to believe that they both see salvation in escape to the West but such deliverance—hazardous and expensive in any case—is vastly complicated by their having two children (ages between 4 and 8) and the fact that his father and mother live with them in the same apartment.

Essentially, Marton's dilemma is that his very coolness in the past has been built on the "normality" of his role as a professional newsman. But as that normality has been steadily deprived of supporting props, it has become more and more a question of personal courage and tenacity. To shrink from contacts with this Legation (and others, notably the British) would now involve a virtually impossible psychic revulsion. Without the moral support and vicarious spiritual sustenance of these contacts with the "West," Marton would feel even more exposed to the somber whims of the regime.

Abbott noted that, apart from my parents, there was only one other foreign correspondent still working in Hungary in 1953, whom Abbott described as "Attila Ajtonyi, a dubious character, obviously unable to support himself on earnings from [journalism]. He is probably a secret police informer . . . and has been successfully stalled off in his requests to attend [U.S. legation press conferences]." Just as they underestimated the potential danger of our French governess, my parents never took this "dubious character" masquerading as a foreign correspondent seriously. They simply felt they had nothing to hide—from anybody. They made no bones about their affection for what America stood for (though neither of them had ever set foot in the United States). American diplomats were their friends. If, once in a while, they could offer advice to their friends—as cut off from the real Hungary as my parents were from the West—they saw nothing wrong with that.

In 1953, an opportunity to help the Americans presented itself. My parents were irritated by the official Hungarian press's continued depiction of the United States as a racist state, where blacks were still subjugated and kept in ghettos. Papa suggested to Minister Ravndal (the senior U.S. diplomat in Budapest) that one way to debunk that charge was to send a black diplomat to Budapest. Ravndal thought this a very good idea and asked if he might pass it on to Secretary of State Dulles, crediting my father with the idea. My father, assuming that all his conversations with Ravndal were secure, approved. A few months later, Rupert Lloyd, the first African-American ever posted to Hungary, arrived. As first secretary and then counselor, he quickly established himself as a respected member of Budapest's diplomatic community. No doubt Lloyd's high-profile presence was a source of annoyance to the regime's propaganda office, and a damning piece of evidence against the man whose idea it was.

By the time Ernest Nagy, a strapping twenty-five-year-old from Cleveland, arrived in Budapest as the new consul, the Martons were "regulars," invited to most American functions, official and unofficial. "We were all aware that there were these unusual people," Nagy recalled in 2008, "who turned up at the legation regularly." At a time when Moscow and Washington were locked in a deadly global struggle, my parents were the American ambassador's favorite bridge partners. "Your parents never seemed timid or afraid. Were they simply that heroic, or were they on the [AVO] payroll? We all made the assumption that, at a minimum, they had to report periodically and say harmless things about all of us. But we never thought they were fellow travelers. After their arrest, it was clear that they were very brave."

Nagy's wife, Helen, adds a vivid memory of my parents. "I will never forget when they walked in to the legation," Mrs. Nagy recalled in 2008. "Here we are in a country where you can't buy *anything*, where everybody looks poor, neglected, and forlorn, and in walk these two Hungarians who look better than any of us. I learned a lot about style and dress from observing your mother."

Mrs. Nagy shows me their family photo album, full of those small black and white photos from the 1950s. "See," she says pointing to my mother, elegant in a dark suit and a small veiled hat, "that was taken at our wedding, in Ravndal's garden. You would never have known she was not *one of us,* would you?"

Perhaps my parents had persuaded themselves that looking and behaving as if they were *one of them* would fool their enemies, too.

Chapter 4

THE AMERICANS

Mama, the fourth from left, at a diplomatic reception in
Budapest—the only Hungarian in the group, as usual.

If Matyas Rakosi—an omnipotent character out of a *Grimm's*
fairy tale—represented Evil in my childhood, the White Knight was
Christian Ravndal, the chief of the American mission in Hungary.
From 1951 until 1956, Ravndal set the mood and tone for the forty-
four adults and fourteen children who represented the United States
in this forgotten corner of Europe. We only really found out what this

deceptively lighthearted man was made of when my family was in serious trouble.

Ravndal's name evokes the most dramatic days of my childhood. Born in Beirut, where his father was the American consul, educated in Istanbul and Lutheran College in his native Iowa, Chris, as he was universally known, had already put his stamp on the State Department before arriving in Cold War Budapest. Starting as a code clerk in the Vienna embassy, he became director general of the Foreign Service in 1947, beginning the transformation of that elite corps into something that better reflected American society. He had already been ambassador to Uruguay when he arrived in the Stalinist capital of Hungary. In Budapest, he defied the climate of fear that prevailed even inside the American colony.

"He was my first chief of mission," Ernest Nagy recalled. "And all the others were a disappointment after him. He was very attached to your parents. He loved to talk to them about music, sports, writers. Your parents were very well informed in all those areas—so there was a real bond there."

Ravndal, like my parents, refused to be hemmed in by the wall of informers and agents encircling the Americans. "He was a Hemingwayesque type," Nagy recalled, "who liked to drink, liked women, enjoyed sports, was brilliant at cards, a gifted musician—loved life!" Ravndal had built himself a four-hole golf course and hired a Hungarian golf pro named Joe. "We were all obliged to play," recalled Jordan Thomas Rogers, economic attaché in Budapest under Ravndal. "And there'd be prizes given out each weekend. I think I got a prize for never winning a prize." A man who turned his passions for bridge, golf, music, hard drinking, and hard partying into tools of diplomacy, Ravndal must have been a bewildering character to the AVO. What to make of a man who much preferred playing four-handed piano sonatas with the wife of the British ambassador, Lady Hankey, to talking politics?

More than half a century later, Tom Rogers still recalled his first interview with Ambassador Ravndal. "Ravndal shared an office with Clare Boothe Luce in the State Department," he remembered. "She was then serving as ambassador to Italy and she was on the phone. Ravndal hadn't said a word to me and I thought he was just waiting for her to end her conversation. But even after she hung up he still hadn't asked me anything, just perused my files. Finally, after what seemed like a very long time he asked, 'Do you play bridge?' I answered, 'Well, my wife, Sarah, loves it and I play more or less.' Ravndal studied me for a while longer, then finally said, 'Well, thanks for coming in.' I thought that was that, but I got the job as economic attaché.

"When I got to Vienna, Ravndal was staying at the Bristol and offered me a lift to Budapest. He had Austrian police escort us to the border and then his Hungarian limo, an old six-cylinder Buick, met us at the crossing. At that point, he opened a picnic basket of sandwiches and uncorked a pitcher of martinis, which we both consumed. After lunch, he fell right asleep and the driver zoomed through sleepy Hungarian villages. By the time we pulled into Budapest, he was ready to go. I was completely exhausted."

Chris Ravndal wasn't the only American who tried to breach the wall of isolation. There was also the CIA station chief, Geza Katona. Katona used his dogs as a cover for contacts with Hungarians: "I used to take them for walks in the City Park. Budapesters like good-looking dogs, and many would approach me for that reason. People were bolder in the open air, and in the park there was little reason to be fearful of being overheard. That was despite the fact that I was often tailed—at times for two or three weeks at a time, after which there would be a short break, then another week—that was how it went. They were rather glaringly obvious in the way they went about it. There was not much traffic in Budapest, so we were already quite familiar with the license plates and would announce any new ones to one another. 'Hey, I was followed by CD600. Make a note of it. It's a State Security car!'"

Political attaché Don Downs's German shepherd, Duke, also played a cameo role in the spy games of Budapest. In 1954, on his nightly walk, Duke sniffed something under a tree. Downs leaned down and found the minutes of a Hungarian Politburo meeting, left for the American. It was the legation's first alert of the impending fall of Rakosi. (Downs and Duke would also play a role in my father's arrest.)

BUDAPEST'S JAZZ life, and its beautiful women, were two other ways some Americans found to break out of their loneliness. "The Hotel Bristol was our headquarters," Consul Nagy, an amateur jazz musician, recalled. "An Oscar Peterson style pianist played and the girls were there. I was in love with one and tried and failed to get her out. We closed many a bar and greeted the morning." Nagy's bachelor days ended in 1954 when he married a dark-haired legation secretary, Helen Stephens.

"Some weeks after Helen and I got married," he recalled, "I was listening to some jazz at the Moulin Rouge nightclub, a small Pest dive. A guy joined us, a burly, muscular fellow, and reached into his pocket. 'Here,' he said, handing me a pile of photographs. 'We took these from the woods across the road from your wedding. You can take a look, but then hand them back.' It turned out that the jazz lover was an AVO officer by day."

NOT ALL members of the American colony adjusted easily to being under constant surveillance. A twenty-eight-year-old code clerk, Josephine Salvatore, arrived in Budapest in 1949 unprepared for the hostile environment. "One night," she recalled, "around 2 A.M., I was woken by a call from the State Department operator. 'You need to go to the legation right away for an incoming coded message,' I was told. I only lived a few blocks away, and there were no taxis. So I walked. Every step I took, I could hear someone's step right behind me. By the time I reached the legation, I was pretty shaken. Then we were told we couldn't associate with Hungarians, that if we did, they would get in trouble. So we never reached out to the people. Meanwhile, we lived in this small, incestuous diplomatic community. A lot of parties, a lot of drinking, and a kind of a forced gaiety. And the stories we heard about Rakosi, about his cruelty to his own people. It was rough living under that kind of pressure."

Adding to the claustrophobic atmosphere of the Cold War capital, Americans were not allowed to travel more than thirty kilometers outside the city without special permission. Most of the country was forbidden territory for them. With the Rakosi regime doing all in its power to keep the "Imperialists" in an airtight box, the diplomats' isolation was greater than ours—but, unlike our family, they had a passport to get out at any time—as, in fact, Josephine Salvatore did, going home early at her own request.

Service in Budapest merited "hardship pay" for American diplomats. Life in the American colony was described in bitter terms in an official legation message on October 27, 1953: "Local transportation facilities are available but policy of Legation is to minimize exposure of personnel to hostility in view of effective anti-American campaign. Legation provides transportation to/from work for American personnel not living within walking distance of the Legation." Not even the spectacular historic sights of the city, which today draw hundreds of thousands of tourists, were available diversions. "Sightseeing," the report continues, "must be done circumspectly to avoid charges of spying." Atop these artificial barriers was a permanent one: the Hungarian language.

The language barrier is a basic one, since Hungarian is unusually hard to learn being unrelated to any other commonly known language, and virtually useless after you leave the post, and few Americans can do more than learn enough for shopping, ordering food, etc. . . . As most of the Hungarian wealthy class who spoke English, French or German are either in prison, deported, or destitute, contact with them is unlikely. Except at of-

ficial functions, contact with any except pro-Western nations is nonexistent.

Inadequate recreation is a hardship since the limited types available and the constant constraint of unfriendly authority prevent personnel from obtaining the fullest relaxation and stimulus. The individual becomes stale and friction between personalities looms disproportionately large.

Isolation is a hardship factor at the post since it limits social contacts to a small group with the result that all entertainment involves contact only with the group with whom you work. Topics of conversation are limited and the lack of fresh stimulus plus constant repetition creates friction.

MY SISTER and I were honorary members of the bubble inhabited by foreign diplomats and their children. We were invited to birthday parties, swimming outings (there was, inevitably, a modest version of an American country club outside the city), and movie screenings at the British or American missions. This is how I saw Disney's *Bambi* and *Snow White* and, the most magical of all, the coronation of the young Queen Elizabeth. When I see pictures of the now elderly queen, I remember my discomfort that particular evening. My cheek had ballooned from a tooth infection so every time the lights in the embassy screening room came on, I dove under my seat in embarrassment. It was bad enough being a self-conscious Hungarian waif (who did not speak English) in a sea of chatty Anglo-American kids.

The little girls wore bright pastels, even in winter, lacy little socks, and white nylon sweaters over their petticoated party dresses. To me they looked like Easter confections. Though I did not speak more than a few words of English, we played "A Tisket, a Tasket," and musical chairs and many versions of hide and seek. I loved the breeziness of Americans: "Hey, girls!" the father would greet us. "Hey, Daddy!" the children would shout back. No standing up, no shaking of hands necessary in adult company. We could sit on the floor, something we did not do in our home. I did not enjoy the prickly bubbles of my first taste of the American national drink, and found their orange-colored, square American cheese tasteless. But how I wanted to be part of that bright, carefree-seeming world. My sister and I were generally the only Hungarian children at such functions, our parents being the only Hungarian adults. Stepping into diplomatic residences was always a thrill for me. They were so well cared for, so bright, and they felt so *safe*. In 1995, when I chose the garden of the American ambassador's residence in Budapest in which to be married, I was again choosing that safety, marrying in my native land, but on safe American soil.

Behind their clipped hedges, inside their imitation American suburban villas, playing bingo on Saturday night or, led by Ravndal, singing the hymns they had sung every Sunday in Columbus, Kansas City, or Fallon, Nevada, the forty-four Americans were prisoners of the system, *almost* as much as we were. The key difference, however, was that their stay behind the Iron Curtain was limited. Anytime they felt the urge, they could jump into their Buick or Chevy, and, five hours later, they would be greeted by the grimy buildings and cobblestones of postwar Vienna. To make that same trip my family was willing to risk everything.

Sometimes, moments of levity broke the tension of daily life in Stalinist Budapest. "One day," Ernest Nagy recalled, "this furtive Hungarian came to the legation. He was carrying a package, and asked to speak to 'someone important.' So we led him to Geza [Katona, the CIA station chief]. 'This fell out of an American car,' the Hungarian told us. 'I did not want it to fall into Soviet hands.' It turned out to be a box of used condoms that Max [economic attaché Max Finger] had tried and failed to dispose of."

My parents were a topic of endless speculation among the Americans. "We assumed that they were routinely questioned by the AVO," Tom Rogers noted. "I can't imagine that they weren't. I never asked them. It doesn't mean they provided anything meaningful to the Hungarians. It's just the way things were. But your parents were doing so many risky things, covering for AP and UP, their social ties with us, which were really quite deep. They came to weddings, baby showers, and went Christmas caroling with us. Sin upon sin."

One American diplomat was deeply suspicious of my parents. Sidney Lafoon, Ravndal's deputy chief of mission, was everything his chief was not. "A mediocre, bumbling fellow," in Nagy's words. "An unimaginative, suspicious, visceral, 'Them vs. Us' kind of guy. There were a lot of them around the State Department in the McCarthy times. Lafoon was a holdover from those days. To me, your father was the product of a Central European education system that was all about creating the well-rounded man, the humanist education which you rarely meet anymore. To Lafoon, your father was 'not one of us'—suspect."

Lafoon was rumored to have a personal fortune and thus able to relieve Ravndal of much of the tedious official entertaining. By a stroke of bad luck, Lafoon, his wife, and two daughters moved into the diplomatic residence next door to our house on Csaba Utca. The problems began immediately.

My grandparents still lived with us, and my grandmother was a passionate cook. The kitchen of the American residence faced our balcony. I remember my grandmother chatting with Francesca, the Lafoons' cook. Francesca would lean out the kitchen window, to discuss the day's menu with "Nagymama." Shortly after the Lafoons moved in, workmen installed iron bars that supported opaque windowpanes, blocking any communication or visual connection between the Lafoons and us. One of the Hungarian workmen commented to my father, "I've only ever seen this type of thing at Kistarcsa," the infamous Nazi and AVO internment camp outside the city.

There would be no further chats between Francesca and my grandmother. Juli and I learned not to let a stray ball fly into the Lafoons' garden, from where we knew we could not retrieve it. "I despised him," Tom Rogers says flatly of Lafoon. "He thought your parents were Communist spies, and basically refused to have any contact with them."

Sometime in the 1970s, when I was a graduate student in Washington, D.C., my father asked me to accompany him to a State Department diplomatic reception. In a jostling crowd of diplomats and journalists, my father spotted a bulky figure. Sidney Lafoon. "Do not smile at that man, Kati. He is a very bad and stupid man." I made a point of squeezing through the crowd to get a good look at this family nemesis, and gave him my best scowl.

My parents did not realize that there was a far more dangerous American *inside* the legation—a man who would do them vastly more damage than this diplomat.

Chapter 5

SIN UPON SIN

A secret police telephoto shot of my parents (my father in the center), which I found in the AVO files.

O N APRIL 30, 1952, the Budapest correspondent of the International News Service, Jeno Szatmary, signed after being tortured a "confession" saying that "Endre Marton and his wife are transmitting intelligence data to the American embassy at their weekly press conferences. In my presence," Szatmary was forced to say, "they informed diplomats about political and economic events, the disbanding of religious orders, and the arrest of Social Democrats and others in Hungary." Shortly thereafter, suffering from untreated stomach cancer, Szatmary died in his cell.

My parents never knew that their friend and colleague had been tortured into a fake confession. But his arrest terrified them. Their anxiety was increased by the brutal treatment of Szatmary's wife, a former silent screen star, who was deported to an internment camp for "undesirables."

In her unpublished memoir, Mama remembered the moment vividly. "The tension for us became almost unbearable. For now we knew beyond any doubt that we were doomed and that our turn would be next. . . . Night after night we lay awake in our bed and made whispered plans for escape. Andrew and I and even the two little girls might not find it too hard to get out of the country alive, but we had Andrew's aging parents to think of. They could not be left behind and neither could they endure the risks of escape that the rest of us were prepared to face."

Of course, Juli and I knew nothing of the immense drama going on in our own home. In retrospect, it's quite miraculous how normal our lives felt to us. Children can adjust to almost anything as long as their parents are close by. My sister and I did. Only when I finally read the files did I realize the full cost my parents paid for this "normalcy." A recently published memoir by Carroll Sherer, wife of American diplomat Albert Sherer, offers more insight into my parents' desperation. Writing in 2007, Carroll Sherer describes a frantic call from my mother. "One day a Hungarian friend, a journalist, asked me to meet her at Gerbeaud, a fancy meeting place, for tea. I was surprised, but delighted, as I was an admirer and of course my curiosity was piqued," Mrs. Sherer recalled. "We chatted for a while and finally she said, 'Carroll, I have a serious request.' My imagination did not stretch far enough to anticipate what she asked. 'Will you take the two girls out?' I was speechless for a long time. I knew I had to say no, but I hadn't the heart or the wits to figure out how to do it. She went on. 'I think Endre and I will be arrested soon, and I don't know what will happen to them.'

"Her husband was also a journalist and a very fine one. What she was telling me was undoubtedly the truth. Finally, I gave the most direct answer, the most truthful answer there was. 'Ilona, if I did what you are asking, I would jeopardize the entire American mission. I think the AVO is waiting for me to do something against the law, something stupid, and Heaven knows I am surrounded by temptations every day.' I would have had to smuggle those children somehow in a diplomatic mail pouch or in the trunk of my car. There was no way to keep it secret anyway."*

The thought of my mother imagining—even imagining—giving up her children, in order to save them, is overwhelming. Such a discovery—long after I can talk to Mama about it—changes my memories of her. My admiration for her willingness to make such a sacrifice blends with horror at the choice she had to make. And then another thought: how might our lives have turned out had Mrs. Sherer taken us with her, raised my sister and me as her wards at various diplomatic posts (Albert "Bud" Sherer, declared persona non grata and given twenty-four hours to clear out of Hungary in 1952, went on to a distinguished diplomatic career, including as ambassador to Czechoslovakia). No amount of security, however, would have satisfied the longing for our parents.

Meanwhile, my father was desperately searching for a way out that would keep our family together. I am grateful that I was too young to understand what was going on. Cocooned in early childhood, I was oblivious to my parents' distress.

Sometime during that awful year, the AP's Vienna correspondent, Richard O'Regan, managed to get word to Papa of a human smuggler—a Salzburg-based army intelligence agent—who might be willing to help us. The problem was that "the Frenchman," as he was referred to, wanted money up front—much more than we had. O'Regan was wary of getting too far involved in this shadowy business. In a letter to the AP's general manager, Frank J. Starzel, in New York, on October 29, 1952, he wrote, "Emotionally, I would like to

---

* Carroll Russell Sherer, *The Great Adventure* (Lunenburg, VT: The Stinehour Press, 2007), pp. 36–38.

help Marton, but judgment tells me it would be smarter if Marton just stopped working for us, found himself another job before it is too late, and stayed where he is. The risks of escape daily become greater, the successful flights less frequent. I can't say accurately how much [Marton] might need. Winter approaches and, in any case, he must now wait until spring. Today, the fee is about $1,500 a head, meaning he probably would need a $3,000 advance from AP if he restricted the escape group to himself, his wife and two children. But by spring, the rate may be higher."

"If I thought the project had any chance of success," Starzel replied, "I would be willing to approve a $3,000 advance, although I would hesitate to go much higher. I doubt very much that [Marton's] situation would be helped any by chucking his job with us. To the contrary, it might make him subject to even more suspicion. Additionally, it is unlikely that he could make as good a connection elsewhere."

That summer, my parents set off on a day trip along the Danube. My sister and I knew that their trip was not a holiday outing, since they had left us behind. By nightfall, they had not returned. I stubbornly sat waiting at the bottom of the stairs leading up to our house. I cannot remember who persuaded me to give up my vigil and come to bed. I suppose it must have been Madame, but I have trouble recalling a single compassionate act from that arch and impatient woman.

The next day they returned, dispirited and bruised, their heads and arms bandaged. Their real destination had been a village on the Danube, their purpose to talk to a boatman who had had some luck hiding people in crates and smuggling them out on one of the riverboats that ply the Danube between Budapest and Vienna. As night closed in over unfamiliar roads, my parents' car lost control and somersaulted into an eight-foot ditch. "For a minute I was stunned," my mother later recalled. "Then, I became aware that I must be very seriously injured for I was covered with blood. A passing motorist stopped and bent over me anxiously, but we could not find my wound. A sudden moan from Andrew and we discovered that I was covered not with my blood but his. An artery on his wrist had been severed. All but unconscious, we carried him to a local doctor while I followed in a State truck. The country doctor could not adequately treat [your father's] injury, but when he was able to ride, we returned to Budapest in a taxi that took us straight to the hospital."

MY FATHER'S last remaining "foreign correspondent" colleague, "Andrassi," reported on January 11, 1953, to the AVO that he "overheard" Papa at the Gerbeaud say, "Everybody's nerves are on edge. Even respected cultural figures, scientists, artists, and doctors are forced to make such grotesque statements supporting the Party that it makes you ill."

On January 21, 1953, based on Szatmary's "confession" and my father's "destructive and damaging statements about Hungary," the Ministry of the Interior "recommends the arrest of Endre Marton, on charges of spying for the United States."

But on March 5, 1953, the miracle happened. Stalin died.

My single memory of that day is of an eerie quiet in the city. Workers dropped their tools, streetcars and buses screeched to a halt, and, in our nursery school, we stood quietly in a circle, to show our respect. My mother recalled the following days: "Men and women who for eight years had not dared to speak their thoughts now talked openly with their friends. . . . People hung over their radios and rushed to their neighbors to repeat the latest news. In the streets and cafés there was laughter and joking." My parents congratulated themselves for having survived the worst.

BUT IN BUDAPEST, Rakosi was still in office and still dangerous. Having given up on the Danube sailor, my father was still working "the Frenchman."

On April 2, 1953, O'Regan again wrote Starzel a note, which he asked "be destroyed." Fortunately, Starzel did not honor that request.

The invitation to the World Peace Council in Budapest certainly compli-cates matters . . . and seems likely to fall about the same time as certain interested parties hope to get Marton out.

As far as Marton is concerned, I believe we should protect his position as long as he is there. I think it is important to maintain that we regard Marton as our Budapest correspondent and that we would only send a second man if Marton wants help. . . .

Marton called me apparently quite by chance last night. (He called to ask if I had received his letter for "medicine." I told him certain people are trying to get it for him. I was shocked to get such a transparent call.)

What Marton's escape would mean to the AP: . . . A story could be written from here saying he apparently has disappeared from Budapest and is assumed to have been arrested.

There remains the possibility that he may be arrested while attempting to break out.

It seems to me that no matter when he is arrested, he is going to be forced to make statements that he had contacts with U.S. and British embassy officials and that he sent letters relative to his escape to the AP and to me.

Personally, I wish he were happy where he is. But the repeated visitors I get and his phone calls make it seem he's scared to death and is praying that something will happen soon. In any case, I think he is safe until at least after the Peace Council meeting and perhaps even longer if the Com-mies are not to upset the propaganda they hope to get out of the Council meeting.

Meanwhile, the general manager of AP had also decided it wanted no part in our escape plans. General Manager Starzel instructed O'Regan, "Neither you nor any other representative of the Associated Press will participate in any activity which would be discreditable to this organization or place us in jeopardy in any manner whatsoever." Stalin might be gone but the machinery of terror, manned by thousands of agents and informers, was still in place. Nobody had instructed those dedicated workers to close their file on the Martons.

But on July 4, 1953, a deus ex machina intervened on our behalf. On that day, at a special parliamentary session, only four months after Stalin's death, Rakosi was dethroned. Stalin's "Best Hungarian Pupil" was forced to hand power to a moderate, reformist Communist, Imre Nagy. Records reveal that Rakosi had previously been summoned to the Kremlin and severely scolded for having lost the support of the Party and the people. Nagy accepted his new post with a promise of a new era of reform. He pledged to end forced industrialization and the collectivization of farms, and the deportation of "unreliable elements" to the countryside. He spoke of "Socialist Legality" and the need to review politically based arrests and convictions. Above all, he promised to do better than Rakosi—without ever naming him. But his much loathed predecessor did not retreat very far. He simply swapped chairs with Nagy, remaining the Party's first secretary, with Nagy as prime minister. Stalin's successors in the Kremlin, themselves jockeying for power, were still hedging their bets.

My parents covered this dramatic change of course for Hungary, and for their own fortunes. "Out in the corridors [of Parliament]," my mother recalled, "men and women swept through, Communists and non-Communists embracing each other. Pressed against the wall, Andrew and I were congratulated by newsmen and politicians who for years had not dared speak to us. 'You were right!' they cried, grabbing our hands. 'Now you are safe. Your worries are over!' I saw Nagy in the corridor. I went up to him. 'Congratulations!' I said with feeling. . . . He shook his head and peered at me anxiously from behind his glasses. 'Please,' he pleaded, 'don't make it bigger than it is.'"

My parents then rushed over to Rakosi, accompanied only by two bodyguards. Seeing them, he stopped in his tracks. "I accepted his fat, outstretched hand," my mother remembered. "'How are you?' I asked him. 'Not a thing wrong with me!' he answered with a jaunty laugh, and vanished down the marble stairs."

The traditional Fourth of July celebration at Ambassador Ravndal's had a very special quality that evening. My parents felt that with

Rakosi's demise, they were celebrating their own liberation. It would turn out to be nothing but a stay of execution.

For one of Rakosi's victims, my parents' colleague Jeno Szatmary, it was too late. On November 26, 1953, Szatmary's widow telephoned my father. Amid sobs, graphically captured by the AVO wiretap transcript, the widow told my father that her husband died in prison on April 6. "How?" my father asks, "and where?" "They aren't telling me anything," the widow replies, still sobbing. "Only where they dumped his body. Oh my God!" she wails. "I am going to kill myself. I cannot bear any more of this. I could bear it before because I thought I would see him again. I was living for him and now it is all over. What should I do? What should I do?"

"They don't give the cause of death?" my father asks.

"The cause of death?" the widow asks. "The cause of death was that they killed him! He was their prisoner for a year, and has been dead for six months, and now they inform me of that fact. I can't bear any more," she cries.

"You have to calm yourself," my father says.

"I need to ask you a favor," she replies. "You have a car?"

"Yes."

"On Sunday," she continues, "will you take me to the cemetery and help me find his grave?"

"Yes, of course," my father replies.

So my father and the widow of the man whose testimony formed the basis of the charges against my parents spent that Sunday searching for Szatmary's grave. No legacy could make a child prouder than this small fact, buried and almost lost in the thousands of pages from the AVO.

Imre Nagy may have hoped to usher in a new era of Socialism with a Human Face, but Rakosi's henchmen were still running the AVO. On February 5, 1954, the AVO once again requested permission from the minister of the interior "to arrest and turn the American legation's most active agent, Endre Marton . . . whom we have on several prior occasions requested permission to take into protective custody, but were denied permission to do so. . . . Marton continues to maintain close personal relations with the American ambassador Ravndal."

Inside the Kremlin, the power struggle among Stalin's heirs continued to rage. Its outcome would shape the course of the Cold War. As it went on, my father provided his enemies with ammunition.

On July 14, 1954, while sitting in the elaborately frescoed grand chamber of the Parliament, my father tore a piece of paper from his notebook, wrote on it, "See if you can get me a copy of the annual budget for this year," and passed it to "Andrassi." The agent had been waiting for many years for such a note, for it had been announced that *this year*—with the economy a shambles—the budget would not be distributed to the press. Journalists could look at it inside the Parliament, but not take it with them. When "Andrassi" informed my father of this, my father, who generally treated his "colleague" with contempt, replied, "Well, if they don't distribute them, I'll just have to steal one." And, with that, he strolled by a table piled high with the annual budgets for official distribution. Picking one up, he casually tucked it under his arm and hurried out of the Parliament.

The American legation on Freedom Square is a few minutes from the Parliament. As he walked the short distance, my father was followed. Waved through by the Marines, my father took the special elevator to the ambassador's second floor corner office. Here, he had always felt on secure ground. Sure, there were microphones all over the place, spotted and removed by regular security sweeps. But microphones cannot pick up dates and names on documents, and everyone in the ambassador's office knew not to utter anything sensitive out loud. Economic attaché Tom Rogers was present when my father arrived with the budget. "He let me take a look at it for a routine report to the State Department about prices and productivity and so on. I asked him if we could keep it for a few days. He agreed to let us have it." Rogers did return the budget after a few days and my father filed his own story about it, a story that was of very little interest to his American readers. But Rogers had also sent a copy of the budget to Washington, via the secure diplomatic pouch. Or so he assumed.

Reading this, I am shocked by my father's irresponsible behavior. Though he did not consider "lifting" the budget theft, it was at the very least a provocative act. By turning it over to the Americans, Papa was handing his enemies the weapon they had been waiting for. It was an act of reckless bravado for which his whole family paid a price.

Finally the AVO had a concrete charge against my father: "stealing" a government document and passing it to the enemy. But what my parents did not suspect until much later was that it was neither our treacherous French governess nor "Andrassi" who provided the most damaging "evidence" against them, but an American who had become an AVO agent.

Richard J. Glaspell had been awarded the Bronze Star for his service in the Pacific theater during World War II. A U.S. Army chief warrant officer, Glaspell was born in Cleveland, Ohio, on August 9, 1918, and arrived in Budapest in November 1952. Glaspell, whose Army enlistment record lists his profession as "decorator/window dresser," was accompanied by his wife, Mimi, son, Gregory, and daughter, Claudia. I do not know when exactly the AVO began to blackmail Warrant Officer Glaspell; the Army buries such embarrassing incidents, and nonfamily members are limited in what they are allowed to access in military personnel records. Glaspell's own children, neither of them alive, never discovered exactly what happened to their father in Budapest.

But it is a fact that Glaspell was booted out of the Army and never received another assignment, nor a pension. That much, the family's sole survivor, their daughter-in-law, Conchita Glaspell, told me. What his wife, Mimi, also deceased, knew, I have been unable to find. Only Gregory's widow and their son are alive, and they were unaware of the reason for Glaspell's sad downward spiral. All they knew is that Budapest was where he had been happiest, and where his professional life ended. "He lost the confidence of his superiors," his daughter-in-law, who is a high school psychologist, told me in 2008. "He returned early from Budapest, and they had no other assignment for him."

It must have broken my father's heart that it was an American who provided the key evidence against him. Papa is deliberately vague in his memoir. "The story is almost always the same," my father wrote. "The foreigner has an affair with a local woman who is either on the payroll of the secret police or was pressed into serving it. Then they are photographed in bed, through a one-way mirror, *as happened in the case of the man who betrayed me* [emphasis added], and the foreigner is blackmailed. . . . The picture would not be complete," my father concluded his painful subject, "without adding that the man who played this despicable role in my case was neither a foreign service officer nor a local Hungarian employee of the legation in Budapest."

My parents had dinner with Glaspell's boss, military attaché Harry C. Fields, the evening of my father's arrest. Perhaps that is why it went off so smoothly. Though my father only learned Glaspell's identity once we were safely out of Hungary, he did share it with his closest American friend, Tom Rogers. "Yes," Rogers confirmed to me in 2008, "Glaspell turned a report I had sent to the State Department over to the AVO. It included a copy of the Hungarian budget for 1954 which your father provided us." That "stolen" budget, and some other items only someone with access to the legation's inner sanctum would have known about, provided the core of the case against my parents.

Ernest Nagy, who also learned of Glaspell's treachery from my father, said that during the Cold War all diplomatic personnel were trained to deal with the threat of blackmail. "I was involved in a similar case a few years before Glaspell," he recalled. "A legation Foreign Service secretary became romantically involved with a Hungarian doctor. In due course, the AVO confronted her with incriminating photos and sought to blackmail her into an espionage relationship. She went directly to Chris Ravndal and told him the whole story. The next morning, Ravndal had me—as the most junior officer there—drive her out of the country. Through prearrangement, I handed her over to people from our Vienna embassy at the frontier. The girl had a complete Foreign Service career and retired honorably. The story is to the credit of Chris Ravndal. He created a climate of trust within the legation, enabling the girl to come to him this way." But Richard Glaspell chose a different route, and thereby provided Washington's Cold War foe that most prized asset: penetration of the Enemy's inner sanctum.

But here I must interject my own reaction to my father's behavior, the details of which I am learning for the first time. Papa may not have known about Glaspell but he knew he was under surveillance. Sharing a restricted document with the Americans was an act that exceeds a reporter's responsibility and, especially from the perspective of the Cold War, could be interpreted as espionage. Papa paid a huge price for his reckless arrogance.

With a growing file of incriminating evidence against my parents, the AVO waited for permission to arrest them. The capstone to the year that had swept both Stalin and Rakosi from power was a telegram from Frank Starzel, general manager of the Associated Press: "Warmest Christmas Greetings to you and yours and my deepest appreciation for consistently excellent performance during past year despite multiple pressures. . . . Best wishes for much happiness in the New Year and full measure of professional success."

Chapter 6

REPRIEVE

Our last day as a family before my parents' arrest was spent trying out our new skis, atop a Buda hill.

I REMEMBER THE TIME between Stalin's death in 1953 and my parents' arrest in 1955 as a happy time. I thought there was less tension at home and in our little world of school and friends. I didn't like Madame any better, nor her partner in infamy, our concierge, Mrs. Priegle. Raw-boned and with a look of permanent reproach for the bad hand life had dealt her, when she arrived each morning to clean and gather my parents' used coffee grounds to reuse for her own cup, I avoided her. But most of the adults in our world seemed more relaxed. They laughed more and whispered less. More Hungarians came to our home now. And, to my mother's absolute delight, my grandparents suddenly received their emigration permits. My parents started sprucing up our apartment. According to the AVO files, Madame and Mrs. Priegle reported that this was "cover" for our imminent plan to flee.

But the reality was more complicated. That year a foursome was formed whose importance in my parents' lives was not apparent to me until decades later. This was a friendship with the British economic attaché, Gerald Simpson, and his wife, Peggy. I remember finding Mrs. Simpson rather frosty and beautiful, in a pale, English rose way. She was strikingly different from my witty and temperamental mother. My father once mentioned that Peggy had driven an ambulance during World War II, which I found surprising from such a seemingly prim lady. The Simpsons had a daughter, Toni, who was as beautiful as her mother and just as intimidating.

Some years after our family had safely reached America, when I was about thirteen, I learned some shocking news. The source was my mother, the subject was her marriage. My father, she told me, had had a romantic involvement with Mrs. Simpson in Budapest, and it had almost ended my parents' marriage. In her own memoir she wrote about how she discovered it.

"It was at the queen's birthday party," my mother recalled, "at the British legation. The guests moved about the garden, sipping champagne, chatting. . . . As I stood in a group, I could see Andrew [Papa] and [Peggy] talking together a few paces away. What they were saying, I did not hear, but Andrew reached out and brushed an insect from her shoulder and at the touch of his hand, she blushed. I stared, astonished at her confusion, and I knew the truth: she was in love."

The first time I felt that there was something amiss between my parents was during the summer of 1954, when we had accompanied my grandparents to the train station, to begin their long journey to

Australia. It was obvious that my father was pained by this parting from his parents. I held his hand after we waved the Vienna-bound train goodbye, but my mother walked coldly and silently beside him. Why doesn't she comfort him? I wondered. As it turns out, she was seething with anger, so much so that my grandparents almost canceled their long-awaited trip.

"My father-in-law has sensed my estrangement from Andrew," Mama wrote. "How could one keep a secret in that overcrowded flat? He said to me in a faltering voice, as if even now he would change his plans and stay behind if necessary, 'Ilona, there is something wrong with you and Bandi [my father's nickname].' He thought I had fallen in love with someone. 'Dear, it's not me, but your son.' His face brightened with relief. 'Well, then,' he said, 'everything will be all right. Bandi will come back. Be kind to him.' What does it matter if he comes back? I wanted to ask him. I don't want him anymore. He's broken my heart."

After my grandparents left, our family went for the last time to a summer vacation on Lake Balaton. We stayed at the Sport Hotel on the water in Tihany and I spent much of my time paddling around on an inner tube in the lake. Juli and I spent more time with my father than with my mother, sailing and swimming. Later, my mother told me she had found a love letter my father had written Peggy Simpson. The letter started, "After four days I am still thinking only of you. Each night I swim out in the lake, hoping somewhere in the middle I shall find you." My mother laughed bitterly at this detail, as my father hated cold water and would never have gone swimming at night. But the worst treachery of all, for my mother, was that he quoted a line from one of her favorite poems, "Cynara," by Ernest Dowson, "I have been faithful to thee, Cynara! in my fashion . . ."

When she confronted him, my father begged forgiveness, promised to break with Mrs. Simpson (who was due to return to London at summer's end anyway), and tore up the letter in front of my mother. "But I retrieved every piece from the wastebasket," she wrote with typical drama, "and put every little piece away to keep forever. . . . I would never forgive him, never trust him again." (Ironically, the secret police put an end to this ridiculous bit of masochism on my mother's part. During their house search, they came across the scraps and took them away for later examination. An unintended favor to all of us.)

My parents left us briefly with a friend at the Balaton and they returned for the Americans' Fourth of July celebration at the legation. There, my mother confronted Mrs. Simpson. I can picture this moment: the melodramatic, outraged Hungarian, aglow with anger, and the cool, reserved Englishwoman, meeting on the fringes of the lush lawn, with all eyes pretending not to be transfixed. Peggy confessed to my mother that she was in love with my father, but had no intention of marrying him. "I already have a husband," she coolly informed my mother. "Then, what about me?" my mother asked. "Well," Mrs. Simpson answered, "you've had ten years with Andrew. Surely, that is happiness enough." My mother repeated these lines to me often as I was growing up, perhaps to inoculate me against male deceit, or possibly to dampen my hero-worshipping of my father. She failed on both counts. But they are engraved on my memory.

In due course, the Simpsons left Budapest. My parents never heard from them again. I always think of them as a dashing, beautiful, and dangerous pair, a sort of Daisy and Tom Buchanan, who left broken crockery in their careless wake. "Goodbye and good luck," were Peggy Simpson's parting words to my mother. My mother never did get over her bruised *amour propre*.

While my parents were living out their domestic drama in Budapest, my sister, Juli, and I were often left in the care of a friend and bridge partner of theirs, Lajos Csery. Tall, athletic, handsome, and in his early thirties, Lajos was a dream baby-sitter. He seemed more like a big child than an adult, and played games with us that our parents would never stoop to (I recall a game he called *Panzerfaust,* where he played a German bazooka and we were enemy targets). In his tennis whites, with long, tan legs, hypnotic blue eyes, and perfectly chiseled features, he was beautiful. As the tension between my parents became more obvious, Lajos became a more important presence in our lives. Sometimes he came along when we were just with our mother. We adored him.

I read now in the AVO files that so hurt was my mother by my father's romance that she wrote her former fiancée, a doctor now living in Sydney, Australia, asking him to forgive her for rejecting him for my father, "a stranger with whom I have spent eleven unhappy years." The AVO must have particularly savored this bit of correspondence, for on the back of the envelope one agent scribbled, "Looks like the shit has hit the fan in the Marton family regarding Mrs. Simpson!"

In the hothouse world of the Budapest diplomatic community, word spread of the Simpson-Marton relationship. "The only thing that really surprised me," Tom Rogers noted, "was when I heard about your mother finding the letter to Peggy Simpson. Your father was such a careful man. It just didn't make sense." My mother punished my father by spending more and more time with Lajos. Perhaps with their most dangerous enemies—Stalin and Rakosi—seemingly defeated, they could indulge their private passions, bottled up during more dangerous times.

All summer, my father continued to woo my mother, to try to coax her out of her cold, punishing reserve. One letter in the files reduces me to tears and to shame. "Dearest Darling, Wife of all Wives!" he wrote to my mother in English, always their private code, during one of their separations of the summer. "Though I decided not to bother you during this brief week, I was so touched by your note which I found Sunday night in my bed. . . . The kids have been angels, helping in every respect, especially Kati. Julika is doing the flowers every morning, giving fresh water and imitating you. . . . How are you? I hope everything is all right and if you have time, please don't forget that I am bored to death without you, and I need and want you." On the margins of this note, an agent had scribbled, "The reformed sinner!"

The AVO took no vacation from its surveillance. Summarizing my father's solitary time on the Balaton, following our departure for school in September, they noted that he "spent most afternoons in the company of Mrs. Endre Kabos,★ with whom he made daily excursions to various places of amusement, cafés, restaurants, the beach. We noticed that in front of other guests at the Sport Hotel, they were very reserved. Outside the hotel, the couple's behavior was quite different, for example they walked arm in arm and sit very close together and engage in intimate conversation." There are pages and pages of detail regarding where they dined, what they consumed (my father, whom I had never known to touch beer, drank beer with her), and even the speed of his car. "When Mrs. Marton and their two little girls reappeared," the agent concluded, "Mrs. Kabos disappeared."

Should I be shocked as I read the surveillance records of that summer and fall of 1954? On the contrary, I am relieved that my father managed to store up some good memories for the long nights to come, the relaxed hours he was able to spend with this lady, described by the watchers as "between 25–30, blond wavy hair, and of medium height," whose usual costume by the lake consisted of "green shorts, white shirt, and white tennis shoes," and with whom my extremely reserved father walked arm in arm and "engaged in intimate conversation while drinking beer, wine, and cognac." This is a side of my father I never saw.

I am strangely moved by the AVO's description of my father in their September 30, 1954, surveillance report: "Based on external surveillance we can say that he is a calm, determined, polite person. . . . He is a strong swimmer, likes women, and is a passionate pipe smoker." (How I miss the rich smell of his pipe tobacco. When I catch a whiff of it now on a city street, I follow it blindly.)

★ Endre Kabos, a friend of my father's, was a triple gold medal–winning Olympic fencer who was killed during a bridge explosion while serving in a forced labor brigade in Budapest in 1944.

Papa was worried that he was under surveillance. "When he first gets in his car," the AVO reports, "he looks around to make sure no one is following him. Then he usually drives around the corner, makes a loop, before he heads off. Sometimes, he parks in front of the market, on the corner of Csaba and Maros Utca, gets out, looks around before he gets back in his car. When the weather is clear, he keeps the roof of his convertible down, so he is able to observe anybody following him. Despite the fact that he has two telephone lines in his apartment, Marton frequently makes calls from public phone booths." If he thought these modest precautions foiled their efforts, my father grossly underrated the AVO.

Under the heading "Family Relations," the agents had this to report about my father in September 1954: "His bourgeois origins are reflected in his family life. His relations with his wife seem superficial, as he is frequently in the company of other women. This is in great contrast to his relations with his children, to whom he is obviously very attached. This is demonstrated by his frequent stops to buy them candy and other treats. When he walks with them in the city, he always holds their hands. When his wife and children rejoined him at the Balaton, he hugged and kissed both his daughters."

How lucky we were—to be oblivious to the twin struggles swirling around us: our parents' complicated marital strife, and the life-and-death struggle for power between their old nemesis, Matyas Rakosi, and the man who replaced him, Imre Nagy.

EVEN KINDERGARTNERS were expected to celebrate the tenth anniversary of our "Liberation" by the Red Army, on December 21, 1954. For an all-school assembly, we had to memorize poems, and rehearse songs of gratitude to the Soviet Fatherland. My parents were invited to a special festive session of Parliament in Debrecen, a historic northeastern city where Louis Kossuth had proclaimed Hungary's independence from another army of occupation, the Habsburgs, a hundred years earlier. My father related his memory of a day that would change our lives.

"We [foreign correspondents] were but a handful and were carefully isolated in a passenger car reserved for us. . . . The atmosphere was relaxed, it was a festive occasion, and no one expected more than a color story to come out of it. How wrong we were. . . . Rakosi was the keynote speaker . . . in the centuries old Calvinist Church. . . . It was a vicious, mean, belligerent speech and the legislators listened like a flock of frightened sheep."* The brief period of reform was over.

At the end of the session, there was an official reception at Debrecen's historic Bika Hotel, to which all reporters were invited. Imre Nagy, now all but officially a dead man walking, was absent. My mother and father approached the triumphant Rakosi, as he was leaving the festivities. Seeing them, Rakosi's usual mask of bonhomie slipped. He cut them off before they could even speak. "Why should I talk to you?" His jaw jutting in defiance, he snarled, "You won't write the truth anyway." My father maintained his composure, but my mother froze. She had never seen an expression of such loathing. At that moment, my parents understood that the reformer Imre Nagy would not be the only casualty of the resurgence of Stalinist stooge Matyas Rakosi.

WE HAD a wonderful Christmas that year. Maybe the best ever. My parents' friends and colleagues in Vienna, London, and New York must also have realized what Rakosi's return to power meant to us personally. Perhaps that accounts for the generous bounty my sister and I found under the tree that year. I dictated a letter to my grandparents in Melbourne, which my father typed. "We had a big Christmas! This is what I got: Austrian skis, real ski boots, a kind of doll with real hair

---

* This and other quotes from my father—except as noted—are from his prison memoir, *The Forbidden Sky* (Boston: Little, Brown, 1971).

that I can comb, and so many, many other things that if I were to list them it would take all night." By way of family news, I provided these details: "Juli is letting her hair grow. It's so long that Papa can't stand it, and told her she had to braid it, so Mama braided it and tied it with two red ribbons. It looks very good on her but she cries when Mama combs it. I will pray for you tonight. Kati."

My parents attended a New Year's Eve party hosted by the Ravndals—a gala affair in an old palace—and danced until four in the morning. Afterward, they went to a nightclub and then to the French ambassador's residence down the street from our home for breakfast. In a good mood after their revels, they started for home just as first light was breaking. "As we crept over the icy pavement," my mother wrote in her unpublished memoir, "with the morning sun glistening over the snow-covered streets, holding hands to keep from slipping, it seemed to me that we had really started off the New Year right and it was a wonderful feeling after all the years of fear. As we came to the stairs leading up to our apartment, we saw an old woman lying on the ice. We rushed to her and picked her up. In tears, she said that her family had warned her not to go out on such an icy day, but that she felt she had to get to early Mass. . . . Andrew brought the car around, lifted her into it, and drove her home. When he came back, I greeted him happily. 'How lucky to start the New Year with a good deed. Maybe now the whole year will be good!'"

The snow just kept falling that winter, which suited my sister and me just fine: snow days at school and a chance for our father to give us ski lessons on our new Austrian skis. But Papa knew he was living on borrowed time, that Mama's New Year's hopes were unjustified. In February, our governess told the AVO that he "has been much more careful and suspicious of [Madame]. For example, on a recent evening the Martons left for the evening but half an hour later Marton returned unexpectedly and looked carefully around the apartment. Lately when [Madame] gets up early in the morning Marton follows her into the kitchen and wants to know what she is doing there. She's overheard him say that he'd really like to get rid of her. These are new signs of suspicion on his part which [Madame] attributes to the fact that at the end of January two agents [of the secret police] met with [Madame] in the apartment of Mrs. Priegle [the concierge] and was seen by the Martons' maid, who no doubt told them about it."

If my parents fired Madame, the secret police would be losing their most reliable agent. But there was always Richard Glaspell, the legation insider who was feeding the AVO incriminating information. The assistant military attaché had informed them not only of the "loan" of the 1954 budget, but had added that my father had frequently provided the legation political advice. (Such as Papa's suggestion to the ambassador that Washington should send a "Negro diplomat" to Budapest to counter Communist propaganda about American racism.)

On February 18, the agents charged with my father's case announced they had finished reading all eight volumes of the Marton file. They drafted a scenario for my father's interrogation. It began with a bold statement:

> *Marton is a skilled spy, with a bourgeois education and a great deal of experience, who has conducted hostile activity since Liberation. He despises the People's Republic of Hungary—its people and politics.*
> *. . . We plan to achieve three goals during the first interrogation:*
>
> 1. *Study Endre Marton's character, resistance, and behavior.*
> 2. *Establish his close relationship with the Anglo-Saxons since the Horthy regime.*
> 3. *Get a clear image of the Hungarians he contacted and continues to contact in carrying out his espionage.*

"The interrogation," the memo's author, Captain Zoltan Babics, concluded, "will proceed in a polite manner, which will only change if Marton is provocative and insolent." In order to tie my father's case directly to the Americans, they planned to simultaneously arrest an employee of the legation, a translator named Bela Kapotsy. A bit player thrown into the production for good measure.

Yet, almost until the last, the AVO's first goal was to turn the "skilled spy" into a double agent. "If he is willing to talk," a memo dated February 10, 1955, reads, "we will recruit and release him."

Chapter 7

THE END OF
CHILDHOOD

My sister, Julia, and me in our apartment in Budapest,
with "Morzsi," who followed me home one evening in
the months before our parents' arrest.

Fᴇʙʀᴜᴀʀʏ 25, 1955. The overhead light in the room I shared
with my older sister snapped on. My mother, a ghostly figure, hovered
over our beds. "Children," she whispered. I lifted my head for an instant, before dropping back on my pillow. "You have to get up. They
need to search your room." Her voice, urgent and weary, was about

to break. *"Now."* I could just about see who "they" were: shadowy figures, five or six of them, forming a dark mass in the corner. Behind them, with their arms folded, stood Madame and Mrs. Priegle, "witnesses," required by law for such operations.

"Get into our bed," my mother said. As we slowly awoke, one of the searchers moved in. Like a hunter stalking big game, he sank his knife into our beat-up stuffed rocking horse. Straw spilled out of my oldest possession, as my sister and I ran to the room next door, and dove into our parents' bed. We were too dazed to ask where Papa was. Or did we know somehow? *"Elvitték,"* Hungarian for "They took him away," was a word I often heard as a child. I did not understand where people were taken *to,* just that they were gone, and not much more was said. So now my father had been *elvitték,* taken away.

Of the few hours left of that awful night, I don't recall much more. My sister and I must have slept through the rest of the search. But I have been told so often what happened from 2 A.M. until daylight that I feel as if I witnessed both my father's "abduction" and my mother's ordeal. Tales of how the AVO ripped apart our home, looking for "evidence" against my parents, were part of my childhood. But only now, thanks to the files, am I able to reconstruct the day and the night that ended the idyllic part of my childhood.

It kept snowing hard. I remember that school was closed. We had fun that day—which would be our last as a family for some time. My parents took us up to one of Buda's many hills to try out our first pair of skis, our prize Christmas gifts. Here is how the agents following us recorded that day, in minute detail:

At 11:10 Marcine [code for Mama], wearing a ski cap and a brown sheepskin jacket, black ski pants, holding a shopping basket, accompanied by her younger daughter, left their home and walked down Csaba Utca to the market where they spent approx. one minute. They then went to the other market at the corner of Maros Ut. where they spent 10 minutes before returning to their apartment.

At 12:20 [my mother] dressed as earlier, accompanied by her husband and two children came out of their house and headed for the nearby garage where they got into their car, with [my father] behind the wheel, and at a speed approx. 50–60 km an hour drove to the Normafa tourist hotel where they all got out of the car, and strapped on their skis. While they skied, we ceased surveillance.

At 14:25 all of them returned to the car and removed their skis, then got in the car and followed the same route back to their apartment.

At 16:00 we ceased surveillance.

How I would have loved it if those AVO agents had included a few details regarding my first ski lesson from my father.

The next day we were back in school. According to the file, my father spent a part of the afternoon in a struggle to get chains on the tires of the Studebaker.

At 7:30 P.M. my parents drove to the apartment building of the U.S. military attaché, Harry Fields, and his wife, Louise, on the Pest side of the Danube for dinner and a bridge match, their favorite game. It was after 2 A.M. when they left the Americans, got in their car, and negotiated the silent, snow-blanketed streets of the city, up to our hilltop home. Later, my mother told me they had been in a mellow mood. Alone in that car that always gave them the illusion of freedom, they probably savored another triumph at the bridge table. The garage where we kept the car was half a block downhill from our building. After parking, my father carried a bucket of ashes to sprinkle on the icy pavement. Papa was coming around to help my mother out of the car when the dark, silent street suddenly came alive with shadowy figures. On each side of my father, and behind him, dark-suited AVO agents closed in on him. Two of them gripped his arms above the elbows and led him toward their own car. Dazed from this scene out of a bad dream, my father thrust the bucket of ashes at my mother, "as though it were our most prized possession," she later said. "But aren't you even going to kiss me?" she cried. His arms no longer free, he leaned toward her and kissed her cheek. Then they shoved him in the back seat. With its headlights off and the engine's sound muffled by the fresh snow, the AVO car rolled silently down Csaba Utca.

Of these details I knew nothing yet. But I had never seen my mother as determined, as much in control, as she was the next day. "You must rest, madame," our nanny urged her, when, at dawn, the five searchers, carrying five suitcases of "suspicious" material, finally left. Piles of books and American magazines, back issues of *Life* (one with Grace Kelly on the cover) and *National Geographic,* were strewn in heaps in their wake. One of the searchers, my mother later told us, had taken his time perusing these forbidden pieces of Western "propaganda," taking his ease in my father's favorite armchair. While the others meticulously shook each book for "secret documents," this agent slowly turned the pages of *Life* and closely examined the lavish layout on the new princess of Monaco, commenting with a sneer, "She's not even that good-looking." Our rocking horse was not the only casualty of their knives. Several old chairs and pillows suffered the same fate. Our formerly beautiful apartment looked like a war zone.

Now it was just the three of us. Mama kept us home from school the day after Papa's arrest. She knew that "they" would come back for her, but not when. She also assumed they would not arrest her in front of her children. Arrests were meant to proceed quietly, with a minimum of fuss. She needed us as much as we needed her. Holding hands we set forth, determined to find out what happened to the man all three of us called Papa. While my eyes said, *Stay with me,* I commanded my mother, *"Szoritsd!"* or "Tighter," as in, Hold my hand tighter. For the rest of her life, that word was code between us for love and fear of separation.

Chapter 8

THE PRISONER

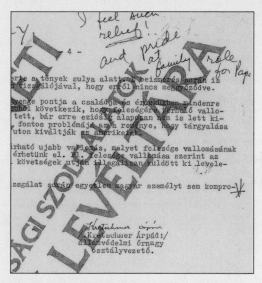

This is the document confirming that my father did not incriminate a single Hungarian during his brutal interrogation. I scribbled my reaction on top when I found it.

Mʏ ꜰᴀᴛʜᴇʀ ɴᴇᴠᴇʀ described what went through his mind when they handcuffed him and shoved him into the back of a black Mercedes—not in his memoirs, not to his children. Wedged between two uniformed agents of the country's most dreaded organization, I assume he rode in silence to the Fo Utca prison. He would not give them the satisfaction of asking questions they would not answer. It was a fifteen-minute drive from our hilltop house to the fortress that had long awaited him, but the psychological distance between freedom and prison is impossible for a nonprisoner to fathom. I have ridden the route, unfettered, in an effort to put myself in Papa's shoes, but it doesn't work—the journey is an interior one.

Even under the Nazis and their local Arrow Cross thugs my father had not experienced this degree of helplessness. Then he had managed to bolt from his forced labor brigade on two occasions, hiding in a drain pipe until he could run for safe haven. Now, jammed between two blue-uniformed, sullen secret police agents, he could not even think of escape.

The brutal swiftness, as well as the precision of his arrest—almost balletic in its choreography—is striking. In an instant a man was separated from his life and his family, with barely a sound uttered. The AVO had waited years for this moment. They were not about to make any mistakes now. Contrary to their custom, they did not ring our doorbell. (There was even an expression in Hungarian for that fear of the midnight doorbell: *csengofrasz*.) They did not allow the prisoner a chance to grab a warm sweater or sensible shoes, or hug his children. A few steps from the garage to our house, in the predawn hours, unseen, unheard, and it was their moment to strike. They wanted a few uninterrupted days before the world—particularly America—noticed. Hence Friday, the start of the American weekend. With Marton's friend, Ambassador Christian Ravndal, back in Washington for consultations, precious time would be gained—time enough perhaps to break and turn the prisoner.

But things did not pan out quite as planned. Overzealous about obeying regulations, an AVO agent stamped our garage door with the Ministry of the Interior's red seal, alerting everyone to what had happened. Moreover, Don Downs, the American political attaché, and our next-door neighbor, saw the arrest. He had just let his German shepherd, Duke, out for a late run in his garden. He remembered every detail more than fifty years later. "I observed cars with their headlights turned off slowly drive up Csaba Utca," he told me in 2007. "The trap was set. I went inside to a room upstairs from where I could see the whole thing. I saw them surround your father. Four or five other agents led your mother into your house. Then, the lights went on in your living room and I could see them ripping the place apart. I sent a cable off that night to Washington describing the whole situation."

My father's arrest affected the American legation dramatically; it was back to the siege mentality of the Stalin era. "From our intelligence sources," a secret Hungarian Ministry of the Interior/Counterintelligence Section memo dated February 28, 1955, noted, "[CIA station chief] Geza Katona, in a confidential briefing of personnel, said that Marton's arrest is no doubt the result of a high-level political decision, since the Hungarian government must know that such a move will create a strong reaction in the West and will damage Hungarian interests. As a result of the arrest, the legation will impose enhanced security measures on all personnel. As an example of the present anxious atmosphere in the legation, when chargé d'affaires Spencer Barnes, who has only recently arrived in Hungary, walked to attaché Don Downs's residence, and when Downs learned he'd come alone and on foot, he became very agitated and reminded him that from now on he must always use a car, as a security measure against abduction."

"EMPTY YOUR pockets!" When my father was stripped of all his possessions (watch, cuff links, wallet, underwear, belt, and socks—all potential "weapons" of self-destruction) except his shirt, dark blue suit, and loafers, two uniformed jailers led him to his third floor cell, slammed the door behind him, and slid the long steel rod in place. Cell 208 was specially outfitted with the most up-to-date listening devices, reserved for a Very Important Prisoner.

Papa walked the five short steps from the door to the wall before collapsing on the wooden plank and its filthy blanket. A bright naked bulb that was never turned off shone overhead, and in the iron door he faced a square Judas, or spy hole, which the guards opened and shut noisily every few minutes.

Ten minutes later, his hands held behind his back by two guards, my father was hurried up silent staircases, through empty corridors, to a well-furnished interrogation room. In stark contrast to his cell and the corridors just traversed, here the lighting was low, all the chairs upholstered, except the suspect's, which was of hard wood and had no arms. The image has haunted me since I read his files: Papa, among the most dignified of human beings, on that hard chair surrounded by his enemies. "Mr. Marton!" Captain Zoltan Babics, in his early thirties, but already well known as one of the AVO's most skilled interrogators, greeted him. "I have waited a long time for this." Portraits of Stalin, Lenin, and Felix Dzerzhinsky, the NKVD/KGB's founder, stared down from the wall; a small bust of Rakosi stood on the captain's desk.

My father faced four of the AVO's most experienced officers. But the first session did not proceed according to the script. "He was careful and gave precise answers," Babics reported. "We could see he was determined to avoid every accusation. He insisted that he had always operated according to the rules of his profession as a journalist. . . . He asked us to tell him what he was being accused of and to ask him specific questions and he would do his best to answer them." An uncooperative prisoner who had the temerity to inquire what he was accused of. No quick confession was forthcoming.

"I was told the first night that I was a spy and a traitor," my father wrote in his memoir, "and that my profession as a newspaperman was only a flimsy cover for my real occupation. I was supposed to furnish them with the evidence."

It was first light outside when they had finished and returned Papa to his cell, where it was dark and cold. "I was shivering. I took off my shoes and lay on the bunk, pulling the smelly blanket over my head to escape the light of the naked bulb, which burned day and night above the door. Instantly the door opened and an old guard entered, explaining in a whisper that I must lie on my back with my hands above the blanket, so that he could see my face and hands through the peephole."

He was, in fact, not alone. He had a cell mate, Sandor Fulop. Of course Fulop was reporting to the AVO. He related that the new inmate spent the first few nights wide awake, but had trouble staying awake (as required by prison rules) during the day. "He does not eat properly," Fulop wrote, "and complains of a nervous stomach. . . . Despite my attempt to draw him into conversation, he is silent. Several times he falls asleep as I question him." Fulop offered my father his sweater, which Papa accepted and immediately put on. (How cold he must have been in that cell, for my fastidious father's automatic response to almost anything ever offered was to decline it politely.)

Oddly, my father barely mentions his cell mates in his prison memoirs. Yet he had a string of them and they played an important role in his incarceration. Not just Fulop, but all of them were informers. One of them tried to lead my father to the gallows. Though his cell was equipped with listening devices, these cell mates were supposed to help the AVO get a confession out of my father and prepare him for a show trial. For their effort they were rewarded with better food (which they had to consume while my father was out of the cell) and ten extra cigarettes a day. If they really performed well, their sentences were cut short. Did Papa suspect this additional treachery, atop other betrayals by friends, foes, and country? I will never know the answer to that; in his lifetime I did not know about his cell mates. Perhaps, as reserved as he was, he just needed to talk to someone who wasn't barking in his ear that he was a liar and a traitor, or to keep his hands outside his blanket. I suspect any human contact was better than none.

Captain Babics and his chief aide, Captain Bela Balazsi ("a former butcher, rude and pompous, a short bundle of muscles," in my father's description), worked on breaking down my father's resistance, rather than on extracting a "confession," which, in the normal course of things, they would compose anyway. On February 28, for example, Balazsi interrogated my father for six hours on his reports on Hungary's bauxite production. "Balazsi," my father recalled, "together with another of his men, an extremely rude major, found special satisfaction in ordering me to stand face to the wall while shouting obscenities into my ears."

When I think of Papa, so courtly and polite to all visitors in his normal life, subjected to the disgusting treatment of these thugs, it still makes me feel ill. I know he resisted them, but what was the effect of this treatment on him? Did it change him forever?

Almost all my father's answers to questions were followed by "You are lying!" or "You are trying to mislead us!" At the bottom of each page of the interrogation records is his familiar signature, "Dr. Endre Marton." That was the law: the prisoner testified orally and an agent took notes in longhand. The typed testimony was ready the next morning for the prisoner to read and sign. "The testimonies, so called," my father noted later, "rarely reflected the prisoner's thoughts, nor even his words. At the beginning I protested against this practice, declined to sign one testimony after the other, and was sometimes permitted to make minor changes. Later, however, I lost interest. The whole thing became a Grand Guignol, terror mixed with comedy. What I had actually said bore no relation to the contents of the pile of papers neatly typed and prepared for my signature." With the passage of weeks and months my father's steady hand gets shakier, and sometimes he no longer bothered with "Dr."

The first of March was a dark day for my father. "Today is his elder daughter's birthday," his cell mate/informer reported, "and the fact that he can't be with her is very upsetting to him. His mood is very depressed, he sees his case as hopeless. He has no appetite, says he is too nervous to eat, and sleeps only three or four hours at night."

Exhausted and increasingly convinced that the charges against him were deadly serious, my father decided on a gamble. In a letter he submitted on March 3, 1955, to Captain Babics and addressed to the Ministry of the Interior, Chief of Investigations, he wrote, "I have committed no crime against my homeland. However, despite my innocence, I now acknowledge that my whole lifestyle was anachronistic and thus had to be eliminated." He now did something quite astonishing for a man with no outside contacts, a man entirely at the mercy of the State. "As I am of no use to my homeland in the present, and as I am finished as a foreign correspondent here, I propose that the Associated Press pay a certain amount—a few thousand dollars—for my freedom and that [in exchange for my freedom] I give you all my possessions, my car, my apartment and its contents. My family and I would be satisfied with a few items of clothing." Surely, he noted, "I am of no use to my country as a convict, with all the attendant bad publicity my case would generate." He concluded with what sounds to me like a sardonic closing note: "As I am the last remaining foreign correspondent in Hungary, my case cannot be used as a warning to others. There are no others left. . . . I would like to spare my country as well as myself from this trial, which, whether open or held in secret, cannot help our nation's image."

What did Papa expect the reaction would be to this letter? His captors had all the power; he was alone and isolated. They were sadistic; how they must have hated their high-value prisoner. I am unclear as to what Papa thought the reply would be—he never told us of the letter and does not mention it in his memoirs. But the reaction was predictably fierce, since Papa's offer was clearly impossible. "Insolent and insubordinate!" the minister of the interior wrote in the margin of my father's letter, in a large, angry hand. "How could you even accept such a letter from the prisoner?" he demanded of Babics and Balazsi. Such arrogance had to be punished, the prisoner more thoroughly humbled. In a fury, Balazsi ordered my father dispatched to the "black room," a windowless, pitch black hole, without even a bed, just some straw to sleep on. (Balazsi must have enjoyed giving this order, as Papa's cell mate had just reported that my father considered his interrogator "a crude peasant, without any education or culture.")

They now denied my father even his usual grim menu of fake coffee (routinely laced with a sedative) and bread for breakfast, and cabbage with the occasional bit of sausage for dinner. When, some time later, he was led back to his former cell, his cell mate reported, "The punishment failed to have the desired effect. Apart from the cold, he said he didn't mind being alone. The straw was more comfortable than this cot, he said, and no one bothered him at night to keep his hand above the blanket."

The interrogators were losing patience as the mysterious May deadline they referred to approached. A silent observer joined the sessions, sitting in the back of the interrogation room. "The single glaring light," my father recalled, "was turned toward my face, so that I could hardly see the other man, who was completely shrouded in darkness. . . . Only much later, after my release, did I find out that the silent man in the corner was a Colonel Ivancov, the 'special envoy' of Moscow's secret police, sent to Budapest to stage the planned show trial of the Martons."

Yet, after nearly seven weeks of brutal interrogation combined with sleep deprivation, my father still denied he was an American spy, recruited by Christian Ravndal. He was supposed to provide the details of how this was done and what secrets he leaked. After nearly two months, my father had not done so.

On March 7, however, during the course of an interrogation, Papa made a shocking discovery. "From the many folders in his safe," my father wrote later, "Babics produced a sheet of paper. 'On June 16, 1954,' he said, 'the legation sent a report to Washington. It was signed, in the minister's absence, by the chargé—Lafoon—and the political officer—Rogers—submitting your recommendation. You still pretend not to know what advice you gave?'" My father could not recall what advice he had given on that day, but he was stunned by the AVO's penetration of the legation's inner sanctum. "No microphone could have supplied that information," he wrote. "I decided that if I ever came out alive, and my chances then were rather slim, the legation must investigate this possible leak."

Nearly two years later he learned the identity of the American traitor. By then the U.S. Army had spirited Assistant Military Atta-ché Richard Glaspell out of Hungary and drummed him out of the service. Though his treachery ended Glaspell's Army career, he was spared the humiliation of public exposure and lived out his life in suburban Washington, his betrayal of his country apparently unknown to his family.

TWO YEARS after Stalin's death, Hungary was in the era of "Socialist Legality"; the AVO could no longer extract confessions from prison-ers simply by beating them to a bloody pulp. In my father's case, the AVO correctly identified cutting him off from any news of his wife and children as the weapon that would be most effective in breaking him. On March 15, Papa told his cell mate how desperate he was for news about his parents and us. His father's birthday was that week, and he wondered if his parents were even aware of his arrest. "I don't think my nerves can take this for much longer," he told his cell mate, who promptly reported that fact to his interrogators. "They told me that they had to translate into Hungarian all my English language dispatches," my father grimly noted three days later. "This will never end!"

"At that point," the cell mate reported, "he dropped on his cot and broke into sobs. . . . Completely broken, he continued sobbing for fifteen minutes."

By the time I read this interrogation report, my father had been dead for two years. But a comment about Rachmaninoff's Second Piano Concerto, a piece we both loved, comes back to me with a new meaning. "To me," Papa once said, "it's the sound of a man weeping." At the time, I wondered, how does he, who never weeps, know this; now I think I know what he meant.

Broken and despairing, Papa still had not signed a confession by April. The AVO decided it was time to change their dramatis personae.

A new, far more subtle, vastly more dangerous cell mate was intro-duced into cell 208. "Ferenc Krassoi" is how he introduced himself to my father, though the AVO files identify him as Mihaly Balogh. By now my father was an easier mark than he had been two months earlier. Desperate and punished for his "insolent" offer, he was out of ideas. Babics continued to threaten that they would arrest my mother if he did not confess to being an American spy. "Krassoi" was full of ideas. First, he gained my father's trust by dropping mutual friends' names. He played the role the AVO assigned him skillfully: as a pardoned political prisoner who would be free in a matter of days. Happy to carry a letter to your wife, he offered. To the American ambassador, too! My father was sorely tempted, but concerned about implicating his cell mate. They are sure to search you thoroughly, he told "Krassoi." What if they find the letter on you? You could land right back here, he warned. (After so many betrayals, he still trusted, he still worried about others.) But "Krassoi" was ready for that. I have a full pack of cigarettes, we won't smoke for the next few days, so they won't be suspicious when I carry out a nearly full pack. You can write your messages on cigarette paper, which we will refill with tobacco. "Krassoi" was an expert.

Playing on Papa's agony about the possibility of my mother's arrest, the skilled agent convinced Papa to confess to save Mama. And so, after two months of interrogation and psychological pressure, my father confessed to being an American agent. But he was still careful in whom he implicated and whom he spared, as he wrote a fictional litany of American espionage. He claimed that press attaché Patrick O'Sheel had been "his closest spying partner," knowing that O'Sheel had long since left Budapest. His "*least* significant contact," he told the AVO, was Ambassador Ravndal.

"My great advantage," Papa's new cell mate reported, "is that I have a personal connection to Dr. Marton, a fact he can use to persuade his wife and Ravndal to trust me. I can prove my familiarity with Marton, how he grips his cigarette in his mouth, what sort of cigarettes he prefers, and so on, to gain their trust."

With the AVO directing this cruel play-within-a-play, the cell mate

was provided the props to set the trap. On tiny scraps of cigarette paper, using the broken stub of a pencil, "smuggled" in by his cell mate,
my father poured his heart into a love letter to my mother. And there
it was more than fifty years later, in the AVO files, where it fell one
day, in 2007, into my lap.

"Sweetheart" (he used the Hungarian *Tunderkem,* which literally
means "my little fairy"),

> *I miss you horribly and am worried sick about you. Under no circumstances*
> *should you ever set foot in this place! Do everything in your own and the*
> *children's interest, as I have explained by messenger, and only then think*
> *about me. I know you are doing everything on my behalf. Forgive me for*
> *the stupid way I said goodbye. There was no time. . . .*
>
> *I love you more than ever, but that should not sway your decision and*
> *please forgive my stubborn stupidity in assuming we would be spared.*
> *Only you three matter. I don't. The children should forget me!*
>
> *I did everything to clear you and told them you were only my puppet.*
>
> *With eternal love,*
>
> *Endre*

Then, with his tiny pencil stub on those flimsy bits of cigarette
paper, he instructed my mother on exactly how to save our family:

> *Sell the car, sell all our property, redeem my life insurance, deposit my clothes*
> *at [he gave a friend's name], then ask for political asylum for yourself and the*
> *children. Start with the Americans, and if they won't, then go to the British,*
> *Swiss, Swedish, or any other Western embassy. Your only goal must be to*
> *leave with the children! Only then will I breathe again. [Mathew] Crosse*
> *[a Labour member of Parliament my parents met during their 1948 Lon-*
> *don trip and who apparently had fallen in love with my mother] should*
> *come and marry you. Or, if a pro forma marriage is more suitable, some-*
> *one—a guard?—who could get you out through the embassy. Don't waste*
> *any time! Your responsibility for the children and for yourself is to leave me.*

*I'm convinced that you could not survive the torment of arrest and prison.
You do not have the right to put the children's lives at risk!*

Once you are safe, you can do the following for me:

The AP should make a great fuss. They should keep my story alive.

*The AP can take measures at the Hungarian embassy in Washington
for a prisoner exchange in my case. I already made an offer here. I offered
the apartment, the car, and a thousand dollars from us. They said that after
my trial they would discuss it. There is some, but very little hope that they
will. The AP should feel some responsibility. . . .*

*If they arrest you, tell them everything, and accuse me and the American
legation.*

*My friend [his cell mate] should meet Ravndal in your presence, but not
with any other diplomats, except perhaps Don [Downs].*

As I read it today, my father's letter is from a man at the edge of a
precipice, who is willing to forsake the thing he values most: his family.
More than anything else in these files, more than the dogged surveillance, the treachery of so many informers, the ridiculous charges of
treason, it is my father's cry of despair that makes me despise "Them."
A system, Communism, that set out to remold human beings into
more perfect creatures, which ended up twisting them into this: a
man proving his love and selflessness by urging his wife and children
to leave and forget him.

Equally desperate is my father's letter to Ravndal, also written on
tiny scraps of cigarette paper:

*Today, after seven weeks, I confessed my guilt as a spy for the U.S. since
1945. They accuse Ilona of the same crime. The source for this tragedy is
inside the legation. The AVO know the contents of your diplomatic pouch.
One example of this is the main charge against me: that Rogers photo-
copied the 1954 budget and sent it to Washington on June 16, signed by
Lafoon and Rogers. There are other signs of penetration which I can only
reveal to you directly. . . . The AVO doesn't deny that a security breach*

inside the legation enabled them to charge us. They have chosen you as the main spy. You are their target.

The same fate awaits Ilona, also because of the legation [security breach]. Your human responsibility is to save her and the children, and then do everything to free me. . . . They regard me as the most important American agent. . . . Against gangsters only gangster measures work. The best way would be to arrest a Hungarian in Washington, who is not a diplomat, but who has a family, and exchange them with us.

A deadly danger threatens Ilona and me. The time has come for the U.S. to show her power.

Every day counts. I have struggled for ten years for the U.S. and still hope the U.S. will save me.

SOS

Andrew

To have written this risky SOS to Ravndal is the sign of a drowning man. There is no mention of these two letters in his own published memoirs, although my mother refers to them in her unpublished journal. She was shocked when he told her. How could he have been so trusting of his cell mate, she wondered. Painful though it is to read this, what it reveals about my father—his character and his love for us—is a priceless gift.

Papa's two letters did not travel further than the desk of Captain Babics—who presumably dreamed up the whole scheme. Babics now thought he had enough to convict my father of espionage, and expected a long sentence, perhaps even his execution. But first he needed my mother in custody.

Chapter 9

THE THREE OF US

My mother, sister, and I formed a tight bond after my father's arrest. But four months later, they came for her as well.

Papa's arrest transformed Mama. I had never seen her as determined as she was during the four months between his arrest and her own. Perhaps because she had lost her primary audience, my father, she also lost her dramatic personality. She had two small children who were now utterly dependent on her alone—and a very shaky sense of her own future. Vanished was the self-indulgence I associated with her, cooking only when she felt like it, letting my father organize our lives and file her reports for the UP. Now, the woman who only recently had been furious with her husband for the incident with Mrs. Simpson, focused all her energy on saving him and protecting us. Her entire life until that moment—a life of loss and survival—had prepared her for this.

She was born into a prosperous merchant family in the northern industrial city of Miskolc. Her father had a weakness for cards, which ultimately ruined them financially. "He came home one night when I was fourteen," she recalled, as if it had happened last night, not fifty, sixty, or seventy years earlier, "and presented my mother with an ebony-handled umbrella. He had just lost his money and his house in a game of cards. All of it. Gone. With his last pocketful of change he bought my mother the umbrella to cheer her up."

Horse-drawn wagons soon pulled up in front of their house to claim the family's valuables. They moved out of their house and into an apartment in town, and my mother, still in high school, started tutoring younger students to help support the family. At eighteen, she went off to Debrecen's Calvinist University, her tuition and board paid for by the sale of the remnants of their former wealth; their piano, silver, and carpets bought her an education. Penniless, but armed with a Ph.D. in history at twenty-two, she married Sandor Brody, a wealthy, much older local landowner. Brody set her up as the chatelaine of his vast properties and showed her the great cities of Europe. But without love she was miserable, and within three years she left him. Penniless once more, she set off for Budapest.

A year later, she met and fell in love with my father. Their love affair, and the marriage that soon followed, took place just as SS Obersturmbannführer Adolf Eichmann and his Judenkommando arrived in Budapest. As their romance progressed, Hungary was living through one of the worst periods in its thousand-year history. Eichmann's fast-moving transports picked up her parents immediately, and they disappeared into the death camp at Auschwitz. My mother in faraway Budapest could do nothing to save them. For the rest of her life, she buried her grief, and tried to bury their memory. She almost never spoke of them, and in our home there were no reminders of their ever having existed—not a single photograph nor memento.

My mother, the survivor, had survived the Nazi and Arrow Cross terror, became a wife and a mother and a foreign correspondent. Now, everything was on the line again, and she would fight to save her husband, and protect herself and her children. She knew the odds were against her, and ultimately she failed, but in the effort, she was magnificent.

During the months after my father's arrest, when it was just the three of us, we spent more time with our mother than ever before or after. When she could take us with her, she did. I remember when we called on her oldest childhood friend from Miskolc. Ilonka Heller was married to a prominent engineer and inventor, sufficiently valued by the authorities to merit a villa on the Hill of Roses. Ilonka, always beautifully dressed, smelled wonderful. Coming from the same home-town, she sounded like our mother and shared her passions for bridge, swimming in the Lukacs baths, and gossiping at the Café Gerbeaud. It seemed natural that she would be our "caretaker," if the need arose. Not that we believed anybody could actually take our mother away from us. But Ilonka hugged and kissed us and assured my mother she had nothing to worry about. She loved us and with no children of their own, the Hellers promised my mother they would take us in "if . . ."

"Tighter," as in, Hold my hand tighter, was my routine command to my mother that spring. Since my father's arrest nothing seemed the same. For the first time since I started school, I was not counting the days until summer vacation.

Together we marched down Csaba Utca to the post office where Mama made her phone calls. (She did not trust our house phone.) Her first call the day after my father's arrest had been to the only person who had given her his name during the long night's search, Captain Zsigmond Feher, of the Budapest Police Department. Or so he had led my mother to believe. In reality, of course, Feher was a captain in the AVO.

The transcript of this phone conversation is just the first installment of the cruel game of cat-and-mouse the authorities began to play with my mother.

> Mrs. Marton: *I'd like to speak with Zsigmond Feher.*
> X: *What division?*
> M: *Well, I think this is it.*
> X: *I haven't heard of him in the Budapest HQ.*
> M: *But he is in the main division of the Budapest police.*
> X: *This is the main division but there is no Feher.*
> M: *But I have his name right here, signed by the Budapest HQ.*
> X: *I never heard of him. No such person here.*
> M: *He was at my home, on a house search, and he signed the report.*
> X: *And his rank?*
> M: *Lieutenant.*
> X: *Then it's not Zsigmond.*
> M: *But it is printed right here. He also signed it.*
> M: *Hello? Hello?*

My mother now inherited the full complement of our father's shadows. On March 1, they reported on her persistent attempt to find someone who could tell her what happened to her husband. She clung to the faint hope that it was a police matter (the searchers had mentioned unpaid customs on some imported tires). The other possibility, that he had fallen into the AVO's black hole, was too terrifying for her to consider, she wrote later, even though it was rather obvious.

> *At 9:50 she took bus #39 to the Foreign Ministry [my poor mother must have missed our beautiful Studebaker, now locked in the AVO sealed garage]*
> *At 11:07 she caught #6 streetcar and got off at the National Police HQ building*

At 11:31 she went into a bakery and bought two brioches which she consumed while waiting for the #12 bus

At 12:46 she entered the Ministry of the Interior on Roosevelt Square

At 13:10 she returned to the National Police headquarters.

For her shadows, "hearts grown brutal" in W. B. Yeats's powerful phrase, in pursuit of their ghastly work, there was no difference between her desperate call to the Ministry of the Interior and her "consuming" two brioches while waiting for the #12 bus.

They were toying with her. But she was determined not to follow the example of the former silent film star (and wife of their colleague Jeno Szatmary) who called all her friends for help when they dragged her husband from his bed at midnight and who, as a result, was deported to an internment camp somewhere in the countryside. My mother would not provoke the AVO. She did not even tell the AP what happened to "Andrew." "I remember," my father's AP colleague Dick O'Regan told me in 2008, "calling him and your mother answered, and she said he was in the hospital."

On March 2, my mother wrote a letter to the minister of the interior, Laszlo Piros, politely requesting his advice as to what she should tell my father's employers, and how to answer a growing number of questions from foreign journalists. She also requests the minister's advice as to whether she should continue to work for her agency, and accept the AP's request that she cover for her "absent" husband. "Our work has not always been easy," she wrote the minister, "but both of us have always been mindful of our responsibility as Hungarian citizens that we would do nothing to harm our country's interest. I would like to continue to work in this vein. I would like to avoid doing anything to harm my country or, for that matter, prejudice the case against my husband. So I must tell you that the present situation, with me having disconnected the telephone to avoid answering questions about my husband's situation, is not a very practical solution and will only lead to further wild rumors about him. . . . I am turning to you, sir, for your kind advice as to how I should handle this situation."

In its own way, the government's response was as repellent as its treatment of Papa. My mother was practicing unusual self-control by not reporting my father's arrest, not turning to the AP or to the American legation. She was behaving the way they always had, "as if . . ." Hungary were a normal country of laws and citizens' rights. Meanwhile, she kept pushing for information from the government about Papa.

Six weeks after my mother's plea for official guidance, the AVO came up with a cruel set of "guidelines." On April 29, in a secret directive, AVO officer Jozsef Turcsan summarized my mother's campaign to learn what happened to her husband. His tone is that of an important official annoyed by a meddling housewife. Turcsan complains about my mother's daily calls to the Ministry of Foreign Affairs, her engaging a lawyer to establish her husband's whereabouts, her attempt to nail down the charges against him, her query as to whether she should continue working for the United Press, and whether she should tell her husband's employers that he has been arrested. She even had the temerity to request visiting her husband, wherever he may be!

The Ministry of the Interior replied with a sinister passive aggressiveness. Do what you think best, these are matters of individual judgment. When may I come back for more information? "Well, it's hard to say, but try again in two weeks."

"She returned exactly two weeks to the day and I told her we had no answers yet," Turcsan noted.

Frustrated and anxious, my mother decided to contact the Americans. "If [she receives] no reply by March 9," reads a secret telegram from the Budapest legation to Secretary of State Dulles,

Mrs. Marton hopes the case can be fully aired in the Western press as the last possible means of bringing pressure to bear on the government. She expressed her personal conviction that no action will be taken against her. She will risk that eventuality for the sake of her

husband *[emphasis added]. . . . Press handling should be carefully tuned. As opener, we would suggest a telephone inquiry to Legation from the AP, based on the inability of AP to contact Mrs. Marton. We would answer that many reports are circulating to the effect that Marton disappeared around February 25, but we know nothing of the circumstances or his present whereabouts. . . . This would be the opening wedge and continued badgering by AP should probably provide essentials for playing case by ear thereafter. . . . Central issue . . . should be fact that* one of two remaining Western press representatives in Hungary has disappeared suddenly without explanation *[emphasis added], once again giving proof to the free world that things have not changed behind the Iron Curtain and especially in Hungary, where fear of free exchange of information still exists and terror based on arbitrary police action continues to reign supreme.*

With Ambassador Ravndal in Washington on home leave, Dulles no doubt had already been primed on the significance of American engagement in my father's arrest. The day after this telegram to Dulles, Starzel, the AP's general manager (who had been reluctant to subsidize our high-risk escape two years earlier), wrote to his Vienna bureau chief, Dick O'Regan. "State Department suggested that I telephone Dr. [Endre] Sik, Hungarian Deputy Foreign Minister, and ask his assistance in obtaining information about Marton. I placed a call and after repeated delays, was advised that a connection could be made at 4 a.m. the next day. At that time I was informed that Dr. Sik 'was traveling' and the date of his return was indefinite. I sent him a message on March 12 expressing concern over our inability to communicate with Marton and asking his assistance."

By the end of April, two months after the arrest of their correspondent, the AP took a harder line. "We have refrained from disclosing for publication such information as we have been able to obtain about Dr. Marton," Starzel cabled Sik, "because we have confidently expected that either the charges would be duly announced by your Government or that he would be cleared of any culpability. . . . In addition to desiring to learn the nature of the charges against our correspondent, I would like to be advised as to the provision for legal defense for him and other pertinent factors."

A week later, without waiting for an answer, the AP again toughened its tone: "We are deeply concerned about Dr. Marton's case because he has not been permitted to communicate with us as his employer. We have been unable to learn the reason for his arrest . . . nor whether he has been able to obtain adequate counsel or legal assistance. . . . Dr. Marton's detention deprives us of his services. This results in a serious loss to our news report. Budapest has been an effective point for an interchange of dependable, objective information. . . . While Mrs. Marton endeavors to act in behalf of her husband, she is understandably preoccupied with other matters and is not in a position to serve us adequately."

I AM IMPRESSED that my mother continued to cover soccer matches, and even the Davis Cup, for two American wire services under these circumstances, and was present for the opening session of the Hungarian Parliament. These, too, are things I did not know while she was still alive.

Our truest friend during these four months, when so many people shunned us, was Lajos, our sometime baby-sitter of the summer before. He was now our constant companion. Our governess reported to the AVO on March 4 that "Csery Lajos is a conspicuous presence at their home. Csery's mother has warned him that he should break with the Martons, as he could get in trouble himself. Csery answered that he was friends with them before they got in trouble and was not going to abandon them now."

Madame filed daily progress reports on my mother's relationship with Lajos. "They went to the movies together. Sunday afternoon they were entirely alone in the apartment. Mrs. Marton is alone with him almost every day and it's likely that their relationship is deeper than merely sexual. In my opinion," Madame ventured, "the relation-ship between Mrs. Marton and Lajos Csery could be exploited."

The AVO agreed. Lajos was eventually summoned and interro-gated. "You know," the agents told him, "while you and Mrs. Marton are having your little tryst, the Americans are choosing bombing targets for the coming war." Did they really *believe* these things, I asked Lajos in 2007, as we sat in a café in Budapest's Gellert Hotel. He was in his eighties and still handsome. "They had to believe them. Otherwise how could they justify what they were doing to people?" In his straightforward way, Lajos told the AVO—and now told me—how his relationship with my mother evolved: "During the summer of 1954," he said, "Marton and his wife had a falling-out which resulted in the two of us spending more and more time together. Marton had fallen in love with a Mrs. Simpson, the wife of a British diplomat. Mrs. Marton and I drew closer, and eventu-ally fell in love around August 1954. We continued to see each other until her arrest."

The AVO ordered Lajos to continue seeing the people he had met through the Martons and to report to the secret police about those meetings. "You know," Lajos told them, "I'm really clumsy at these things. I'm a very poor liar and I don't think I would make a good agent for you." With that, somewhat inexplicably, he says the AVO let him go. He never heard from them again.

As THE weeks since my father's arrest passed, my mother grew more confident. Perhaps they would not come back for her after all. She put away the pleated Scottish tartan skirt she had picked out as her "prison uniform." Using her recent accreditation to serve as both AP's and UP's correspondent, she made more frequent calls on the American legation, calls that provoked the following secret cable from Washington to the American legation, on April 27, 1955: "Legation's comments requested on possibility Mrs. Marton acting under police compulsion to implicate Legation." Cold War suspicion was not restricted to one side of the divide.

Ravndal had no such concern regarding my mother. "Mrs. Marton reported this morning," he cabled Washington on May 3, "that her husband will be brought to trial charged with conspiracy and/or espionage. . . . Appears worst fears . . . may come to pass. . . . Such a trial now could be timed to coincide with the conclusion of Eastern Bloc defense agreements in Warsaw with the aim of proving the existence of a US directed conspiratorial organization of such scope that Hungarian request for Soviet assistance in form of maintenance of Soviet troops . . ."

Ravndal maintained steady—and sometimes creative—pressure on the Hungarians to release Papa, or at least news of him. On May 7, he reported to Washington, "Conversation [with the deputy foreign minister] . . . led naturally into Marton case . . . believe AP should continue to demonstrate its interest in Marton by pursuing direct inquiries at the Foreign Office. Recommend that action to blow up case in press be held in abeyance pending signal from Legation."

Partially declassified State Department files reveal heavy cable traffic from Ravndal spurring both Washington and the AP into action. In early May, every major Western news organ carried this long-delayed report of my father's arrest:"The Associated Press has received information indicating that its resident correspondent in Budapest, Dr. Endre Marton, has been arrested by the Hungarian secret police. Communication from Marton . . . ceased late in February. . . . Efforts to learn the nature of the charges against Marton have been unavailing. The Foreign Ministry has not responded to several letters and messages in the past two months. Marton, 44, is a Hungarian national. He was educated in England and holds a doctorate in Economics from Budapest University. He is married and has two children. Marton's by-line became well known in Western newspapers through his coverage of the Cardinal Mindszenty trial in 1949 and other outstanding events."

On June 9, in another secret cable, Ravndal suggests linking my father's case to Hungary's desire to host the 1960 Olympics. Ravndal proposed that the State Department plant a question regarding Papa at the upcoming press conference of Avery Brundage, the head of the International Olympic Committee: "[I]n connection with Hungary's Olympic games pretensions, a widely circulated Hungarian sport sheet printed article May 17 marshalling claims for selection of [Budapest] as games site and (probably inadvertently) quotes Marton on the same subject . . . to the effect that awarding games to Budapest is 'only decision this little sports loving country would consider sportsmanlike.' Marton arrested by authorities of 'this little sports loving country' and no one yet informed of reason or his whereabouts. Suggest you inform Brundage of this incident as further background material."

"Strong impression gained," Ravndal wrote Washington, following a May 20 call on the Hungarian Foreign Ministry, "that AP's needling has been effective that the Foreign Office is attempting to use the Legation in an effort to have 'the dogs called off' and that the Foreign Office concerned re possible implications of publicity. Believe AP should continue its needling of Foreign Office."

DURING those spring months we formed a tight little trio. Mama did not socialize much. There was one notable exception—kept alive over the years as one of her prized anecdotes: her triumph at the British mission's birthday party in honor of Her Majesty the Queen. My mother looked so glamorous in a wide-brimmed hat and a fitted gray silk suit that I assumed Queen Elizabeth herself would be in attendance. But afterward she regaled us with the details. "I arrived late, deliberately," she said, green eyes flashing, "to make a grand entrance. The embassy garden with its spiral marble stairs is suitable for such an entrance. The ambassador [George Labouchère] mounted the stairs to greet me. Together, we slowly descended the white marble steps. After kissing my hand he handed me off to Ravndal, who led me down toward the diplomats and officials gathered on the lawn. As we passed [Erno] Gero [Rakosi's number two] and Endre Sik [the deputy foreign minister], Ravndal mischievously said to them, 'You have to come fishing with me sometime in America. I hope the Martons will be there too.'"

Later that month, Mama was invited to Ravndal's residence for dinner. All of us kids in the house gathered around the huge, shiny black ambassadorial limousine he sent to pick up my mother. She later said how much fun it was to see the AVO follow car try to keep up with the speeding limousine. Ravndal himself escorted my mother home. "When the chauffeur opened the door," my mother recalled, "Ravndal stepped out and ostentatiously kissed my hand. 'I hope my shadow saw you,' I whispered to Ravndal."

I'm doing this for Papa, she told us the next day, reading our thoughts as to how she could be parading around in her finery while our father languished who knew where. But her triumph was brief. A week or so later, the AVO arrested my father's former secretary, our friend Marika Hallosy, who had been recruited as an "informer" years before. My mother's determined good cheer was suddenly deflated, like air out of a balloon.

On May 3, Madame reported that she overheard Mama on the phone receive the news that "Her husband is accused of serious political crimes and will receive a very severe sentence. She seemed very shaken and asked whoever was calling to come over right away. . . . She later said that everything she had been told at the Ministry of the Interior had been a lie. Since receiving the above news she has been extraordinarily agitated, more frightened now than when her husband was arrested."

My mother was preparing for prison. But how does one do that? As with a fatal illness, I suppose, you make arrangements for your loved ones.

Sometime in early June, my mother took my sister and me on a yellow tram to the end of the line, to a place on the outskirts of the city called Adyliget. There was a summer camp for children there,

My mother—some months prior to her June 1955 arrest—giving me a knowing look. I am wearing an American T-shirt, a hand-me-down from a U.S. diplomat's child, which made me stand out in school.

My father as a young dandy. Budapest was still an open, prosperous, and tolerant society for a few more years after World War I, and the Martons were part of its thriving upper middle class.

My father in a characteristic pose—
always elegant—in the late 1940s.

My father beams at his first born
daughter, my sister, Julia, in 1947.

Mama in her tennis clothes in the late 1940s. She was a strong tennis player—but brilliant at cards.

My sister, Julia, and I in the early 1950s, dressed, as always, in identical clothes, though we were very different.

After my father's arrest, I drew very close to my mother, who showed great courage during this terribly stressful time, awaiting her own arrest. This was taken by her friend Lajos.

My parents, my grandmother, and me at an excursion a few years before my grandparents emigrated to Australia. The man sitting somewhat behind my father, Laszlo Heller, and his wife, had promised to look after my sister and me if our parents were arrested. When the time came, they were too frightened to keep their promise.

My beloved grandfather, Nagypapa, and me at his farewell lunch in the summer of 1954, en route to Australia. I never saw him again—and never stopped missing him.

My sister, Juli, and me in front of the big, white American convertible we drove around in—and which was such a thorn in the eyes of the Communists. When they arrested our parents, they took the car too. Painted black, it was used by the State as an official car.

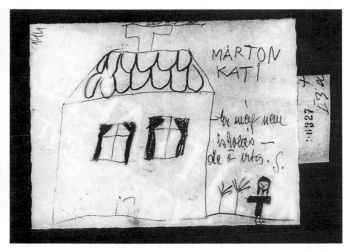

My art work and "signature," which I found in the AVO files. My grandmother had written, "She isn't even in school yet and she did this."

My mother (left), my Aunt Magda, Julia, and me at Lake Balaton in the mid 1950s.

My favorite summer pastime during our final family vacation at Lake Balaton. I was oblivious to my parents' marital problems and to the State's plans to arrest them.

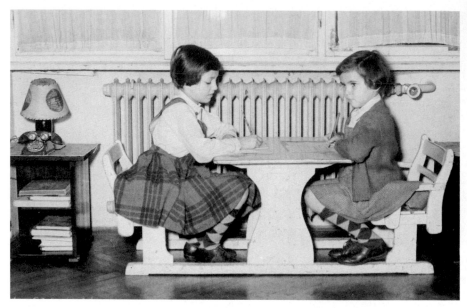

Juli and I doing homework in the room—and at the desk—we shared in our Csaba Utca apartment.

A 1954 dinner at Csaba Utca for various American foreign correspondents. My father is sitting on the floor, I am next to my mother, on the lap of an AP photographer. My grandparents are in the corner.

In 1995 Richard Holbrooke and I were married in the American Ambassador's residence in Budapest, where my family spent happy times in the 1950s.

My parents loved covering sports for their wire services—a break from the otherwise gloomy political news. Here, with the AP's Vienna Bureau Chief, Dick O'Regan, they covered the opening of the People's Stadium in 1953.

The most universally despised figure in Hungary: Communist Party Chief Matyas Rakosi, who loathed my parents and ordered their arrest. My father secretly photographed him with a hidden camera at a Party meeting in Debrecen in 1954.

Lajos, Juli, and Mama—the summer before my parents' arrest, when my parents' marriage nearly broke up—at the Balaton.

A posed photo with Juli and me doing our best to look happy, sent to our jailed parents in 1956.

This was taken the day Papa was suddenly released from prison in August 1956. He is back at his desk and wearing his favorite seersucker suit—but the dark circles under his eyes tell a different story.

Freedom fighters during the October 1956 Revolution, many of them teenagers, male and female, holding arms for the first time.

With our house in the background showing scars from mortar fire during the October Revolution, my sister and our playmate Sandor Liptay-Wagner drag our sled up the field during the uprising.

Soviet tanks in our neighborhood during the uprising. Schools were closed, and my sister and I were largely unsupervised by our busy parents covering "the story of [their] lives."

A Hungarian soldier observing Soviet tanks take Budapest in November 1956.

My parents—safe at last—in Washington, D.C., sometime in the 1970s. They had survived the Nazis and the Communists and they considered America the greatest country on earth.

My daughter, Lizzie, and I in Budapest in April 2008, on my final research trip, to meet "Flower."

and my mother wanted us to see it—and to like it. I hated it. It was a sleepaway camp, and, to me, used to summer vacations with my parents at the Balaton, there was nothing appealing about it. Strange children milled around in a dusty field, throwing balls over nets. I gripped my mother's hand tighter and smiled grimly. I could tell she was even less happy than I was, so I did not cry.

UNDER THE heading "Action to Be Taken," the AVO called for "Tighter security surrounding Mrs. Marton, and [Madame] is instructed to immediately notify us if she sees anything suspicious."

Later that week, Madame notified the AVO that my mother received a call from the post office inquiring about a malfunctioning telephone. "There is nothing wrong with the telephone," my mother answered. The post office insisted that there was, and that a repairman was en route to fix it. "The next day," Madame's report continued, "the phone was pulled out of the wall and I asked Mrs. Marton why. 'That phone is not to be used anymore,'" my mother told her. In the same report Madame noted that she had "asked the Marton children what was wrong with the phone and the children answered that their mother told them their phone was not only for speaking, but was also used for listening into their apartment. The children said that from now on their mother had been told by friends to whisper."

At the bottom of that report is this: "Notice: telephone listening device no longer functioning at Martons'."

On June 3, a secret Ministry of the Interior memorandum states that "Several of our agents ["Andrassi" and Madame] report that Mrs. Marton has been visibly nervous. She informed our agent [Madame] that she plans on visiting Bela Hallosy and that if no one is available to drive her home, she will spend the night there. Our agent was told not to call her at Hallosy's. Our agent believes that her real plan is not to visit Hallosy but to see her friend [Lajos] and that she is making plans to escape."

Reading this, I am struck by the AVO's delusional paranoia. How on earth would someone living inside a country that was itself a large prison, behind mined fields and barbed wire, stalked by secret police agents, whose phone was tapped, and whose inner circle were informing on her every move, *escape*?

A June 9 surveillance summary of my mother's activities reveals that she still kept up her dangerous bravado with "Andrassi," who reported that she planned to maintain contact with the American legation, "and if her husband is freed, says they will both do so." The AVO records that it has "documentation of her continued visits to the legation and that she participates in the weekly news conferences. . . . We also have information that she has made plans to send her children to a camp for the summer and that she is about to dismiss her household help [Madame], thereby leaving herself entirely free."

A June 10 memo entitled "In the Matter of Mrs. Endre Marton" concludes, "Our present case against Endre Marton is still fairly weak. To help us confirm his testimony and strengthen his confession [of spying], we request the immediate arrest of his wife, Mrs. Endre Marton, United Press correspondent, age forty-three, from a bourgeois background."

Chapter 10

A TERRIBLE SUMMER

My sister and I were unaware that our parents were
front-page news everywhere but in Hungary.

We were still a family—shrunken in size to three—when the Main
Division of Investigation of the Ministry of the Interior issued its "Plan for
the First Interrogation of Mrs. Endre Marton." It was dated June 20, 1955.

"Our goal," the memorandum explained,

*is to prove her and her husband's spying. Through this we can demonstrate
the destructive work of the American legation against our People's Republic.*

We have concrete evidence in the case of Marton and his wife: the budget, Marton's letters [to Ravndal and my mother]. . . . Because the case of Marton and his wife is time sensitive and we can expect the intervention of the U.S., it is imperative that we discuss Mrs. Marton's spying during the very first interview.

We shall discuss three questions during the first interview:

1. *Her biographical data, her friends, family, and past with a focus on her wealthy lifestyle, her marriage to a landowner, and her year spent studying in England.*
2. *Her connection with the Americans and her spying.*

   - *The people she has met since 1945 and what sort of connection she formed with them.*
   - *We shall observe the way she reacts to this question.*

3. *Proving her antidemocratic orientation.*

Here we will refer to her and her husband's derisive reports and her love of the Western way of life.

We shall maintain a polite tone with her and make it clear that her husband is cooperating with the investigation and that we are convinced that she was also an active spy.

Signed,
Major Tamas Gero

Three days later, in the late afternoon of June 23, our doorbell rang. Entirely absorbed in my long-awaited play date with Zsuzsi Kalmar, the older girl next door, I waited for my mother to answer it. Zsuzsi and I were cutting up an old dress of my mother's—a silky thing with giant green polka dots—which we planned to turn into doll clothes. It was not by chance that Zsuzsi had chosen that afternoon to visit me. We only learned much later that she had been enlisted to play a small part in my mother's arrest: keeping me occupied during its smooth execution. At the time, I was excited to have this serious older girl's company, and reluctant to get up and answer the door. After the second ring, I did. Three men in worker's overalls peered down at me. "We came about the meter," one of them lied. "Your mother had rung. Please get her." I had a feeling they weren't who they said they were. Even to a child's eyes, these men did not belong in those too clean overalls. But I was eager to return to Zsuzsi. Now, I wonder: what did it feel like for those secret policemen to be masquerading for a child? Did they feel anything at all? Were they fathers of little girls?

"Mama!" I called out. But by the time she emerged from behind her closed door, I had already returned to my room and to Zsuzsi. When, sometime later, the apartment seemed strangely quiet, I peered out. "Mama," I called. "Mama." No answer. The apartment was empty. I had never before been alone in a place that just months before housed three generations, my grandparents, my parents, and us children. I had never before noticed how the floorboards in the dark foyer creaked. As I rushed from room to empty room, I was aware of my heart, pumping, for the first time in my life. My mother was gone. How could she have left without calling out my name? Without kissing me?

Crying and calling out "Mama!" I ran down the three flights of stairs that led to the street. My sister was sitting on the curb, crying, her bicycle lying next to her. She had seen the men in overalls holding our mother above the elbows shove her into the back of a Mercedes. But the car had pulled away before my sister could get off her bike. So we sat there, the two of us, and waited. For the first time in our lives there was no one to comfort us. And I really have no memory of what happened next.

Even now, half a century later, I feel guilty about my mother's arrest. I had called out to her too casually, when her jailers came for her. I hurried back to Zsuzsi, when I should have made a fuss. I knew instinctively that those men with their expressionless faces hated a fuss.

DON DOWNS, our next-door neighbor, recalls more clearly than I do what happened to Juli and me. Fifty years later, he remembered still driving his Chevrolet up Csaba Utca and seeing my sister and me sitting on the curb. "Nobody was looking after you and you were crying," he remembered. "My first thought was to get you into the car with me, take you to the legation. I spoke no Hungarian, you spoke no English. But you would not move." I must have been in shock because even now the memory of that early summer afternoon of my childhood has a powerful physical effect on me.

Madame, who had been absent during my mother's arrest, finally arrived and—no doubt under instructions—called Aunt Magda, my mother's younger sister. The files report that an AVO Lieutenant Gyula Petrovics "Handed two Marton children to Mrs. Laszlo Pless [Magda]. We gave them 2,200 forints left by Mrs. Marton. Mrs. Pless will take care of the children during the day, and Gabriella Guillemet [Madame] will look after them at night." Lieutenant Petrovics included a receipt for both the money and for the children in the files. He lists twenty-five items taken from our home during the house search, items I suppose his comrades had missed earlier, when they arrested my father. Of this second search, I have no memory.

The idea of Aunt Magda taking care of us was either amusing or alarming, depending on one's point of view. This beautiful, flirtatious woman, with her saucer-size blue eyes, was almost comically unsuited to be anybody's mother or caretaker. She had no interest in being ours, but there was simply no one else available. (How often during that year I wished my grandparents had not left for Australia. How different things would have been for my sister and me.)

The next day, Magda finagled a ride in a nice AVO car (a Mercedes, I think) to the Hill of Roses villa where she and we hoped we might find shelter. (There was nothing that my aunt, with her blend of equal parts humor and sex appeal, could not accomplish if a man was somehow involved.) My mother's friends, the Hellers, lived there, and Ilonka Heller had promised my mother she would take us in, "if ever . . ." No doubt it was the sight of the AVO car and the uniformed agent who escorted us that turned the normally vivacious

Ilonka sheet white. I can still picture her round, panicked eyes as she surveyed the scene in front of her. To this day, I have never seen the face of terror more nakedly exposed. "Let me know where I can send the girls' things," she spluttered. "And you can drop their laundry off here, anytime," she offered, before hissing at Magda under her breath, "And don't ever come here in that car again." Ilonka did pay for our room and board with the strangers we were eventually placed with, though I don't think she ever came to visit us. Among my mother's first acts when she was freed was to pay off every penny she owed her oldest friend.

Many, many years later while signing copies of my latest book in a Philadelphia bookstore, a book is thrust before me. "I am the nephew of the people who looked after you," a well-dressed man says. I look up. "Ilonka and Laszlo Heller." I smile and nod and sign the book without comment. I am far enough along in my research to better understand the nature of fear, and to have no ill will toward those who succumbed to it.

That day, June 24, Downs sent Washington the following cable, marked "Secret": "Mrs. Marton believed arrested last night. Her apartment which adjacent to my house and on same level shuttered until 10 this morning when 2 men and woman with typewriter observed taking what appeared to be complete inventory of house. Visitors departed at 2 p.m. Mrs. Marton's sister, with whom she planned to leave 2 young daughters in event anything happened to her, seen with girls, but Mrs. Marton not in evidence."

With my mother's arrest, the American legation shifted to a tougher tone toward both Washington and the Hungarian government. The following day, June 25, Downs sent another cable: "Arrest of Mrs. Marton 6 p.m. June 23 confirmed. Information suggests she will appear as witness in the trial of her husband which reports indicate will occur within next two days. Whether she will be charged is moot point, but today's communiqué strongly suggests she will be. Today's development would appear to negate completely theory that use of tact or the avoidance of provocation on our part

is going to have any effect on the ultimate outcome of this affair.
. . . Whether recent general terror tactics and actions aimed against
this Legation are internally or externally motivated and inspired, it
is clear that this policy is increasingly at variance with surface international developments of past months. . . . We should now go all
out and seize publicity offensive . . . to hit Hungarian pretensions to
eligibility for UN membership."

The following morning, the Hungarian state news service, MTI,
announced, in reference to my parents, that "State Defense Organs of
the Ministry of the Interior have detained American spies and sabo-
teurs . . . recruited and trained for subversive activities against the
Hungarian People's Republic by the American spy organization, CIA,
and so-called Radio Free Europe, an Imperialist propaganda and spy
organization."

The Western press now had a bigger story: the human drama of
a husband-and-wife "spy team," their small children left alone. The
State Department tried to control the news, but did not always succeed. "Vienna Reuter quotes reliable Budapest sources on arrest of
Mrs. Marton," reads a cable from the U.S. embassy in Vienna addressed
to the secretary of state, dated June 29, 1955. "Reuter has been requested [by the embassy] to withhold the news, but has already filed.
Also, New York Times has also filed the story. . . . Timely advice might
permit guidance of all Western news agency reports for maximum effect on Hungarian Government."

On July 9, the AP carried the following story, picked up by newspapers around the world: "The Hungarian government today confirmed reports that Endre Marton and his wife, both correspondents
for American news services, had been arrested on charges of spying
for U.S. Intelligence. Marton had been Budapest correspondent for
the Associated Press since 1947. Mrs. Marton had been correspondent
for the United Press, since about the same length of time. Both are
Hungarian nationals. The announcement said two other Hungarian
nationals, employees of the American Legation in Budapest, also had

been arrested on the same charge. Marton, 44, apparently had been arrested last February. The Associated Press had been unable to reach him by normal telephone or telegraph channels since that time. The last telephone call from Vienna to Mrs. Marton in Budapest was on June 18."

Though my sister and I were oblivious to the deadly serious charges against our parents, we were miserable enough. In a bizarre twist, we were driven to summer camp by the agent who had helped "unmask" our "saboteur" parents. As I recall, Attila ("Andrassi's" real name) had a shiny face, a year-round tan, and was a flashy dresser. Since I had heard my parents refer to him in the most dismissive way, I was confused as to why he was performing this service. My mother's prison memoir explains. "It was generally accepted that [Attila Ajtonyi] was a police informer. I was not sure and I did not really care. When [my husband] was arrested and our car confiscated, the young man, who had a car, offered his services as a 'good colleague' to take me anywhere I wanted. To everyone's embarrassment, I accepted his services. 'Don't you realize he is doing it only to report everything you do?' I was asked. 'Of course I do. But why take a cab or walk miles when he has a car? What can he report? That I covered the session of Parliament? Or the basketball world championship? Let him report what he likes. For me the main thing is that I can get to places easily.'"

Again, my parents underestimated the damage a shard of "evidence" could do in building the mosaic of their "treachery." What for my mother was an innocent quip, for the State was another instance of my mother's hostility toward the "People." Compliments of "Andrassi."

The children's camp at Adyliget looked even bleaker now than when we had visited with my mother a few weeks earlier. I had never felt so exposed in my life. I assumed everyone—fellow campers and supervisors—knew we were the offspring of Enemies of the People. I made no friends in the nearly two months we were there. I had no sense of fun or play. Without my parents beside me, I had no idea who I was. No one was reassuring me that things would be better when school started, or ever again. I'm sure I was an embarrassment to my sister, as I was continually on the edge of crying. I recall a long wooden picnic table where all of us "inmates" consumed dark bread smeared with sour cream and paprika, which I found tasty. I also recall a sort of camp warden who tried to rouse me from my reverie during one lunch by clapping her fat hands right next to my ear. This caused me to burst out in tears, and she in great guffaws. I wonder now why any adult would do that to a traumatized child. Had people become so coarse that a miserable child was an object of fun? But back then, I felt that I was the one who was out of step and underperforming, as I was so obviously not enjoying myself the way everybody else, including even my sister, seemed to be.

Another memory from that summer: I am walking with two or three other little girls on a field, near the camp. It is Sunday and we have no scheduled activities. Suddenly a group of men—laborers or miners—in workmen's clothes, appear and shout, "Surround them! Get them from both sides!" My camp mates and I scatter. I start running down that steep hill so fast that my feet barely touch the ground. My chest feels like it is about to burst when I spot a small cottage with the door open. I fly inside. A woman is sitting on a sagging daybed, very slowly unrolling her stocking up her skinny, veiny legs. Without a word, I dive under her bed. Minutes later some men peer into her door, "Seen a little kid come down the hill?" No, the woman shakes her head and continues her business with the stockings. Not here. With my heart still wildly pumping, I wait for silence and then crawl out. I thank the woman, who nods as if this were a normal event. After a few minutes, I start back toward the camp. I admit, this memory sounds as if I had lifted it from a fairy tale or a surrealist film. If my sister, who was one of the other girls in the group chased down that steep hill, and who found her own hiding place, did not confirm my memory, I would write it off as a lonely child's wild imagining. It is still unclear to me what it was that the old woman had saved me from.

But something—which deepened my sense of feeling exposed and utterly unprotected.

"I SAT in the middle with my two escorts still holding my arms," my mother recalled her arrest in her memoir. "In five minutes we reached the great fortress of the AVO." (During their entire imprisonment, I had no idea my parents were so close, on the same bank of the Danube as my sister and me. They had vanished into thin air. They might as well have been on a Siberia-bound transport.)

"I was hurried from the car down a flight of stairs," Mama wrote, "into a shabby office in the cellar of the prison. I was struck immediately by the dreadful silence. Except for a few uniformed guards loitering in the courtyard and manning the high watchtowers with submachine guns and searchlights, the whole building seemed to be abandoned. Two uniformed jailers took charge of me. Everything was emptied from my pockets, I was permitted to keep only one handkerchief. They took my watch, my wedding ring, and, astonishingly, my bra. This I later discovered was considered a possible suicide tool."

"Well, Mrs. Marton," AVO Major Tamas Gero greeted my mother with a smile. (Gero's name was a familiar one from my mother's prison memories. In my research I discovered that Gero was notorious, even within the context of the AVO's brutal standards, for a near perfect record of breaking prisoners.) "Here you are at last," signaling for her to sit on the only wooden chair in a room full of upholstered easy chairs. "We have been waiting for this occasion for a long time," my mother recalled Gero's taunt. "But I must confess I am disappointed. Yes, we had been told to expect a pretty woman, and I now see that this is not the case." "If you'd given me one more day," my mother quipped, "I could have kept my hair appointment, and I'd look a lot better." That was the end of the banter. Asked to sign a warrant for her arrest (dated one month prior to the actual event), she saw for the first time that the charge against her was espionage for the United States.

"This is ridiculous!" she blurted out. "Sign it," the major commanded. "I can't," she replied. "It's not true."

"Now," she wrote in her memoirs, "from behind the desk, a beefy man, addressed as Comrade Colonel, wagged his finger at me, and shouted that I should sign or face the consequences. 'You are a spy,' he bellowed. 'Why else would you have visited the American legation every week for years?' 'It was my job to attend weekly press conferences,'" my mother answered. And then she made her first mistake.

"Suppose," she reasoned, "that instead of working for the American press I was a reporter for *Pravda* and had to attend press conferences at the Soviet embassy. Would I then be considered a Russian spy?"

"It was," she recalled, "as if I had lit a firecracker under the angry man. He flew into a rage and shouted, 'How can you be so insolent? To compare your unspeakable activities with that of an honest comrade who serves one of the peaceful nations? Such comrades are the country's heroes. Don't lie to us like a whore on the street!'"

The colonel leaned in close to my mother and, breathing hard, warned her, "If you don't sign the warrant you can spend the rest of your life here. We don't care," he said with a shrug, "we have plenty of time. Remember: it's in your interest to sign. Now." He then stormed out of the interrogation room. Left alone now with the "good cop" Gero, my shaken mother was given a lesson on the fundamentals of the world as seen from the darkest, most paranoid corner of the Terror State. "Gero took a piece of paper and drew two lines on it. The world, he said, was divided into two camps. Between them (he pointed to the space between the lines) was a battlefield. One must stand on one line or the other. 'No one,' Major Gero said, 'can stay in the middle. Everyone who did not fight on his line was an enemy, and even neutrals must be annihilated.' We had sided with the West. Our clothes, our way of life, our friends, and our jobs were all Western. We made weekly visits to the American legation, where we gave aid and comfort to the Enemy. How could I not see that in Communist eyes, I was a spy?"

"Had we been spies," my mother protested, "would we have gone openly to the legation, parking our car at the front?" That, the major agreed, "'was a smart trick. For a long time my own informers were misled thinking that since the Martons were so openly trafficking with the Enemy, they surely were hiding nothing.' But now they realized that this had been part of our cunning. And anyway, the fact remained we sided with the West and therefore we were Enemies." Enemies of the People.

My mother was a different sort of inmate than my father. She told her cell mate, a Yugoslav serving a life sentence as a "Titoist," that she would tell Major Tamas Gero whatever he wanted to know because, "They already know everything." Besides, she said, "I have nothing to hide." She said she had no fears about implicating American diplomats, whose worst punishment would be expulsion from Hungary. What she would *not* do is compromise any Hungarians. Hundreds of pages of her prison testimony and interrogation as well as her cell mate/informer's reports in the AVO files confirm that she did not. She also had a distinct advantage over my father: she was armed with knowledge he, a prisoner of more than four months by then, and under a much harsher regime, did not have. "Powerful friends in the free world," she wrote in her journal, "were working for our release. I had complete confidence in their eventual success."

Her challenge was to somehow transmit this message to her husband, languishing somewhere in the same fortress. While this knowledge filled her with hope, a Communist prison during the Cold War was still no place for a pampered, self-indulgent woman—no place for anyone, really. The purpose of the Fo Utca—as of every other prison in the vast Gulag across the Soviet empire—was to break the prisoner. And so they tried to break my mother.

It is virtually impossible for me to imagine my mother, whose morning ritual of coffee, newspapers, and silence no one in our family dared shatter, adapting to the prison routine, which she described as, "At five o'clock every morning the guards went from door to door banging and clapping, 'Get up!' This was reveille. The guards opened one cell after another and we inmates rushed through the corridor to the lavatory to pick up the tin washbasins of water and return with them to the cell. When the cell door was closed the guard opened the next one, so that there would never be more than one inmate on the corridor at a time."

Her cell mate/informer (whom my mother seems to have totally trusted) reported that "During the first days she was broken in spirit and seemed very frightened and would not even answer my questions. 'I don't want to break any rules here,' she says. She weeps frequently regarding her children. But after the third interrogation she returned to the cell in a good mood. . . . When I asked her what she is being charged with she said, 'Spying. The things they accuse me of are technically true but I was not aware that everything I said to foreign diplomats is considered spying, even things which have been reported in the press. I now see that from their [the AVO's] perspective I am guilty and I am doing my best to be straight with them so that they will let me return to my children.'"

Major Gero was deft in wielding his cruelest weapon against my mother. She could not long bear up without a word about us. On July 7, she "confessed" to spying for the Americans. "I had to do it," she told her cell mate the same day, "to save my children. If they don't have a father, at least they should have a mother." My mother alternated between her wish to save her husband and waves of rage against him, blaming him for what happened to us all. "My husband forgot that he was a father," she told her cell mate, "and blindly served the Americans. He dragged me down with him. But I will not forget that I am a mother first of all."

With her confession she was certain that she would soon be free. "As of the last two days, she is a different woman, cheerful, very witty, and announced that only with humor can one survive such an ordeal. She says she has faith in the Geneva four-power summit's outcome and that Hungary will be admitted to the U.N., which will lead to her and her husband's freeing."

She was, above all, a survivor. My mother adapted, and even bent the prison rules to fit her own needs. When she was in a good mood she turned her tiny cell into a workout room. "My most satisfying achievement," she recalled, "was persuading [her cell mate, a former nun] that keeping her body fit was as important as keeping her soul fit. I taught her to do gymnastics every morning. The cell wasn't large enough for us both to exercise at the same time, so I would do a routine and then climb up on the bunk and encourage her to copy it." I cherish this image of my mother, working out in prison.

But instead of allowing her to rejoin her children, as she had been promised, on August 29, the AVO asked for and received permission from the Ministry of the Interior (though in reality the secret police were accountable only to Rakosi) to keep her in "indefinite custody pending the investigation of her case." Feeling betrayed, she was in no mood to cooperate. My mother's cell mate reported on August 30, "Her mood in recent days has shifted dramatically. She says she feels closer each day to her husband. All her hope is with the Americans, that they won't abandon [the Martons]. She says her only wish is to get out of this country, where there is no life, no freedom. 'They have killed off beauty, and art, and literature and all that is beautiful and good in life. Press freedom? This is what they call press freedom! If someone has the courage to write things as they are, prison is the result,' she says. She tried to persuade me that it is different in the Western democracies where people have basic human rights. She doesn't even say anymore that, yes, from their point of view, I can see that I am guilty. Today, Mrs. Marton said that everywhere else in the world where there is civilized life . . . these are not crimes, and it is natural to have contact with foreigners. Only here behind the Iron Curtain do they make a crime out of such things."

Through their mindless cruelty, the AVO had managed to turn a cooperative prisoner into an angry and defiant one. Their dilemma now was what to do with the Martons. By late July, with the Eisenhower-Khrushchev Geneva summit deemed a success, Moscow no longer wanted a public show trial implicating the American mission in Budapest. Out beyond the borders of the "greater prison," as Hungarians referred to their country, prospects for Stalin's "Best Hungarian Pupil" were dimming. If Rakosi thought he could revert to his mentor's old ways of running the Terror State, that was not the Kremlin's plan. It was an uncertain time for the Moscow leadership, as Stalin's heirs jockeyed for power. Mixed signals were being sent to the satellites. Beneath the surface, seismic shifts were taking place—shifts that would culminate in Nikita Khrushchev's "Secret Speech" to the 20th Party Congress in February 1956, officially burying Stalinism. But what did two inmates of a maximum security fortress know of such things?

Even with his prime targets, my parents, in jail, "Andrassi" was still serving the AVO. On July 4, he reported on the talk of the Café Gerbeaud regarding the Martons. I can picture the group, inside the false sanctuary of this ancien régime artifact, with its vaulted and frescoed ceilings, the ladies wearing shabby remnants of their prewar elegance, little hats, suits with the buttons recently moved to accommodate ever fuller figures, as new suits were out of the question, and the well-dressed agent leaning in, committing every sigh, quip, and comment to memory, for later transcription, while stirring whipped cream into his espresso. Aunt Magda and Mrs. Kokas (the mother of our playmates Peter and Balint), "Andrassi" reported, protested that the authorities had brutally emptied our apartment of all its contents. *What will happen to the children? What will they live on and who will support them?* our neighbor "boldly" asked the agents who had come to strip our home. Surely a few valuables could be spared for the children's support? Everyone at the Gerbeaud nodded in agreement, "Andrassi" reported. The State is making the Martons into the [Julius and Ethel] Rosenbergs, the group agreed. The Marton children will be orphaned, just like the Rosenberg kids. Magda added that the children had received a letter from their mother telling them to stay calm, she had seen their father [not true] and she would soon be home. Everyone at the Gerbeaud seemed aware that the Hellers refused to take us in, and that we were at a summer camp in Adyliget. As to what would happen to us at summer's end, no one had a clue.

IN THE FARAWAY city of Washington, D.C., news of our sad summer reached the office of the secretary of state. On July 22, Budapest chargé d'affaires Spencer Barnes, in a secret cable entitled "The Arrest of Press Correspondents Mr. and Mrs. Marton," informed him that "The [Marton] children were sent away immediately after the arrest of Mrs. Marton to a summer camp not far away from Budapest. Upon their return they will be taken over by Mrs. Marton's sister, whose husband is a leading Budapest opera conductor. The Legation understood from earlier conversations with Mrs. Marton that she had made other plans in preparation for the contingency which unfortunately developed, that close friends of the Martons (who are in better financial circumstances than her sister) were prepared to take over and adopt the children if necessary."

"MARTON'S sole weakness," Major Arpad Kretschmer, who took over Papa's case that summer, confirmed what others had already noted, "is his family. In their interest he is capable of doing almost anything." The final line of the same document, dated July 14, 1955, washes over me like a balm: "Endre Marton in the course of his interrogation did not compromise a single Hungarian citizen." So now, my greatest fear regarding opening this "Pandora's box" put to rest, I forge ahead.

I find reading and rereading these thousands of pages of secret police records deadening to the spirit. Though I am reading the most painfully personal revelations about my parents, the language of the AVO—and undoubtedly secret police records in general—is utterly detached from flesh and blood. People are reduced to a single dimension: "accused" or "suspect" or "informer," scrubbed clean of their human substance. The most poignant moments, endlessly repeated in memoranda, summaries of memoranda, and action proposals, are drained of meaning or drama or connection to actual living beings. Is that how thousands of agents and loyal officers of the AVO, the tiny cogs that made the wheels of the Terror State turn, is that how they coped? By never calling anything by its name: the arrest of a patriotic Hungarian, who was also a husband and a father, the imprisonment of a wife and mother, the abandonment of small children? And what is the most generous, selfless act a man living under such a system can bestow on his wife and children? Rid them of the burden to which the State has reduced his life. Urge his wife to divorce him and his children to forget him. More than this he could not do for those he loved. That was the ultimate result of one of the twentieth century's bold experiments on humans.

Chapter 11

MY FATHER IS BROKEN

I read and translated hundreds of pages of surveillance and interrogation records that revealed the AVO's full brutality toward my parents.

MY FATHER HAD lost hope. His bold offer of a deal had only provoked the authorities into greater brutality. His attempt to warn my mother and get help from "the Americans" had failed—and given the AVO more "evidence" of his treachery. By April, he had run out of ideas. He knew his wife and his children were more vulnerable than ever as a result of his reckless letters. "They are accusing me of treason and spying," he told his new informer/cell mate, Dr. Leo Benko,

133

when he returned from yet another interrogation. "Apart from six spoonfuls of soup [such precision, this informer was clearly a pro] he did not touch his lunch. . . . During the daily walk in the courtyard, he never looked up, his head hung low and he was silent. . . . When the guard reprimanded him for walking so slowly he answered that he had broken his leg and he was exhausted." (My father had indeed broken his leg in 1946 when his motorcycle was run over by a Soviet transport truck. So mangled was his left leg that only his stubborn refusal prevented its amputation. He was left with a slightly shorter left leg, a fact I never heard him mention. Apparently, the cold, damp cell, with his bare feet in his dress shoes, was causing him pain.)

"His long periods of silence," the cell mate reported, "are interrupted with the following refrain, 'I just can't believe the whole thing. It can't be happening. The whole thing is like a nightmare from which I will wake up.'"

Now my father sunk into the black pit of self-reproach. "He is constantly blaming himself," Dr. Benko reported on May 3, 1955. "How could he have been so deluded and so blind not to have foreseen his fate. That he should have learned from his colleagues' arrest and the fact that there is not a single Western correspondent left in any of the People's Democracies, because they all feared working in these countries.

"He doesn't understand why *now,* after ten years of doing his job without any problems, they are charging him with spying. He claims that he is being 'blackmailed' by the authorities to implicate his wife as a spy. If he doesn't implicate her they are threatening to arrest her as well." So my father was presented with a Catch-22 situation: implicate your wife or we arrest her. The cruelest possible choice. (I wonder, did AVO agents, like Hollywood producers, sit around long tables, dreaming up sinister scenarios, tossing around plots, before consensus was reached?) For my father, most unbearable of all was that he had virtually provoked the AVO into arresting his wife. The letter he had been tricked into writing, by which he hoped to save her, had warned her that she "would not survive a day" in prison. So he had made the AVO's job easier.

He saw no future for himself. He had covered enough spy trials to know that his options were a very long prison term, or execution. What was the point of life as a broken prisoner, or even, if eventually freed, a former prisoner, unable to ever again provide for his wife or children? There *was* no point. It was agony for a proud man to contemplate that life, stripped of all the things that meant anything to him. Entirely powerless now, he had one last weapon to use against his captors, and to spare himself. He began to plan and attempt his own death.

"One evening after an unusually long and stormy day with [Captain] Babics," he wrote later, "I staggered back to my cell. It was a cold night and sticking my hands, covered with cold sweat, into my pockets, I pricked my finger on something. It was a small pin. How it got into my pocket, and why I discovered it only then, I could not explain. That night on my bunk, I tried to pierce the vein on my left wrist. It was a hopeless effort. The pin was too small. I could not hold it firmly between my fingers. I tried again and again, always watching the Judas on the door for the jailer who made his rounds on the corridor. I struggled for an hour and then gave up."

But he did not give up on the idea of suicide. Communist prisons were lavish in distributing sedatives to prisoners, whose daily coffee was already laced with a tranquilizer. Now my father requested sleeping pills from the prison medic. "He prescribed two tablets of Sevenal, a medium strong sedative. Every morning a medical corps subaltern made his rounds along the corridor carrying a large tray suspended from his neck with all the medicines the doctor had prescribed and with a list showing who should receive what. . . . The prisoner had to swallow the medicine right there, opening his mouth and showing his hands afterwards to prove that he had done so. Well, I did not. . . . I took two pills in my left hand and pretended to throw them immediately into my mouth, grabbing the tin cup with my right. But I kept the pills in my left hand, and while drinking from the cup, I quickly pushed the pills into the pocket of my jacket—showing immediately, as required, that my hands were empty and opening my mouth for inspection. For storage I tore a little hole in the pocket of my overcoat and collected the pills in the lining. Though I had never taken sedatives before, I had a notion that a dose of about a hundred would be enough, and that meant fifty days of deception."

Thus Papa kept a scrap of control over his fate. That my father would even contemplate the possibility of not seeing the little girls he left become young women, adults, mothers, and professionals—all those stages in our lives he would have missed—reveals a level of despair beyond my imagination, and that he never discussed later in life.

The very next day, the AVO had further proof that the indignities they had inflicted on my father had achieved their aim. He was no longer the same proud, somewhat haughty figure they took into custody on that snowy night in February. Between 9:45 A.M. and 1:45 P.M. on May 14, 1955, Captain Babics extracted from my father his life story. My father rarely looked back, and when he did, he liked to recall only brave moments of his own history. But in captivity, he saw his life in the darkest light. The fifteen-page transcript of those four bitter hours makes for heartbreaking reading. For the first time, I can understand something that used to be a source of frustration for me. For I am an American, with all our country's optimism and, yes, sometimes naïveté. I have always believed that the healthy approach to the past was to remember it. My parents held to their right to forget. The only way my father could bear the weight of the past was to never talk or think about it, to recall only bright, gallant moments. These fourteen pages of forced biography explain why.

In plain, unembellished Hungarian, he describes his life as a young man, thwarted at every turn by the metastasizing virus of hate: turned down for university (though he graduated with top honors from his *Gymnasium*), he was compelled to abandon his original plan to study law, and accepted a slot in what he considered the less desirable faculty of economics. After earning his Ph.D., he was fired from one job after another, due to ever harsher anti-Jewish laws. Finally, he was reduced to making a living tutoring the offspring of the wealthy, in German and English. At this point in his summary, Captain Babics sharply interrupted my father. "Just *where* did you acquire such good English?" I can almost hear the agent, a mechanic by training, voice dripping with sarcasm and loaded with innuendo: *Aha, now we are getting somewhere—the spy's early training by the Enemy.* "In my parents' house," my father answered. "From age ten onward, an elderly lady named Miss Langreuter came to our house in the afternoons and instructed me in German, French, and English, all the way until I graduated." A whole lost world of "high bourgeois" family life, in a villa on a Buda hill, with parents grooming their firstborn to speak the great Western languages—a bright future glistening before him—suddenly collides with Babics's universe, where to learn the language of the Imperialists was itself a potential crime.

But it is my father's account of his work in the anti-Nazi resistance that is most surprising. In the same matter-of-fact way that he described the arc of his thwarted academic and professional lives, my father told Babics about his life in the resistance—none of which I had heard. In the summer of 1944, at clandestine meetings in the Hill of Roses home of Bela Hallosy, my father volunteered to lead French officers, hiding in Budapest, to Slovakia, to participate in the only armed anti-German uprising in the region. He also offered to participate in a secret mission to Tito's Yugoslav headquarters. Both missions were ultimately canceled as too hazardous. At this point in his account, Babics interrupted my father to demand the names of others in the resistance movement. Of his two closest comrades, my father answered, one had defected to the West, another had already been sentenced to a prison term. Lastly, himself: "arrested and charged with treason and espionage." Unspoken, but implied by my father, was the obvious conclusion: thus did Communist Hungary reward its resistance heroes. "Continue with your life story!" Babics barked.

And so, my father unspooled a detailed account of how he and my mother eluded the Nazis and the Arrow Cross, with the help of Christian friends and fake IDs. He defied the call-ups for Jews for forced labor. He was denounced by a neighbor for holding resistance meetings in his apartment. "Were you hiding because of your leftist politics?" the AVO officer bellowed. "I practiced neither leftist, nor rightist politics," my father answered, no doubt to the bewilderment of his interrogator, to whom all the world was divided into leftists and rightists. My father tells him that at one point during the worst of the Eichmann/Arrow Cross terror, he and my mother were hidden by Christian friends in the Gresham Palace. By an odd quirk of fate, I am reading this file for the first time, sprawled on a bed, in that sumptuous former insurance palace, which once sheltered my parents from the hunters, today converted into a Four Seasons Hotel—one of Europe's grandest.

The rest of Papa's "life story," as extracted by Babics, is a portrait of two clashing worlds. "Who ordered you to do this story? Who called your attention to that one? Why did so-and-so trust you with that information?" Babics hammered away at my father, incapable of acknowledging that a journalist could function as an independent, inquisitive human being, not simply the paid vassal of one of the two titans in the Cold War. The actual news content of the "news" behind the Iron Curtain hovered around zero. Even weather reports began inside Hungary and then stretched to the Urals, without a cloud ever straying into capitalist Austria or Italy. There was no bad news: no crimes were committed, no one ever died, so no need for obituary pages. My father once told me of sitting in a Communist official's office, when he noticed a plume of smoke rising in the distance. "Where is the fire?" Papa asked the official. "What fire?" she asked. "I don't see any fire." Bad news did not happen in the People's Republics. The AVO did not consider what my parents did to be journalism: to them, it was espionage.

So my father, broken and beyond caring, said he was a spy. But,

Babics wrote in his report on May 14, "He has not implicated any-one. He defends himself by saying that it is only in custody that he has come to realize that he committed espionage." Now, this memo-randum continues, "with the arrest of [his wife] we have the means to fully unmask both of them and expose the espionage activities pursued by the American embassy." The behavior of the uniformed thugs—Babics, Balazsi, Gero, and the others, trained in the fine art of breaking humans—is less shocking than the more inspired cru-elty of the amateurs, the less-well-rewarded semipros. Take Dr. Leo Benko, for example, my father's second cell mate (after the "letter smuggler"). He seems to have skillfully ingratiated himself into my father's confidence at this desperate time. "After three weeks with Dr. M.," he wrote, "I can report the following: he is extremely culti-vated and worldly, and at the same time very vain about his knowl-edge and his appearance. He is almost pathologically Anglophile, and enthralled by all Western ideas, but especially those related to England and the U.S." With these words, Papa's cell mate was more or less sealing his fate. Anybody possessing those qualities was as-sumed to be guilty. But Benko wasn't done yet. "He is constantly re-peating that Communism is bound to fail, if not by its own weight, then it must be destroyed with atomic weapons. He speaks of all things connected to the Soviet Union and the People's Democracies with loathing and contempt.

"I do not perceive the slightest trace of regret in him. During our first days together he was quite worked up, but lately he is rather bro-ken in spirit and apathetic and doesn't seem to notice anything around him." Benko then went to the heart of Papa's greatest vulnerability. "In my opinion," he wrote, "if he is still withholding any secrets, then, knowing his nature, there is only one way to force him to confess: by threatening his wife, and, even more, his children. I am certain that if his wife and, even more, his children, were placed in harm's way, there is not a secret that he would not disclose to save them."

So now I know that if my father did not express his feelings for us it was because they were too strong, not too weak. How ironic that the deepest proof of his love for us was provided by an AVO informer.

HAVING HIT a wall with my father, bad cop Babics was replaced by the good cop, Major Arpad Kretschmer, later that summer. A barber by training, Kretschmer, a slightly built man with thinning red hair and a low-key manner, took over when the brutal Babics failed to get my father to implicate others in his "nest of spies." Moreover, to get some peace and quiet, Papa had begun to invent accomplices, dead people. In later years, my father would say that Kretschmer saved his life—a favor he would return during the Revolution, the following year.

As "humane" as Kretschmer seemed to Papa compared to his thuggish predecessors, it was the major who dealt him the most devastating blow. "One morning," my father recalled, "going through the daily opening routine of reading my testimony of the previous day, I found a page of testimony among the others which did not belong there . . . it was signed by Ilona." And thus he learned that his wife had become a fellow inmate. "Marton returned from his interrogation," his cell mate reported on July 7, "sobbing . . . he says they lied to him, when they promised she would not be harmed. He plans on exposing the whole sham at his trial. He will tell the court that he is innocent and that he was forced to sign a phony confession."

That my father still trusted his captors to keep their word, still trusted his cell mates with his confidences, was still shocked and appalled when they did not, is a hallmark of a man who seemed incapable of recognizing the full deceit of the regime he hated. He simply could not participate in their universe of lying, cheating, betraying, torturing, and subverting. What bad luck for such a man to have been born into this corner of twentieth-century Europe.

Thus began a period of pure torment for my father. Until now he could imagine his family was living their lives in relative freedom, while he absorbed the indignities and cruelties of jail. Now his wife was suffering the same fate. What had become of his children? He had no idea. Partly from fear of the answer, and partly blocked by his fierce pride, he could not bring himself to ask.

On July 18, his cell mate reported that my father had told him the most serious charge against him: that he had advised the Americans to dispatch a "Negro" diplomat to Budapest, to undermine Communist propaganda regarding "racist America." (When the files refer to this charge, as well as the "theft" of the budget, they attribute it to unnamed, classified channels. The actual source, Warrant Officer Richard Glaspell, is never mentioned.)

On July 22, his cell mate reported that Marton was so agitated that "He said he wanted to kick the door down. . . . He is sick of being a captive and sick of my company day and night for the past two months."

In despair, my father continued collecting his sedatives, the only way he saw out of his nightmare.

By the end of July the Foreign Ministry had finished translating into Hungarian all my parents' reports, and sent the following verdict to the AVO: "From the material at our disposition we can conclude that the reports contain no data . . . which would be considered illegal. However, all the Martons' reports violate the national interests of the People's Republic, and fail to convey an objective view of the situation here. . . . There is no factual evidence to confirm the charge of spying, but in my opinion, it is probable that the [Martons] conducted such activity. Signed, Jozsel Szall, Ministry of Foreign Affairs." What a marvelous piece of bureaucratic sleight-of-hand, practiced by a man who no doubt lived through periodic attempts at "reform" only to see them reversed. Szall was taking no chances.

August brought fresh anxiety, reported as though it were a soap opera by the AVO agents. Summer vacation would soon end—and then what would happen to his children? "He is worried as to who will enroll the children in school," reported a new cell mate, "Tibor," on August 13, "and will their friends the Hellers honor their promise to look after the children? He says he really couldn't blame them if they didn't want the children of two Enemies of the People, though Heller's high position would shield him against repercussions." My father's greatest fear, however, in his cell mate's words, was "that his children will be placed in a State institution and raised as Communist Janissaries."★

Papa's fears about us were not invented. In a memorandum dated September 8, 1955, entitled "In the Matter of the Children of Dr. Endre Marton," Major Kretschmer wrote that "a solution to the question of the [Marton] children is politically important. . . . Marton should empower his attorney to act on behalf of the children, on transferring funds and valuables to their account." But this was just another meaningless, pro forma nod toward "Socialist Legality." There were no such funds available, for, as Kretschmer well knew, the AVO had seized all our possessions and frozen our bank accounts. Kretschmer concludes by recommending what Papa feared most: "The children," he said, "should be placed by the authorities in a state-run institution."

IN NEW YORK, that other bureaucracy, the Associated Press, was hardly more sympathetic to the plight of the "Marton children." "I think it is inadvisable," wrote general manager Frank Starzel to Vienna bureau chief Richard O'Regan on August 3, 1955, "to take any action on the suggestion that we do something in behalf of the children. As you know, these family pleas can be essentially spurious in that the intended recipient receives no benefit from the money. There may be a bona fide need in this case, but I would like to have it investigated further before authorizing any transfers."

Meanwhile, Major Kretschmer was making preparations for my

★ Janissaries were Christian children, seized by the Ottomans, forced to convert to Islam, and pressed into the sultan's service. They became the elite force of the Ottoman army.

parents' upcoming spy trial. In a memorandum dated August 29, 1955, he noted that "The Court cannot make use of our *secret sources* regarding the Americans' use of Marton's recommendations." The next day my mother's cell mate reported that "Mrs. Marton finds it puzzling that her interrogator shows not the slightest interest in any information regarding the American military attaché. She claims that every time she mentions this subject they move on to something else."

With the end of summer, and still no news of his children, my father's cell mate reported on August 30, "[Marton] says he has no hope left, since he is kept in the dark about his children, and only hopes that during his trial, he will at least find out why he and his wife were arrested *now*, after ten years [of working for the Americans]. . . . At the trial, he will use his right for the final word to defend his wife, which he feels might do her some good. As to his own case, he has no hope."

Chapter 12

OUR NEW FAMILY

The Hellei family were strangers paid to look after Juli and me by friends. Everything about them made me long for my parents and our old life, but the older sister, bottom row left, was very sweet to me, bottom row right. In this "family" photo, my sister and I both look like we are in shock.

Aunt Magda, Juli, and I drove through neighborhoods that did not seem attached to my Budapest at all: twisting, narrow country roads with barely room for a single car, overgrown with drooping hedges, and fewer and fewer streetlights or any other signs of city life. When our taxi arrived, it was dark, and country-quiet. I had spent my entire life atop a Buda hill from where we could hear the low hum of the city and see—however dimly—its flickering lights, surrounded always by noisy neighbors and children calling out from one apartment to the other. Now I felt utterly cut off from everything that was familiar. My parents, my grandparents, my playmates, my dog, my house, my toys—all gone.

By the time we reached the house on Csermely Utca, in Zugliget, I had no sense of where we were. I remember crossing what seemed like a long stretch of an overgrown field, a statue of a saint in the middle and a large house at the end. This would be our new home. Neglect everywhere: peeling plaster and the smell of used cooking fat in the front hall. And cold! Sheltered and spoiled by our parents' unusual circumstances, my sister and I had never been exposed to real *want,* real poverty. We were looking at it for the first time—and we weren't just there to visit. We had our suitcases with us. We had been told we had nowhere else to go. Magda did all the talking. She had found this family, friends of friends, the Helleis, willing to take us in for a certain monthly sum. They were poor, but "genteel." I could see that from the old oil paintings and bits of antiques and the remnants of Herend china here and there. I knew we were there not out of sentiment, but as a matter of mutual needs. We had no place else to go and they were strapped for cash. A mother and father, Sari "Neni" (aunt) and Andras "Bacsi" (uncle), their two daughters, Andrea "Rici" and Maria "Cunci" (who would become my special friend), teenagers, a generation older than my sister and me, and their grandparents, and uncle and aunt, all living under one roof. All barely surviving. Later, we learned that Andras Bacsi had been fired from his university teaching job when the whole family was caught at the Austro-Hungarian frontier, trying to escape. Meanwhile, friends and relatives, thinking the Hellei family were gone, had hauled away many of their worldly goods. The family were brought back to Budapest by the authorities, forced to live the reduced lives of internal exiles. Under constant surveillance, they lived on the grandfather's pension and the mother's part-time work. So they could afford to shelter two children of Enemies of the People. They had nothing left to lose.

Sari Neni worked at the nearby Makarenko Orphanage. That name has stuck in my memory, as it was the first time I heard it and the story that Sari Neni told us seemed somehow to resonate with our own sad circumstances. Anton Makarenko was a KGB officer who designed institutions such as the one where Sari worked, meant to raise "Socialist orphans"—in other words, kids like us, only less lucky. Their role model was a boy who had informed on his own parents' anti-Soviet behavior to the authorities, leading to their arrest and his being made a Young Hero of the Revolution. A role model for all of us. Unbeknownst to me, my father, in the misery of his cell, was having nightmares about his daughters being raised in a place just like the Makarenko.

"The first thing that struck me about you," the older sister, Maria Natali, a doctor now living in Rome, recalled in 2007, "was your bright pink sweater. We had not seen bright colors in a long time. You were coming from a different world! But you did not complain. I do not remember you ever crying." In fact, my sister and I had made a pact that the two of us would never cry at the same time. We would take turns, and only when we were by ourselves.

"We had been living in such misery," Dr. Natali continued, "my dream was to have an egg all to myself. But things improved for us once you arrived. We ate better. We had new playmates. We hoped you would stay forever."

We had no time to feel sorry for ourselves. School started almost immediately, and we stood out in our custom-made pleated skirts and handmade soft leather shoes and those bright pink sweaters (from some American diplomat, no doubt). We had no parents to walk us to school or to occasionally visit the teachers. So everybody knew something was wrong with us. But the other children knew better than to ask, while the teachers let us know *they knew* in their own way. (I remember once whispering a compliment to Mrs. Barna, my teacher, as her starched white coat—for teachers wore coats like doctors—brushed past my seat. Something about her pretty shoes. In a voice the whole class could hear, she scolded me for wasting time on such trivial things, when I did not know my multiplication tables. That ended my charm offensive.) In a generally poor country, the children in this school were desperately so. This was one of the city's most neglected neighborhoods, with a high rate of tuberculosis. Our schoolmates were the children of alcoholics, misfits, and castoffs—people left behind by the Socialist Revolution—and the dirty-faced children went barefoot in the spring and their noses leaked all winter. So we stood out.

Mostly I remember being cold. It always seemed to be warmer outside than inside that unheated, cavernous house. So we stayed out-doors until the very last moment, building huge mountains of leaves and jumping from one to the next to keep warm—and also because, however miserable, we were kids and full of play. At night before go-ing to bed we would warm our covers on the big green tile stove, for which everybody took turns hauling coal from the cellar. Nobody mentioned our parents—it seemed to be an embarrassing topic for the grown-ups—except when the four of us children said our nightly prayers together and always included a line asking little Jesus to take care of them. That was it. Nobody from our old house—our gang of kids—ever visited us. (Now, when I ask my old friends about that, I get two different answers. We didn't know what happened to you. We were told you were with your godfather, Bela Hallosy. Just another family that disappeared. *Elvitték,* as they used to say in Budapest in those days. Taken away.)

Children are resilient creatures. We were famished at the end of the day and relished dinner, consisting most nights of either bread with plum jam (made from the fruit of plum trees that grew in abundance in the garden), or what they called "polka dot bread," bread and butter topped with little dots of salami. I remember my sister and I briefly exchanging looks when this "main course" was served in the same plate as the soup we just had, but after a while, we didn't even notice. Once a week the grandfather left the house before dawn to line up at the butcher shop for whatever cut of meat was available. There were too many of us at the table for meat days to have been special. The family were kind to us, but they were strangers. *"Bei Tisch singt man nicht!"* the grandmother once chided me for humming at the dinner table. *No singing at the dinner table.* (She had a repertoire of such German sayings.) I knew she was right, but she wasn't *my* grandmother. In Cunci—the older sister—I found a surrogate mother. She was about sixteen and all soft curves, long blond hair, and warmth. Like a lost kitten, I liked to curl up next to her. She seemed as unhappy as I was, so in our shared misery, we drew close. She and her father were at war. She was a rebellious teenager and he was a Victorian autocrat. I recall that he would schedule her weekly spanking for his convenience. This, I found shocking. As a mischievous child, my father had delivered a smack or two to my bottom, but always out of temper. To administer a spanking in the cool aftermath of a fight disturbed me. I also recall that Andras Bacsi—a talented painter as well as an academic—painted my beautiful aunt's portrait, enticement, I assume, for her to visit us. She was always entertaining and turned even her interaction with the AVO into humorous anecdotes. I recall her asking the authorities permission to send moisturizer for my mother. "What do you think we're running here," Major Gero answered, "some kind of spa?"

The greatest excitement of our sadly reduced lives was when, periodically, an enormous, shiny black limousine rolled up in front of the overgrown garden and Ambassador Christian Ravndal himself alighted. This elegant, dark-suited, tall figure from a universe that now seemed as remote to us as Atlantis always brought gifts. The most memorable were identical aqua nylon party dresses, with net petticoats stitched inside. My sister and I wore them for years. (Even once we were in Washington, and still poor, I turned Ravndal's gift into a sort of a strapless party dress for my first dance—so it lived on.) I don't remember anything much about those visits except the flutter they provoked in our shabby little household and the thrill of seeing the forbidden Stars-and-Stripes snapping off the enormous front hood of Ravndal's Buick.

"RAVNDAL DID NOT wait for instructions from Washington," Tom Rogers recalled. "He just decided this was the right thing to do. And that he would go himself, the chief of mission, flags flying."

Tom Rogers's wife, Sarah, a woman whose mere presence always made me feel better, also came and brought her daughters, Elinor and Arabella. In 2008, Arabella Meadows-Rogers, now an ordained Presbyterian minister, recalled that visit. "We brought you oranges, my mother's definition of infinite goodness. I remember that as a difficult visit. It was a dark, cold house and we didn't know you, or your foster family. It felt awkward. We did not play with you." I recall feeling a great gulf between us and the Rogers girls, a gulf I had not felt to such an extent when my parents were free. They looked so bright in their American cotton dresses, and by then our arms poked out of the sweaters we arrived in. We had started wearing track suits like everybody else in school. Seeing these carefree American kids, I felt that we were from different worlds. I knew they would get into their paneled Ford station wagon and drive away, relieved to have done their bit of charity work. I loved them for coming, but the visit made me remember how much we had lost.

Another regular visitor who trekked out to this sad suburb of Budapest was Hungary's most famous opera star: Mihaly Szekely. He was not an intimate family friend, which made his visits even more remarkable. Was he just a very good man bent on defying the regime? He died in 1963, and today a street near the Budapest Opera bears his name, but I never saw him again after that year. (I see in the AVO files that they were constantly noting that he must be brought in for "questioning," but he was too prominent and too valuable to the State for the AVO to intimidate.) Mihaly had his own car, and he and his wife, Piroska, also came bearing gifts. Their best gift of all was taking us (including our new "sisters") to the opera. After such trips to that distant, fabulous world in the heart of Pest the four of us children would stage our own operas. I remember a performance of *The Magic Flute,* when we used the long insulation padding that kept the cold out of our room at night as the snake. And I remember raiding the grandmother's attic chest for dusty old frocks for our performance of *Faust.* My sister played the male leads, I the female, and Magda and her husband, our Uncle Laci, the opera conductor, were reliable audience members.

Christmas without parents was too sad to have been Christmas at all, and I have wiped those memories clean. My sister and I avoided recalling the previous Christmas when the world had seemed so bright. We did not talk about the family outing after a fresh snowfall just one year earlier, when we tried out our first pair of skis.

Our best presents were letters from our parents. And for the first time in nearly a year since our father's arrest, we were allowed to send letters to them, and even posed for photographs to accompany them. Looking at those pictures today, they seem extremely forced and cheery, and I think our letters were the same. Those letters are lost, but here is how my mother recalled them:

I can never describe what these letters meant to me [in prison]. I read them a hundred times, wept over them, kissed the pages, slept with them in my hands. They were cheerful, newsy, infinitely careful letters, revealing nothing of their sadness but telling me so much either in words or between the lines. They were well taken care of, they said. They listed their visitors so I would know and be cheered by the roster of those who cared and dared to show they cared. They spoke of their schoolwork and said that the teachers liked them, so that I would know that they were not being persecuted at school for their parents' crimes. The children looked fine, they were clearly well fed, they had grown. I looked at their feet and saw they were wearing shoes made of the leather given me by a diplomat and which I had left with the shoemaker but had been arrested before I could pick up. Now I knew some brave soul had picked them up and that they dared wear them though they were made of "capitalistic" goods. In one picture they held oranges in their hands. Oranges are almost unheard of in Hungary so this meant they had American visitors. In another picture they sat in front of a piano. This told me they were keeping up their music lessons. In another picture they wore ski outfits and I knew they were having fun. . . . I made the pictures serve as a calendar. Each night I turned over the top picture as if it were the page of a calendar. . . . This made the days go by and I looked forward to the next day's photograph.

Another trick from my mother's prisoner survival manual.

The letters we got from our parents were as careful as the ones we had sent. From my father it was mostly about the books we should be reading: Dickens, Kipling, and, an odd note, a book about Erasmus, called *The Cloister and the Hearth,* he had found in the prison library. Not a word about his own pain or uncertainty. I recall my mother's letters as more emotional and personal. She missed us terribly, she wrote, and prayed each night around the same time she knew we would be praying, so in that way we could be together.

Chapter 13

MY PARENTS' TRIAL

O N SEPTEMBER 2, 1955, my father, ever more despairing, wrote
Major Kretschmer a heartbreaking letter which begins:

> *There are people who cannot speak about themselves, who are pained*
> *when they are forced to ask for something (yesterday I was unable to ask*
> *for a few matches, though I needed them desperately) . . . forgive me for*
> *thinking out loud in this way. . . . I am taking advantage of this typewriter*
> [temporarily in his possession for some English translations he had
> been asked to do]. *It is easier for me in writing. I will not ask what has*
> *happened to my wife . . . though for the last months this is what has ago-*
> *nized me most. I am simply not able to ask. . . . I know nothing about*
> *my children. Yesterday was the first day of September, and fortunately I was*
> *not interrogated, because all I could think about was that it was the first*
> *day of school and I don't know a thing about [them]. Since June I haven't*
> *asked about my financial situation, the only thing I had, and which I had*
> *hoped to provide my wife and children. Once before, ten years ago, we lost*
> *pretty much everything we owned and I have absolutely no hope that in*
> *my lifetime I can start to rebuild again.*

Yesterday, I could not find words when I was told that the first time I would see my wife will be at our trial. This will not be good for anybody— as much as I fear my emotions at such a meeting—it won't be good for that very reason. My wife and I have so many things we need to discuss. What possible danger would this pose to anybody? What is left for us to "conspire" about?

And what will happen after the trial: if they immediately send me away from here—which is what I expect. Will I have a chance to see her then? Will I have a chance to discuss with you my proposal regarding the AP and the Americans [for the deal to exchange my parents for money and property]—*though with the passage of time I have less and less faith in anything, especially since my wife is also in custody, and she would have been the only one able to carry this through.*

And then there are the "trivial" things! Things I would want from my apartment [before he is shipped off to begin to serve his sentence]— *my children's photographs from my desk, some warm winter clothes, shoes, etc., and—if my wife is also sentenced—which I cannot bear to even think about—she will need these things, too. I cannot ask anyone to look after these things. I have no one. I wonder if I still have a home?*

Even if I can bear to think about every soul-crushing detail of what is surely coming—years of being locked up—which I now know I have a harder time accepting than most, what then? *I will be an old man, who had caused nothing but trouble for his family and those few people with whom, willy-nilly, I came in contact. I was not able to stand by my family, when my children had the greatest need of me. Should I now turn to them as a broken old man, with empty hands? I cannot even imagine such a thing. Why, then, bother with the whole thing? The answer to that lies only with me.*

All of this would be more bearable if through all these months I wouldn't keep agonizing over "Why?" Why, why was it necessary to eliminate us, now? I would not be asking this had we been arrested between 1950 and 1952. But in 1955, with the beginning of a much improved international situation? I haven't committed any "crimes" that I did not commit then. I never made a secret of my work, everything I did was open, and well known to the authorities.

Cui bono? . . . This is what I agonize about? Why now? . . . The West will never see my wife and me as anything but fresh "sacrifices." There is no diplomat or journalist who knows us, who will ever believe that we are spies, especially not if the charges against us are publicized. How will this make the TASS correspondent in Washington feel, as a regular visitor to the Soviet embassy, where presumably he is speaking of things other than the weather?

And all of this could still be repaired, if the AVO does not make it about their "prestige." Why does the regime need two more prisoners and the negative publicity this will provoke in the West, and not only in America, and especially not in 1955, when these two people could be of so much better use to the country?

I am ashamed that I have not even asked about my parents, though I know Captain Babics had news of them as well. And perhaps in an hour I will be ashamed for having written at all.

It breaks my heart to read this letter. My father, blameless, apart from recklessness in lifting the budget, wrestled with a sense of guilt. For surely he must be guilty of something to deserve this fate. This is the ultimate triumph of totalitarianism: the victim who seeks blame for himself. Papa did not understand the charges against him. What crimes had he really committed, and why *now,* after so many years of performing exactly the same role as foreign correspondent? So, as a rational man, he searched for *something* he had done to justify his punishment by the State. This is the psychological effect of isolation, the unbearable pressure on the individual to find some fault within himself.

But, at the same time, a wonderful man emerges, a man who cares as much about photographs of his children left on his desk as about his bank account. A man who just wants to be able to support his family, but fears being a burden to them more than he fears death. A man who is incapable of *asking* for anything for himself. It is moving to discover, thanks to the AVO, this side of Papa, which (as he told his jailer) he always concealed.

September 1955 was perhaps the cruelest month he passed in captivity. Contemplating what he was certain would be a very long sentence, he told his cell mate on September 9 that he hoped he could work as a prison translator—but would not mind working in the mines. He just wanted his case settled and this period of agonizing uncertainty over.

On September 12, the cell mate/informer reported that my father was hallucinating about his "old life." "Many times he thinks he is hearing his wife's voice, or his father's." Papa's mental state must have been very fragile after so many months of interrogation and captivity. Perhaps, too, those hallucinations were a relief from the monstrous present: the stench of the disinfectant with which he had to scrub down his cell each morning, the sound of the guard slamming the peephole open and shut every few minutes, the craving for real food and cigarettes, the shooting pain from his chronic glaucoma, which had reappeared in prison.

Two days after my father's hallucinations, his cell mate reported that he still had not received an answer to his letter, and that he was "bitter" that they wouldn't tell him about his children. While awaiting his trial, my father was asked to submit descriptions of all the Western diplomats and journalists with whom he had contact in his years as AP correspondent. This forty-six-page document actually makes enjoyable reading. Papa, who always seemed slightly detached and even remote, comes across as a sharp observer of the world. What he provides the AVO is a sociological and psychological profile of a world as foreign to the nasty, brutish, paranoid universe of the secret police as life on Mars. With tantalizing detail, he describes characters the AVO could only glimpse through a telephoto lens. By my father's lights, these diplomats seemed to spring from Somerset Maugham's world. Politics, and the deadly Cold War chess game, seem of little interest to these ladies and gentlemen. Giving the AVO nothing incriminating about his friends, Papa spends more time analyzing various marriages, individuals' relative aptitude for bridge, and their peculiar wardrobe choices than anything useful for a spy trial. How exasperating it must have been for the AVO to get this intimate a look at their Enemies, without any useful political content. Thus did Papa outwit his captors, seemingly fulfilling their command for a full report on all his "spy contacts"—in reality providing nothing of the sort. Here, for example, is his description of the CIA station chief in Budapest, Geza Katona: "He is second generation Hungarian-American, of medium build and with a Hungarian-style handlebar mustache he grew when he arrived here. He speaks pretty good Hungarian and loves to sing Hungarian folk songs and dance the *czardas*."

And again about Max Finger, the economic attaché from 1951 to 1953: "A typical New York Jewish intellectual, good-looking with perfect command of French. His first marriage was unlucky, but he himself seemed well balanced, always charming—a man of few words. . . . He was passionate about Hungarian history and before he was transferred began weekly seminars on the subject at the legation, to which he planned on inviting Hungarian guest lecturers." About George Abbott, the legation counselor, he wrote, "A tall, severe man of fifty-five, whose health issues did not inhibit him from being a passionate golfer, tennis player, drinker, and bridge player. He lived a very full social life. Abbott was, without a doubt, one of the great intellects of the mission, ambitious and capable. Other diplomats shared this view: British economic attaché Simpson once noted that 'Those were the days, when Abbott, [British ambassador Lord Robin] Hankey, and [Israeli ambassador] Avner, retreated from the party and put their heads together.' . . . Abbott liked to drink and got drunk quickly and once in 1953 under the influence he demanded to know how come I hadn't been arrested yet! I am sure it was only partly a question and partly a suspicion that I was working as a spy for the Hungarian authorities." (Clever touch, that last item.)

In this vein my father describes a group of people far from home, but making the best of it. Flirting with beautiful women (the Hungarian wife of the Argentine ambassador, Mrs. González, was the most spectacular), matching wits across tennis courts and bridge tables, while the AVO crouched in the shrubbery.

Papa deflated the case against the chief of the American mission, with his description: "In my opinion," he begins the profile the AVO was most avidly awaiting, "Ravndal is always and without exception kind, and makes everyone feel that he or she is the most important person in the world. . . . From his earliest youth, he aspired to a career as an opera singer [what could the AVO do with that?] and studied music in Vienna. It was there that he met his wife, a fellow music student, rumored to be the daughter of a baron of Jewish origin. . . . As far as I know, he is quite religious, a strong-willed, many-sided personality, fond of smoking and drinking. Whatever he undertakes, he does wholeheartedly, and then drops with equal speed." And, in a final, tantalizingly useless detail, my father makes this pronouncement about Ravndal: "Among all the diplomats I have ever known, he and his wife are the most formidable bridge partners." Did the AVO realize Papa was playing with them?

I read with the greatest interest my father's impression of assistant military attaché Richard Glaspell: "He arrived in 1953 with his wife, Mimi, a rather showy blonde, and the two of them have kept the company of a younger set, since both of them like to sing and dance and enjoy themselves. They have two children, a boy and a girl." Hardly the profile of a dangerous agent, which is no doubt one reason why Warrant Officer Glaspell was able to get away with his treachery for as long as he did.

I hope that writing this report, laced with irony and wit that the AVO could not decode, provided my father momentary escape from his bleak cell.

ON SEPTEMBER 17, my father's informer/cell mate did something that may have saved Papa's life. On that day, "Tibor" reported, "I noticed a number of white tablets on the cell floor. After tasting one, I realized from its bitter taste that they were sleeping pills. Marton said he didn't know where they had come from, maybe left behind by the former inmate. But I noticed him patting the lining of his jacket. When he was taken to the washroom I called a guard and suggested he do a thorough search of the cell. They found sixty Sevenal tablets in the lining of Marton's jacket. Marton admitted that he had been collecting them for the purpose of poisoning himself, but since his wife's arrest, has given up on the idea of suicide. He kept them in case he is ever put through the brutalities of his early period."

"Tibor" reported that he "sternly" lectured my father on the immorality of a family man considering suicide, and what a tragedy it would have been if he had gone through with it, "leaving his children in the most desperate situation, now without either parent." Was Tibor rewarded with extra cigarettes, I wonder, for saving a prisoner who was still useful to the State?

Was it a rare trace of humanity that prompted my parents' jailers to allow them to see each other before their trial, after all? More likely it was fear that their first meeting after nine months might explode into something unplanned and emotional, disturbing the proceedings' smooth choreography. My mother prepared for the first meeting with her husband in a characteristic way: she tried to improve her appearance. "At breakfast," she wrote in her memoir, "using the coffee in the bottom of my mess tin for a mirror, I 'prettied' myself for my husband. . . . I combed my hair carefully and dressed in my nylon blouse, washed for the occasion."

My father, however, was not allowed to shave his stubble before the guard led him to Major Gero's office for a meeting he both feared and longed for. "There she was," he wrote later, "smiling with arms outstretched, but with tears in her eyes. . . . I knew that she saw on my face what I had gone through in the nine months that we had not seen each other." Indeed my mother was shocked by her husband's appearance. "I was not prepared for the enormous dark eyes in wells

159

of purple shadows. I was not prepared for the sadness and fatigue that shone from those eyes. I gasped with shock and sorrow and then I rushed forward and we embraced and kissed each other, weeping, despite the major's orders. I told him about the children, where they were and who was helping them and their school and their health. He asked me about my own health and I realized for the first time that he was as shocked at my appearance as I was at his. . . . Suddenly, the major, who had been fumbling with some documents on his desk, rose, and mumbling, 'Excuse me for a moment,' left the room, leaving the door open behind him. This, I knew, was Opportunity. 'Listen to me!' I whispered in English. 'The Americans will free you!' It was as though I had thrown a rope to a drowning man. His wide eyes became wider and he stared at me like a deaf person trying to identify a sound he cannot understand. 'Darling,' I repeated, taking his hands and whispering, forming the words carefully with my lips, 'the Americans will free us.'"

"The major returned," my father picked up the narrative at this point, "and Ilona continued her report about the children. There was one more thing I wanted to tell her before the thirty minutes allotted to us were over. I tried to be casual when I told her I believed she would be free soon, at least many years before I would, and that I wanted her to divorce me. I would be an old man by the time the Communists let me go, no longer of much use to her and the children. She laughed me off and the major smiled, too, but made no comment. Then the thirty minutes were over, and, escorted back to my cell, I cursed myself for not having used the time more wisely— and especially for not having asked her to explain what she meant by the mysterious message."

"Marton returned from his meeting with his wife," "Tibor" reported to his masters, "and cried. He said he was reassured that she is not angry with him and doesn't blame him for what happened to them. He says he still wants her to divorce him. But he was happy that the children are well looked after. He is afraid, however, that the imprisonment of their parents and their separation from them is psychologically damaging to the children, a fact that is already evident in his younger daughter." (What, I would love to know, had my father sensed about me, separated as we were by the thick walls of his maximum security fortress?)

Shortly after this meeting, my parents were led into one of the stark courtrooms, located inside the prison complex, to face the most notorious of the AVO's handpicked "justices," Dr. Bela Jonas. Judge Jonas, known as "the Blood Judge," dealt exclusively with cases of conspiracy, espionage, and treason. By 1952, the period of greatest terror, Jonas had sentenced fifty people to death. Unlike most judges, Jonas liked to attend his victims' execution. Having covered a number of his trials, my parents were well aware of his record. Mama and Papa stood before this nondescript, balding little man, not as journalists this time, but as his victims.

How satisfying at long last for Jonas to face two such flagrant and persistent Enemies of the People. And yet, how disappointing, too, that when he finally had the Martons in his court, executions at the slightest murmur of "disloyalty" to the State had fallen out of favor.

"I was only allowed to read the long and boring document which accused me of being a spy and a traitor once," my father would write. "I could not make notes and was really not too interested in the whole farce . . . convinced that the only thing they could do with me was to let me 'rot' in prison for many years, to use one of their favorite expressions."

The charges against my father were serious: he had been a "permanent advisor" to the Americans. Specifically, he advised them to send a black diplomat to Budapest, and on how to improve broadcasts of the Voice of America. He had "stolen" the Hungarian budget and given it to the American economic attaché. My father pleaded not guilty.

The charge against my mother was, even by the AVO's standards, laughable: discussing the price of eggs (and meat) with the Americans. A treasonable offense in Rakosi's Hungary. "All the facts in the indictment were true," my mother recalled. "I myself had given them to Major Gero during those weeks of interrogation. But everything I assumed to be so innocent turned out to be treason according to paragraph such and such in the great legal code." She pleaded partially guilty. "Partially," she explained to her cell mate/informer, "because I feel guilty toward my children."

This was what the Communists deemed a "fair trial": no evidence of the crimes, nor witnesses, and the defendants, cut off from the world for almost a year, not permitted to use their own counsel. Preserved as a sort of quaint and harmless period piece was the right of the defendant to a "final word." My father used this "right" to plead my mother's innocence.

Facing the icy gaze of Judge Jonas*—beneath portraits of Stalin, Lenin, and Rakosi—my father began his "final word" to the People's Court. "I would urge the court," he said, "to bear in mind that my wife's parents were murdered." Reading this blunt statement of fact regarding my grandparents comes as a shock. Their deportation was kept hidden from us children. I was thirty before I learned from a virtual stranger that my grandparents were exterminated in Auschwitz. My parents never discussed it. Seeing it in an AVO document, so plainly stated by my father, leaves not a trace of the doubt that floated around this unspoken subject, when it arose, painfully, twenty-five years later in the safety of our Maryland home.

"I would also like the court to take into account her two small children," he pleaded. "I am, have always been, and will stay, a patriot." He concluded: "The 'crimes' I am charged with are inextricably connected to the practice of my profession."

The sentence—like everything else in these proceedings—was preordained. "There we stood," my mother recalled, "and for a minute I remembered the many others I had seen standing in similar courts before us, and who had heard the same words from the judge:

---

* Jonas committed suicide a year later, during the October 1956 Revolution.

'In the name of the People's Republic, we find you guilty.'" My father was sentenced to thirteen years of prison, my mother to six. Had
they served those sentences, my parents' worst fears would indeed
have been realized. They would have missed our childhoods. Raised
by strangers, we would be strangers to them. My father would have
emerged from prison a broken old man of fifty-nine, my mother pre-
maturely old at fifty.

Only one part of this ordeal would they easily talk about in the
coming years: their walk back to their cells. "Of all the walks we took
together," my father recalled, "in the tree covered hills of Buda, or
among the azaleas of Chevy Chase, this one through the dark deserted
corridors of Fo Utca I will always remember."

"On the long walk," my mother remembered, "I held Andrew's
arm and whispered to him why I was sure we would be freed. I told
him that the American legation was in constant touch with the AP in
New York and that they were merely waiting for the trial to take place
before taking any steps. . . . I told him that Ravndal had promised that
the United States would do its utmost to help us and that the British
and all the other Western diplomats had called on me not only to offer consolation, but to promise help. I kept on talking and talking, in
a low voice, to raise his spirits and to give him some hope if I should
be freed before him.

"On the third floor [of the prison], we turned in the corridor. Our
guard knocked on the door, the jailer in charge opened it, and there
was the familiar sight of two rows of cells, the three guards making
their rounds—the dead silence. Now I knew Andrew was kept on this
floor. I was on the fifth. We stopped in front of a cell on the corner. I
looked up: number 12. In front of the opposite cell there was an extra
guard peeping in the Judas. 'Gabor Peter,' Andrew whispered." I suppose there was some poetic justice in the AVO's founder occupying
the cell next door to my father's, a victim of Rakosi's need for purges
in the brief post-Stalinist "thaw."

Now that they were sentenced, my parents were allowed under

the law to receive one visitor a month. But even that law was circumvented, as my parents appealed their sentence, and thus the authorities found another excuse to keep them isolated. But my ever-enterprising mother found a way around this hurdle. "If I could not have a visitor from outside," she protested, "I should have one from the 'inside.'" And so on Christmas Eve 1955, "when the whole building was deserted and only a few AVO men were on duty, I was allowed a meeting with Andrew. It was our twelfth wedding anniversary. We sat in Major Kretschmer's office and talked for one hour. We spoke of the new year that would soon begin and speculated on what it would hold for us. 'Good things, I know,' I told him. Andrew smiled ruefully, and reminded me of New Year's Eve a year ago."

It is particularly poignant for me, their child, to read this description of Mama and Papa's closeness. They had traveled far since the summer of Papa's flirtation with Mrs. Simpson, and Mama's affair with Lajos.

Chapter 14

FROM THE OTHER SIDE OF THE WORLD

That winter, my sister and I settled into our sad imitation of family life with a family of strangers. For my parents, too, now serving time as convicts, prison held fewer surprises or shocks. It was a place without seasons or color or, in my father's case, hope. There was one improvement in their prison routine following their conviction. They were put to work as translators—a welcome distraction from the sea of empty hours of prison life. With this new role came the astonishing "gift" of a small wooden table and a chair—a huge event for convicts such as my parents, accustomed to squatting on their bunks. Best of all was the portable typewriter my father was given to facilitate his work. It turned out to be his own, appropriated along with all our other possessions.

For his first assignment, my father was handed several pages torn from a magazine, the title and the author's name carefully cut out. "It was a wonderful new pastime for me," my father recalled, "obviously written by an atomic physicist, discussing in philosophical terms the morality of using nuclear weapons in the light of . . . Nagasaki and Hiroshima." My father deliberately took his time. "That evening I ate my dinner sitting on a chair, with my tin bowl on a table, turning my back to the Judas." (I wonder now if perhaps some of Papa's subsequent distaste for informal, buffet-style dining was a result of prison.)

Just as in my own attempt to decode AVO documents, I found human error that revealed the actual names of those they were shielding under code names, so, too, did my father in his translation for the secret police decode the author of his work. "Several weeks later," he wrote, "they brought similar pages, obviously from the same magazine; again everything that might have given me a clue to their origin carefully cut out. . . . The article was an answer to the previous one and whoever wrote it referred in the text to Leo Szilard and to the *Bulletin of Atomic Scientists*."

My mother, too, was put to work translating scientific articles from British and American publications. When she asked for an English-Hungarian dictionary, Webster's was promptly produced. "Your husband's been using this one," the guard let slip. "I scrutinized every page," my mother recalled, "certain that he would not use a pencil, but certain also that he would manage somehow [to send her a message]. . . . At last I found it. On the last blank page he had scratched with his fingernail a prison love letter: 'More than ever.'"

Each of us dealt with the trauma of that year according to our temperament. My father prepared himself for the abyss of endless incarceration by not allowing hope to seep into his cell. He still contemplated suicide. My mother alternated between optimism and crushing despair. My sister always seemed up to something with the younger of the two Hellei sisters, Rici, staging operas, playing dress-up with the attic collection, chiding me to stop acting like a baby. As I search my features in the "family" portrait from that year, my sister and I surrounded by strangers, pretending to be a part of this family, I cannot find the chin-out, feisty little fighter my father had dubbed "Dennis the Menace" the year before. During this year, I made up my mind to smile at the world. What other weapons did I have, but to be irresistible to adults?

Silenced in their own country, my parents were beginning to get the attention of the world beyond Hungary's borders. In late 1955, following the success of the Geneva summit, Hungary began to grant visas to a handful of foreign journalists. Three American newsmen arrived in Budapest: Jack Raymond and John MacCormac of *The New York Times,* and Seymour Freidin, European correspondent of *The New York Post.* In a confidential memorandum to Washington, chargé Spencer Barnes noted:

> *Two important subjects each correspondent brought up [with Hungarian officials]: the fates of Cardinal Mindszenty and of the two Martons. With regard to the Martons, the official line seemed to change between Raymond's visit and that of Freidin and MacCormac just a short time later. Raymond was told . . . in the Foreign Ministry that the Martons were being held for anti-State activities, and this coincided with a statement made around the same time by Mr. Rakosi to Senator Estes Kefauver. Both Freidin and MacCormac were given to understand that the main grievance against the Martons was their allegedly unpatriotic and biased attitude toward the new Hungary. When asked how this relatively minor transgression merited such harsh treatment as has been given the Martons, the Hungarians referred the interlocutors to the Ministry of the Interior!*

Two months after their actual trial and sentencing, a front page *New York Times* story, dated January 15, 1956, under the headline "Hungary Sentences AP Man and Wife," featured a photograph of our still intact family, before my parents' arrest. "Budapest radio announced tonight," the article read,

> *that Endre Marton, correspondent for the Associated Press . . . has been sentenced to six years in prison* [in December, following their appeal, my parents' sentences had been halved] *on a charge of espionage. His wife, Ilona, who worked for the United Press was sentenced to three years, the broadcast said. . . . Dr. Marton dropped out of sight eleven months ago. The last telephone contact with Mrs. Marton from Vienna was June 19. The Martons have two young daughters, Kati and Juli, who were reported*

to be living with a pensioned Hungarian university professor in a suburb of Budapest. . . . Frank J. Starzel, general manager of the AP, issued this statement today: "Endre Marton is a distinguished Hungarian journalist. His activities on behalf of the Associated Press were those normal for a foreign correspondent except that his scope was sharply limited by the restrictions imposed in police states upon news sources and reporters. . . . In totalitarian states an individual can be convicted of espionage merely because he showed interest in subjects which the regime has decided are its secret property. That apparently was Marton's crime, in addition to having been an outspoken anti-Communist."

On February 4, 1956, *The New York Times,* in yet another front-page story, headlined "U.S. Again Forbids Trips to Hungary," reported, "The United States today banned travel to Communist Hungary by American citizens and called off proposed talks with the Hungarian Government. It also informed Hungary that it would impose new travel restrictions on Hungarian diplomats in this country. . . . The action arose from the Hungarian government's arrest in Budapest of Endre Marton, Associated Press correspondent and his wife, Ilona, United Press correspondent in Hungary."

At the same time, Ambassador Ravndal urged Secretary of State John Foster Dulles to adopt a tougher line toward my parents' captors. In a secret telegram dated January 16, 1956, Ravndal wrote:

I earnestly recommend the [State] Department exploit all available media to give world wide publicity to Hungarian violations of human rights. . . . I also recommend that I be authorized to send a note to Foreign Minister . . . stating:

- *U.S. immediately endorses American passports as* nonvalid *for travel to Hungary, which of course involves cancellation of* Porgy and Bess *visit* [a much publicized State Department project].
- *U.S. immediately subjects Hungarian Legation in Washington to same travel restrictions that apply to American Legation in Budapest.*

• *U.S. is abandoning preparation for talks re expanded trade and related credits.*

The State Department followed Ambassador Ravndal's suggestions and delivered a stinging note to the Hungarian legation in Washington and, simultaneously, to the Foreign Ministry in Budapest. The State Department found a clever way to censure the Hungarian government for its treatment of two of its own citizens, without seeming to intervene in the country's "internal affairs," by raising the issue of freedom of the press.

The protracted detention incommunicado of Associated Press and of the United Press of the legitimate professional services of these experienced local reporters, have also prejudiced free access to news sources within Hungary and must therefore be regarded as an abridgment of freedom of the press. . . . For many years now the Government and people of the United States have looked in vain for sole slight sign that the present leadership of Hungary might one day be disposed to act like an independent and responsible government, to honor its international obligations, and to show a decent respect for the rights of the Hungarian people. Whatever its pretensions to principle, the Hungarian Government can command no credibility in its words and no confidence . . . in its actions.

The following day *The New York Times* again picked up the story, this time as an editorial. Entitled "Truth vs. Totalitarianism," the *Times* noted,

One common superstition of totalitarian governments is that people will be more contented if they don't know the unpleasant things that are going on and that a regime will be admired in the outside world if it conceals its sins and stupidities. This is true in the Communist totalitarian countries where a foreign reporter does not know from day to day how long the policy of leniency toward truth telling will last. . . . This is what has happened to

Endre Marton . . . serving a six-year sentence for espionage. This is what happened to his wife, Ilona Marton, a Budapest correspondent for United Press. Mrs. Marton is serving a three-year term. Espionage in such a country is what the Government says it is. When used as a trap for journalists it may cover the kind of information any good journalist gets and publishes simply because he is a good journalist.

This concerted official and media pounding on behalf of two prisoners stung the Hungarians. On February 7, the Hungarian Foreign Ministry returned Dulles's note, calling it "an insult to the Government and People of Hungary."

WHILE OUR playmates and my parents' closest friends were too afraid to visit my sister and me, in a distant place called Salt Lake City, in the state of Utah, a doctor who knew us only from the newspapers was making a desperate attempt to save my sister and me. In a letter dated January 30, 1956, addressed to Secretary of State Dulles, Dr. Henry R. Plenk, the director of radiology at St. Mark's Hospital in Salt Lake City, made an offer. "Mrs. Plenk and I," the letter began, "were shocked to read of the arrest of Dr. and Mrs. Endre Marton, correspondents for the United Press and Associated Press, by the Hungarian Government. We understand that their two daughters are living with a pensioner Hungarian University professor in Budapest. We would be delighted to welcome the two children into our home for whatever period of time may be necessary, and would be happy to adopt them if their parents would wish us to do so. . . . We have sufficient space in our house and adequate resources to guarantee the children's support. Would you be kind enough to advise us what steps we could take to succeed in bringing the children to this country?"

Unaccustomed to dealing with adoption issues, the State Department was thrown into confusion by Dr. Plenk's letter. After meetings between Undersecretary of State R. M. McKisson and officials in the visa and consular divisions, including Allyn C. Donaldson, the director of the Office of Consular Services, the following reply was sent to the Salt Lake City doctor nearly a month later: "The circumstances of the Martons' arrest and the publicity which the case has received would undoubtedly prove insurmountable obstacles to any willingness on the part of the Hungarian authorities to permit the children to leave the country on other than Government business. [What sort of government business would two little girls be used for, I wonder, in the mind of Mr. Donaldson?] It is most probable," the head of Consular Services asserted, "that prospective emigrants of this age are among those least likely to be granted permission to depart in as much as they are viewed by the Communist regime as having potential value as economic and political assets."

So much for a bold and humane offer from Dr. and Mrs. Plenk. Mr. Donaldson was perhaps unfamiliar with the lowly status of children like us. Children entering school were classified into six categories according to "class descent":*

1. Worker
2. Peasant
3. Intellectual
4. Petty employee
5. "Other"
6. "Class enemy"

Categories one and two had an easy pass through high school to university, while the third, fourth, and fifth, in descending order, received university education in very rare instances. Juli and I were "class enemies," dealt with almost as strictly as were Jews in Nazi Germany.

Yet another road not taken in my life: as the adoptive daughter of a

---

* George Paloczi-Horvath, *The Undefeated* (London: Eland, 1993), p. 280.

Utah radiologist and his child psychiatrist wife, herself of Hungarian background. What remarkable generosity of spirit—and in what stark contrast to our fellow Hungarians!* But every dictator knows how to use fear, one of the most potent of all human emotions, to suppress compassion or even love.

---

* I recently located the Plenks (both doctors, he a radiologist, she a child psychiatrist) in Salt Lake City and called to thank them for their long-ago efforts on our behalf. The Plenks, now in their nineties, stilll remembered their touching offer to adopt us, and I was profoundly moved to talk to these almost-surrogate parents of fifty years ago.

Chapter 15

REUNITED

Papa is free! My mother had been released from jail for a few months already—but this was the happy day of our family reunion in August 1956. (We are wearing the party dresses given to us by U.S. Ambassador Ravndal.)

I T WAS THE early afternoon of April 3, 1956, my birthday. I had rushed home from school because my "big sister," Cunci, had promised to accompany me to our old house, on Csaba Utca. I had not been back since the summer before, and I longed for a glimpse. I hoped I would find my old playmates at home, maybe even peer into our apartment, whose front door had been sealed with the State's red stamp. I wanted to see everything we had left behind, even if for only a few minutes, and to show Cunci my lost world.

I held her hand as we walked toward the Zugliget bus stop for the long ride down to Csaba Utca. Suddenly, a car pulled up next to us, which I recognized as belonging to our occasional visitor, Mihaly Szekely. My Aunt Magda sprang out. "Look in the back seat, Kati," she said, "it's your birthday present." It was my mother. I jumped in her lap and we both burst out in tears. Mamika, Mamika, I kept repeating. She looked haggard and much older than when I last saw her, nearly a year before. As with her arrest, there had been no warning. But I had my mother back! The blast of joy was as powerful as the earlier pain. We drove back to Cunci's house and to the kind people who lived there, and I knew that never again would I have to pretend that this was my home, that they were my family.

My sister was hanging from the thick branch of a tall tree when she spotted my mother and promptly fell to the ground. So my mother switched back to the consoling role, kissing my sister's bruised knee. Juli laughed through her tears. For children fortunate enough never to have endured an open-ended separation from their parents, there is simply no way to describe that feeling of being whole again. For the rest of that evening and the night she spent with us (though she joked that her cell had been warmer than our house) we competed for my mother's attention with our stories of a year's worth of triumphs (my sister) and tribulations (me). My mother laughed and cried and told us about her last day in prison.

Summoned from her cell by Major Gero a few days before, she was instructed to draft an amnesty appeal to the Ministry of Justice. Momentous events had roiled the Soviet Empire in the weeks since Khrushchev's 20th Party Congress speech, revealing some of Stalin's crimes. Almost overnight, Mama's appeal was approved. Gero called my Aunt Magda, who at this point picked up the story. "Do not even think of calling anybody with this news!" the major instructed Magda. But, true to form, by the time my aunt arrived to the Fo Utca to pick up Mama, "half the city" had been informed.

Washington learned of my mother's liberation, indirectly at least, thanks to our concierge, Mrs. Priegle. In a confidential memorandum Ravndal wrote Dulles on April 7, "Housemeister in Marton apartment has reported to servant Legation officer who lives next door that Mrs. Marton was released from prison April 3 and release confirmed by chance meeting between Legation officer [Tom Rogers] and Marton children. . . . Recommend no publicity re Martons until release of both confirmed, more substantive information re his prospects become known, or until her release becomes matter of public information."

Mama moved fast to recover our apartment—but not fast enough for her impatient children. Now every additional day and every night at our foster parents' seemed unnecessary. We wanted to be with our mother, in our real home. Our apartment had been left vacant—another sign of the uncertain political climate—but everything in it now belonged to the State. My mother was informed that she had the right to buy it all back, if she could raise $2,000 for the contents. "I wrote the Associated Press," she recalled, "and told them they were my only hope. . . . They came to my help. Moreover, they assured me that Andrew's salary, which had never stopped, would continue. In return for this generosity, I offered my services as correspondent in Andrew's place. At the same time, United Press received permission from the authorities to rehire me. I was back in business." A good thing for the American wire services, as historic events were soon to unfold in Hungary.

A tightly sealed country had begun to open its door to the West, but very slightly. *Time* magazine bureau chief in Vienna Simon Bourgin was issued a visa. On July 5, after a seventeen-day trip, Bourgin reported on Radio Free Europe:

I found that the political situation had changed considerably. Hungarians were debating openly about Rakosi, and it wasn't even so much of a debate. They were saying that Rakosi had to go . . . and this was the sort of talk you heard from mechanics in garages and middle class people and hotel porters—anybody you could manage to take aside and talk to for a bit. . . . The events that started in Moscow with the de-Stalinization pro-

*gram . . . are traveling at a pace where the results cannot be predicted. . . .
Mrs. Ilona Marton, whose husband, Andrew, is still in jail, and who was
released some weeks ago, was reaccredited as the American news agencies'
correspondent on Saturday night, and wrote her first story about this on
Sunday, which means, incidentally, that one should pay rather more attention to the American press agencies' dispatches that come out of Budapest,
because Mrs. Marton is an extremely competent reporter.**

Of course, I was too young to understand anything about Khrushchev's stunning speech about Stalin's crimes. The Hungarian press was
forbidden by Rakosi from printing the speech, but soon copies were
circulating in Budapest and causing great excitement. To me, it seemed
that the whole city was celebrating with me over my mother's return.

The good news continued to break, carrying us like a friendly
wave all summer long. In July, the most loathed and feared presence
of my childhood, Matyas Rakosi, was fired by the Kremlin, dispatched
to early retirement in the Soviet Union. His deputy, Erno Gero, succeeded him. A faithful servant of his departed boss, he was too gray
a figure to cause fear and trembling. Virtually overnight, Stalin's and
Rakosi's images disappeared from public places.

By early May, we had moved back to our hilltop apartment, with
our toys miraculously back on the shelves as we had left them. Only
a few valuable items—our car, my father's camera, my mother's dia-
mond ring, which we always blamed on Madame, herself gone forever
from our lives—were missing. We were too happy to care about any
of that. The other kids in our old house acted as if we had never left,
as if no one had seen the AVO grab our parents, carry away our possessions, and seal our front door with its red stamp. No questions were
asked. We were back. Everybody picked up where they had left off.

We had new playmates next door. While we were gone, the Rogers
family had moved into the diplomatic residence (previously occupied

---

* *New Hungarian Quarterly,* vol. XXXVII, No. 142, Summer 1996.

by Mr. and Mrs. Don Downs). Best of all, they had four daughters of roughly our ages. "I remember the street play," Arabella Meadows-Rogers recalled in 2008, "the gang of kids from your building, the bicycles. We all played in our yard and on the hill behind your apartment. We climbed trees, jumped in and out of the fishpond in our garden."

Just as fast as I got my mother back, I dropped the good behavior I had imposed on myself during the past year. What relief to revert to my former, more authentic "Dennis the Menace" self. "You and I took up smoking that summer," Arabella said. "Both cigarettes we'd stolen from my mother and twigs. Our maid, Ann Nadasdy [a countess from one of Hungary's oldest aristocratic families, reduced to working as a chambermaid], found us in one of the unused maid's rooms upstairs, and got really mad. Juli was our 'big' sister and we weren't allowed to cross the street without her," Arabella continued. "I picked up that Zsuzsi [Kalmar, the daughter of the AVO officer across the hall from us] was to be spurned and that Erzsi and Magdi [Mrs. Priegle's daughters] were to be felt sorry for. Even at that young age, there was something special about being in the street playing with Hungarian children. So different from hanging out only with Foreign Service children. I felt very honored to be included. I remember your little red kerchiefs on your school uniform."

That summer, I recall Arabella's younger sister, Louisa, shouting across the fence between our two homes. "Mrs. Marton!" the four-year-old bellowed, "where is your husband?" No doubt she had heard her parents, Tom and Sarah, whispering about my absent father. We wondered, too. But with each passing week, my mother seemed more like herself. We resumed our summer routine: took the tram to the Lukacs baths, or the bus to Margit Island for a bigger treat, swimming in the Olympic-size pool. I held my mother's hand tighter than ever, and I was happy.

In June, after weeks of tireless effort, my mother was allowed to visit my father in prison. Sitting in the old familiar interrogation room, awaiting my father, she asked Major Gero if her husband knew she had been freed. Gero shook his head. "But you promised you'd let him know!" she cried. We had other orders, he replied. The AVO's operating principle was still to resist every opportunity for a human gesture. When they finally were allowed to meet, my father, in my mother's words, "nearly broke down with happiness," at the sight of his obviously free wife. "When I told him that I had even gotten back my old job, he was upset." You must not go to the American legation, he admonished her. You must not take such risks. "I wondered how I could convince him that the climate of the country had changed, that I and everyone else now enjoyed relatively much greater freedom. I had been warned in advance not to speak [to him] about such things. Then, suddenly, I thought I found a way. . . . I had dinner with John MacCormac last night, I said casually. He could not believe it. Mac-Cormac, a *New York Times* correspondent, a dear friend of ours, had been expelled from Hungary in 1948 and told never to come back. Now, in 1956, he was not only back, but came and went whenever he wished. This, more than anything else, was proof of the changed political situation for Andrew. 'It won't be long,' I told him when I left."

Sometime in August 1956, as we waited for the light to change to cross the street to the Palatinus swimming pool on Margit Island, I broke free from Mama's hand. "Kati!" she shouted. "Stop!" The next thing I knew I was lying between the front wheels of a car, strangers peering down at me. "Are my red sandals okay?" was the first thing that popped out of my mouth, for I had just received the sharpest sandals from the AP's Vienna correspondent. The sandals were intact, but I suffered a concussion that kept me in the hospital for days, crying for Mama the whole time. Even with her husband still in prison, and working for both AP and UP, she was at my bedside every evening. How selfish children are. It never occurred to me to thank her or to apologize for my willfulness, then or later.

AND NOW I learn from the AVO files that Mama's freedom came with strings. They still had the power to wreck lives. Nobody had ordered AVO agents to look for another line of work. (As of July 1956, 31,000 agents kept watch over a population of under ten million.*) Every ten days or so Mama was obliged to meet with an agent in a "safe house." According to the AVO files, she did not submit written reports but summarized her activities, whom she had seen, what she had learned, particularly during her visits to the American legation. This condition belatedly fulfilled the Americans' expectation of the price exacted from my parents during the worst terror. I recall the two American diplomats, Ernest Nagy and Tom Rogers, both telling me that, even before their arrest, "For their good and ours, we did not tell them things that were sensitive."

Learning of this string attached to my mother's freedom pains me. My memory of that summer shimmers still with happiness; her freedom, our reunion. But it is clear that once the AVO got their teeth into you they would not let go—ever. Those interrogators enjoyed harassment of my poor mother as she tried to piece her life back together, while her husband was still in prison, and with her daughters needier than ever of her presence. I wish I had known this while she was still alive, so I could have told her how much I admire her spirit and her courage—knowing now what I did not know when she was alive.

On a damp, overcast November day in 2007, I head out of the Archives in search of the Ady Cinema, which had been the location of my mother's forced meetings with the AVO. I want to retrace her steps, and thus, somehow, lamely, to share her burden. People along the way tell me, yes, there used to be a movie theater in the neighborhood, but no more. It has started raining and the gleaming new Budapest looks like the gray city of my childhood. My anger at the AVO—and, I am ashamed to admit, with Hungary itself—grows with each block. Along the way, I have taken the wrong turn and I am now

---

* Paul Lendvai, *One Day That Shook the Communist World* (Princeton: Princeton University Press, 2008), p. 107.

in Jozsefvaros, a neighborhood unfamiliar to me. Soot-blackened wrecks, seemingly untouched since World War II, sit side by side with freshly restored pink and white eclectic buildings on the narrow streets of this still raw neighborhood on the edge of the city's new prosperity. A man in a green loden coat, a cigarette in one hand, a large dog on a tight leash in the other, asks me if I'm lost. His tone is not friendly. This is a neighborhood where strangers are noticed—like in the old days. Sweat and rain drip from my face. Dark is falling, and there are no taxis in this part of town. I walk for a long time, searching for some familiar landmark, my rage at the AVO and irritation with myself mounting with each step. But I cannot find the old Ady Cinema.

In April 2008, I return to Budapest. This time I am accompanied by my own daughter, Elizabeth. I am calmer now, having, since my last visit, assimilated the latest revelation thrown up by the files, that my mother was forced to maintain contact with the AVO after being released from prison. On a sunny day, holding hands, Elizabeth and I find the former Ady Cinema, above which those meetings took place. It is across the street from the fabled Café New York, which, it turns out, also played a role in the AVO's post-prison harassment of my parents. My daughter's pride at her grandmother's courage in "facing down" the AVO soothes my own anger. Elizabeth takes pictures of the spot where her grandmother was humbled. I head back to the Archives for another trove.

ON AUGUST 13, 1956, with Rakosi already gone, and the city buzzing with new freedoms and a tentative self-confidence, an AVO officer named Rezso Kovacs, in a top secret memorandum addressed to the minister of the interior, declared: "The crimes committed by Dr. Endre Marton—treason and espionage—are sufficiently demonstrated by evidence to prompt us not to recommend that his sentence be lowered. Marton should continue to serve his sentence," Kovacs concludes, "unless issues of the highest national interest deem otherwise." A deft way for Major Kovacs to express his own disposition against freeing such a proven traitor, while covering his bureaucratic backside, just in case the winds continued to shift.

Indeed, the very next day, the winds did shift. On August 14, *New York Times* correspondent John MacCormac sat down with Erno Gero, the new Communist Party chief, for a rare interview. On August 15, the *Times* carried MacCormac's story on its front page under the headline "Hungarian Asks Closer U.S. Ties." "The Hungarian government would like to improve relations with the United States," read the lead. "'We would like far better relations with the United States. How highly we value America, both past and present, is shown by the fact that the statue of Washington still stands in Varosliget [a Budapest park]. But, as a Hungarian proverb says, "For a love affair you need two people."'" On my father's fate, however, Gero was opaque. "He was asked why Hungary did not initiate better relations by freeing imprisoned former employees of the United States Legation in Budapest and Endre Marton, former Associated Press Correspondent here. He replied that these persons had been tried as Hungarian citizens and their disposition therefore was a Hungarian issue."

On the same day as MacCormac's article appeared, my father's day had started exactly as every other since his conviction, utterly without hope. But at noon on August 15, the heavy steel door of his cell was unlocked and the jailer told him to get moving. In the interrogation room, he faced Major Kretschmer and a man wearing civilian clothes. "Colonel Jambor," Kretschmer nodded toward the stranger, "from the Ministry of the Interior." Then, Kretschmer proceeded to read the lines that, though my father was too stunned to follow at first, told him that he had been officially pardoned. He snapped to when the major said, "We want you to pick up your life where it was interrupted." Do you mean go back to work for the Associated Press, my father asked, in disbelief. Yes, go out there and see things for yourself. And report to the world. "You will be surprised by the changes," the colonel assured him.

In a state of shock, the prisoner was led back to his cell for the final time. He broke the convict's first rule, never to address the guards, when he whispered to his jailer, "I'm going home." The sergeant nodded with a grin. A new world indeed.

"I will give you one and a half hours," Major Kretschmer gruffly told my mother on the phone that same morning. "You must announce your husband's release to the Associated Press and the United Press. After you have done that, come at once and pick up your husband." Her heart pounding faster than her fingers raced over the typewriter keys, my mother did as she was told. "Then I ran into the street and flagged a taxi. When I told the driver my destination he looked at me in surprise. 'How can anyone look so happy going to prison?' I told him why and when we reached the prison I said, 'Wait for me.' 'Oh no,' he answered, 'I've seen too many go in and not come out. Pay me, lady, and get another cab when you come out.'"

By the time my mother's taxi dropped her off a block from the Fo Utca, my father's shirt, underwear, necktie, watch, and wallet had been returned to him. The prison barber had cleaned his face of its week-old stubble. My parents' reunion was restrained. She gave him one of her I-told-you-so smiles, and the rest they would save for later, away from this place. All that remained was for Major Kretschmer to give my father Ambassador Ravndal's Christmas presents, eight months late: cartons of Pall Malls and my father's favorite pipe tobacco. My mother magnanimously distributed the prized packets of American cigarettes to the secret police officers. Kretschmer then hauled from his large wall safe suitcases full of the photographs, correspondence, and files taken from our apartment on that long-ago night. Since my mother had already regaled the secret policemen with the story of the scared cabbie, Kretschmer offered an official car to drive the two ex-convicts home.

"Our house stood on a hillside," my father recalled, "and about two dozen steps led up to the entrance. I will always see my daughters—how small they were then!—running down the stairs in the warm summer afternoon, with their arms stretched out toward me, and crying in my arms."

My young and handsome father looked like an old man to me. His coal black hair was matted and flecked with gray. The pallor of his complexion I had never seen outside a hospital. We did not let him get much past the front door before my mother ordered him to remove the shiny, frayed suit he had been wearing since his arrest. My sister and I took it down to Mrs. Priegle to throw in the furnace. By now the whole neighborhood knew the prisoner was home, but everyone kept a respectful distance. While my father retreated to his bath, my mother and I ran down the hill to the open-air market on Szena Ter to buy the biggest, fattest goose we could find. By the time we returned, my father was wearing his favorite seersucker suit and tie and on the phone to the AP in Vienna, dictating the story of his own liberation.

Once again, Papa made the front page of *The New York Times* on August 17, under John MacCormac's byline, with the headline "AP Correspondent Freed by Hungary." "It was partly because of the arrest of the Martons," MacCormac reported, "that the United States banned travel to Hungary by Americans other than newspaper men and business men. This ban has tolled heavily against the tourist traffic that Hungary has been seeking to promote. The thaw in East-West relations and particularly Mr. Rakosi's disappearance from power apparently also operated to bring about Dr. Marton's release. This correspondent," the article concluded, "mentioned Dr. Marton's imprisonment in the course of an interview last Tuesday with Erno Gero, Mr. Rakosi's successor as Hungarian Communist Party chief. Mr. Gero said the case . . . was being reviewed."

A picture of Papa, movie star handsome, his thick black hair brushed back, his face unlined and his trademark pipe jutting from his lower lip, accompanied the article. He no longer looked like that picture, but in his seersucker suit, he was beginning to look more like himself. Today, I have that front page of the *Times* framed in our New York apartment

School was still out. Holding Papa's hands, Juli and I went almost everywhere with him. Like a famished man approaching his first meal, he inhaled the sights and smells of his city. He was stunned by the new freedoms—his and the city's. "There was no more looking back over one's shoulders," he recalled, "there was no flinching when I told those who did not know me that I was an American newspaperman." (To the end of his life, my father referred to himself as "an American newspaperman"—there was so much pride in that.) One of his first stops was to his old barber, a scene he described in his memoirs. "'I read in the paper that you were free,' the man said, working on my head with angry grunts, cursing the prison barber for what he had done to my hair. 'I have been expecting you for some time.' The barber's indifferent attitude amused but also annoyed me. People, I thought, should be more surprised to see me alive. I had no better luck when I enjoyed the unheard of luxury of a manicure after the old man got through with my head. I did not know the young manicurist and I warned her that I needed special attention because for eighteen months I had to bite off my nails when they became too long. 'Prison?' she asked without surprise. 'I know what you mean. They all come in with the same problem.'"

In my ecstatic state, I did not then wonder what it was like for my parents. What was it like for Papa, putting on his old clothes, when he was no longer the same man? The shock of his freedom—he had no warning, no time to prepare emotionally, must have been overwhelming, akin to a soldier's abrupt demobilization. Invisible to the world—and, in truth, to me—were the psychic and emotional scars of nearly two years of constant browbeating and humiliation. And, as painful for this most private man, the indignity of never having an instant alone, the watchers observing his most private moments. When he revealed his despair in the night, in his prison cell, it was under watchful eyes. He had been pushed to the edge. He had urged my mother to divorce him, for us to forget him. He had not only contemplated but methodically over several months planned his own end. Because of us, he had resisted. But he was not the same proud, debonair man. No barber, manicurist, or tailor could erase those invisible bruises. Not even his wife and daughters possessed such healing powers.

At the same time, prison had strengthened my parents' marriage.

Later, my mother would say that it saved it. It was something they had shared and survived, as they had shared and survived the nightmare of the Nazi occupation. They were welded together by loss, confinement, war, jail, and, finally, love. My father understood his debt to my mother. Not only did she ignore his advice that she leave him and flee the country, she continued to practice their dangerous profession and fought fiercely for his freedom. She had put steel in him when he was on the brink of despair. "The Americans will free us," she had whispered during their melancholy walk back to their cells. And in a way they had.

The files reveal one more secret my parents thought that they had shared only with each other. As with Mama, Papa's freedom had come at a price. From the time of his freeing, until the outbreak of the Revolution on October 23, my father had to meet regularly with an AVO agent. His contact was Colonel Arpad Jambor, to whom my father was introduced when he was informed he would be freed. The AVO described their relationship as "social." They met in the open—in fact in the most open and showy place in Budapest: the Café New York. So, while black-clad waiters served espressos to customers sitting at immaculately set tables, my father had to account for his days to Colonel Jambor. Though my father's amnesty was directly related to Hungary's desire for improved relations with the United States, permission to resume his work as a foreign correspondent depended on his contact with Jambor.

That my father made a strong impression on Jambor is apparent from the agent's own description: "Marton's contact [Jambor] found him to be a man of his word, who does not care for cheap little lies. He is upright and honest, and has no moral weaknesses. As to his passions, we are unaware of them. His courage has been demonstrated by his behavior before arrest and under interrogation. He loves his wife and his children and supports his parents and brother [in Australia]."

So freedom for both my parents was conditional. It was partly this that the head of the Archives, Dr. Katalin Kutrucz, referred to, when she told me to come alone to the meeting with which this chronicle begins. But as I write this, I have spent enough time studying the AVO and its sealed universe, built on equal parts paranoia and ignorance, to be less prone to outrage. My initial "How *could* they!" has been supplanted by another question. How would *I* survive under such a system? What price would I pay to preserve my own freedom and my children's future? I think about this a lot these days.

In a strange way, I suppose I owe the AVO a debt of gratitude. The man and woman who emerge from the AVO's failed attempt to crush them are admirable people. I would have liked to have known them, even had they not been my mother and father. And without those files, I would not have known so much about my parents.

Ambassador Ravndal, who had spurred Washington to stand behind my parents, and never forgot their children, had been transferred to his next post, as ambassador to Ecuador. It was not just my family that missed Ravndal. The stunning challenge to the Soviet Empire that began in the streets of Budapest that late summer and into fall would happen without the presence of a senior American diplomat. John Foster Dulles, the Cold Warrior who had trumpeted rolling back the Iron Curtain, chose not to send an envoy to replace Ravndal until the explosion of freedom he had encouraged was extinguished in blood.

A search of records turned up another departure from Budapest. The passenger manifest of a Pan Am flight from London to New York, dated August 22, 1956, lists Richard J. Glaspell, his wife, Mimi, and his children, Gregory and Claudia, on a one-way ticket to the United States—exactly one week after Papa's release.

Chapter 16

REVOLUTION

Hated members of the AVO—the Hungarian secret police—led by Freedom Fighters in October 1956. A number of such agents were lynched by angry mobs during the Revolution.

My memories of the Hungarian Revolution are tied up with the reuniting of our family. I felt that I had been restored to the little girl within a tight family that I had been before they took my Mama and Papa away. I look back on those days when the world watched the drama in Budapest as a thrilling time, even though it ended in tragedy. I had no notion that I was living history. We were a family again—Mama-Papa-Juli-Kati—the old unit reconstituted. Nothing would break us up again. But by chance, Mama was in London when the Revolution erupted. As part of the sweeping new reforms and in a final attempt to placate a population that was at the boiling point, the government was issuing passports, not to whole families, but to individuals. My father urged my mother to have some fun "in the West." So Juli and I had our father all to ourselves.

On October 23, my father and I took a yellow streetcar to Bem Square. It was too jammed with people for me to see the large statue of the Polish general that occupies the center of this normally quiet spot on the Buda side of the Danube. Students poured out of side streets and more and more people—workers and even uniformed soldiers—joined the crowd. I wanted to hold my father's hand in the tumult, but he was busy scribbling in his reporter's notebook. There was a cheerful, holiday feeling to the crowd. Everybody was shouting and excited. Even a child could tell that this was a different sort of demonstration than the sullen, robotic May Day marches. The trams stopped running because people jostled them. This was unplanned, spontaneous, and remarkable. A woman appeared from a balcony waving the Hungarian tricolor with a large hole cut in the center where the hammer and sickle had been. Everybody cheered. The symbol of the Hungarian Revolution—and so many others to come—had been born. Cutting the hated Soviet symbol from the national flag was an irreversible act. A line had been crossed. I looked up at my father, a cigarette perched on his lower lip, a smile spreading across his face. I had never seen that smile, but I understood that something tremendous was happening. Then someone called out, *"Ruszkik haza!"* "Russians go home!" Wilder cheering. This crowd would not be cowed. The electricity in the air and the unaccustomed expression on my father's face made my heart beat faster.

An elderly man appeared on the balcony of the parliament later that day. I recognized him as the man on the bus my mother had spoken to some weeks before and who, shaking his balding head, had told her, "Your arrest should never have happened." That's Imre Nagy, my mother had whispered to us, a good man, a good Hungarian. He looked very ordinary, sitting on that bus with us, a retired school-teacher perhaps, with a big handlebar mustache and old-fashioned round little glasses. Now the crowd looked up at him expectantly. "Comrades," he began. Everybody booed. "We are not comrades!" they shouted. The Revolution had begun and it was already far ahead of this good, patriotic, but uninspiring man.

Revolutions begin with symbolic acts. I was not there, but Papa was. The crowds needed to destroy the most hated symbol of the Stalinist era, and headed to the edge of City Park, where a twenty-six-foot statue of Stalin stood. My father and his photographer, Andras "Bandi" Sima, were with them. Working with torches and ropes, the crowd struggled to bring down the giant bronze.

It took hours because nothing was planned. To topple the bronze colossus was not a job that young university students, armed only with high spirits, could accomplish. But help came from the facto-ries. A truck drove up with workers carrying acetylene torches and other equipment. My father told Sima not to budge until he got the picture of the falling statue. "The poor man stood there for hours," Papa would tell us later, "but we got the picture." Finally, with the immense crowd roaring, Stalin crashed to earth. Only two gigantic boots remained on the pedestal. Sima's photograph flashed around the world.

That day, October 23, 1956, the Ministry of the Interior declared Personal File #10-30084/950, of Dr. Endre Marton, officially closed.

The Revolution spread to our peaceful Buda hill. We could hear the pop pop of gunfire coming from Szena Ter, our neighborhood bus and tram terminal. With schools closed, Mama in London, and Papa constantly gone, my sister and I were left unsupervised. We ran down the hill to inspect the "front." "Freedom Fighters," as they were now called, had overturned trams as barricades. Most astonishing, some of them were neighborhood teenagers, fourteen and fifteen years old, dragging what seemed like oversize weapons. Full of grim purpose, they had no time for us.

Back home, our dining room turned into a sort of newsroom, and Juli and I bustled around, playing "hostess" to Jack MacCormac of the *Times,* Ronald Farquhar of Reuters, and Tom and Sarah Rogers. (I think secretly we were pleased our mother was away so we could fill in for her.) We had never seen grown-ups so excited.

On October 25, the festive mood turned. My father and MacCormac were the only newsmen present on Parliament Square when a Soviet tank opened up on an unarmed, peaceful demonstration. "We hit the ground," my father recalled, "demonstrators were running to find shelter . . . others were lying prone on the square. I did not know whether they'd been hit or were paralyzed with fear. The craziest sight were . . . the tanks. Their turrets were revolving rapidly in all directions, as if looking for the enemy, and their guns were firing wildly. Who had started the shooting? Certainly not the demonstrators: they were unarmed. Suddenly, MacCormac grabbed my arm and pointed at the roof of one of the six story buildings at the square's southern end. There was a plume of white gray smoke slowly rising from behind the parapet on top of the building. . . . When it was all over—ten minutes which seemed like hours—Jack and I counted about fifty bodies in a small section of the square." A final count revealed that seventy-five people had been killed and 282 wounded. The plume of smoke from atop the nearby building was thought to have been an AVO sniper. This act of senseless slaughter abruptly changed the mood of the city and the nature of the Revolution.

For Papa, covering what he called "the story of my life," the frustration was not finding a working telephone line to get his report out to the world. "I knew that the communication blackout was not total," he recalled, "that the government maintained some thin lines of communication open to the West. I knew the president of one organization which I suspected had its lines open. I decided to try."

As a boy, my father had ducked Horthy's right-wing thugs, when he and his mother huddled in the tunnel leading to the Chain Bridge. In the last days of World War II, he had outrun the murderous Arrow Cross. He knew his way around the city. He would dodge Soviet tanks and AVO snipers.

In half an hour, my father reached the government office with the last functioning phone line in Pest. He gave the numbers of several AP European bureaus to the night clerk. And waited. "The night-time silence of the room was suddenly broken when my telex sprang to life. . . . And then, miraculously, the words appeared on the paper. 'Associated Press, Vienna.' I sat there with trembling fingers and punched back, 'AP Budapest.' Back came the message: 'Endre is that really you?'"

The next day, my father's story of the massacre at Parliament Square was on the front page of *The New York Times,* and most other major dailies. Thanks to my father's bold trek across the city, Budapest had the world's attention. When he crept back home at dawn, I raised my head and whimpered, "Why can't you stay home, like all the other fathers?" To console me, he tore a piece from the freshly baked bread he had bought from the bakery he passed on his way home. It smelled and tasted wonderful.

Sometime that week, when the Revolution was spinning out of control, the population, angry and afraid, turned on the most loathed symbols of the old order: the AVO. As they scurried for cover, AVO agents shed their blue uniforms, but their boots often gave them away. They were dragged by lynch mobs dispensing a brutal justice. Their bodies soon hung from lampposts in Pest and a few on Szena Ter. We avoided looking up at them. My parents (Mama had returned from her brief trip to London) were repulsed by this bloody excess, and feared it would damage the Revolution in the eyes of the world. Somehow, Major Kretschmer found his way to our home. He spent a day hiding in our maid's room. This man, just recently my father's all-powerful jailer, now looked small and, even to my child's eyes, frightened. My father hung the American flag on our front door, so the searchers would not bother us. Then Kretschmer was gone. Only years later did the full irony of his seeking sanctuary in our home hit me.

My father later told me that his interrogators, Captain Balazsi and Captain Babics, fled Budapest around October 24 and headed toward Czechoslovakia. AVO agents were ordered to disperse and wait to be summoned back to Hungary when it was safe. Somewhere along their route, a former inmate of the Fo Utca, a farmer, recognized the pair. The village elders resisted the hotheads' demand for summary execution. Instead, they formed an escort and the two secret policemen were led back to the Fo Utca, this time as inmates. Their incarceration ended when Soviet troops returned in force.

The Revolution slowly ran out of oxygen. The Western powers were otherwise engaged. Britain, France, and Israel attacked the Suez Canal on October 30—with no advance warning to the United States. Eisenhower and Dulles were furious. The 1956 presidential campaign was in its last week, Eisenhower against Adlai Stevenson. Dulles was suddenly hospitalized for cancer. The Soviets charged that Washington raised the Hungarian situation at the Security Council to divert attention from its allies' maneuvers in the Middle East. Outraged, Moscow charged the West with hypocrisy and vetoed a call for it to stop its intervention and withdraw Soviet forces from Budapest. By the time Dulles's envoy, Edward T. Wailes, reached Budapest on November 2, it was too late. Washington praised to the skies the first armed uprising against Soviet rule and would leave it to die.

EARLY ON the morning of November 4, Mama woke us up. We could hear the pounding of gunfire. Our house trembled from the reverberations, but we were too frightened to cry. Our parents looked stricken. The Russians were back. The four of us huddled around the radio in our living room. "This is Imre Nagy," came the old man's voice. "Today at daybreak, Soviet troops attacked our capital with the

obvious intention of overthrowing the legal Hungarian democratic
government. Our troops are in combat. The government is at its post.
I notify the people of our country and the entire world of this fact."
This melancholy final plea for help was followed by the playing of
the mournful Hungarian national anthem. My parents, momentarily
forgetting my sister and me, were feverishly dialing, trying to find a
telephone operator awake somewhere in Europe. Finally, an operator
picked up. "It's too late," the operator wept into the phone, "I can't
connect you anymore."

Unable to send his report out, uncertain as to our own fate, my
father looked up and saw his daughters, "without tears, without signs
of panic, without asking unnecessary questions, like two little soldiers
waiting for orders. What should the orders be?"

I was less afraid this time than after my mother's arrest. Yes, the
Russians were back, and how long could teenagers with Molotov
cocktails withstand long lines of monster tanks? But this time, I had
my parents.

As first light broke over the city, we hurried out of our apartment, carrying small overnight bags. On our way down the stairs, our
neighbor, the wife of the AVO officer, Mrs. Kalmar, looking distraught
and unkempt in her dressing gown, intercepted us. "What is going to
happen now?" she asked. "Madam," my father replied, "you have no
reason to be afraid anymore. They are back and they are your friends."

My parents bundled us into the Volkswagen Beetle loaned to us by
the AP, and we headed for the river, toward Pest. No one said a word
in that crowded little car. We did not know where we were headed,
but almost any place was less exposed than our hilltop home, from
where my parents had been dragged not so many months before. We
reached the Danube and faced a frightening sight: two Soviet tanks
barred the mouth of the tunnel that led to the bridge. My father
quickly made a sharp right and headed down the Danube to the next
bridge. Liberty Bridge was still open. As we rolled off the bridge on
the Pest side, we could see in the car's rearview mirror Russian tanks

rumbling into the square behind us, in front of the Gellert Hotel. My father noticed that these were not the tanks used earlier by the Russians. These were brand-new and much bigger, T-54s, brought in to crush the Revolution.

Our family joined a group of foreign correspondents gathered in the lobby of the Duna Hotel. As usual, we were the only children, my mother the only woman, in the group. My father immediately offered to lead the reporters on a reconnaissance through the city. My mother and sister and I, a sleepy mass huddled on a couch in the dingy hotel lobby, were much relieved when they returned after a few minutes. Apparently one of those T-54s turned its gun on the little party of newsmen. The hotel shook from the tank's powerful fire. Only eleven years after the Second World War, Budapest's splendid old buildings were again being pounded into rubble.

The foreign newsmen scurried around, looking to evacuate the exposed hotel. One by one, they ducked into telephone booths off the lobby, calling their embassies or friendly Western missions. Where would we go? My parents were again caught between two worlds— safe in neither. Only now, reading the diplomatic cable traffic between Budapest and Washington, do I learn how we were saved from gunfire or my parents' certain rearrest.

Ambassador Edward Wailes, on his second day in Budapest, cabled the State Department from his besieged legation on Freedom Square: "Five American journalists now downstairs and want to press with me their desire to bring Endre Marton and wife AP-UP Hungarian correspondents recently released from jail with worldwide publicity. I don't like taking in Hungarians," Wailes continued, "but inclined to go along as I believe this is the last non-American press we will be asked to take in. If we do take them in, I believe we will have to make it clear that we cannot guarantee protection from Hungarian authorities. Have you any thoughts?"* he asked his superiors in Washington.

---

* *Foreign Relations of the United States, 1955–1957,* vol. XXV, pp. 382–83.

"Regarding question about American newspapermen," came the reply, "you may give shelter to German and other non-Hungarian nationals . . . though this not considered asylum."

Wailes returned to the classified telex machine to continue his real-time continuous dialogue with Washington. "Press delegation really up in arms at Endre Marton, wife and kids, who seem to be the only Hungarians directly reporting for American press. Furthermore, they point out that the Martons were jailed because of alleged assistance to US (I have not mentioned to press consulting Department, nor will I do so). I am now inclined that lesser evil is to take these people in. Do you wish to comment or leave it to me?"

"Leave it to your judgment," came the laconic word back from Washington, approved by Undersecretary of State Robert Murphy.

With those five words our fate was secured. It was the beginning of our American journey. We did not know it yet, but we were in from the cold. Edward Wailes would not let us down.

I have only happy memories of the days and nights we spent in the legation. It was like a first trip to America. My sister and I were the only children, as all nonessential diplomats and their families had already been evacuated to Vienna. We were treated like curiosities by the reporters (some of whom I would later meet again when I began work as a journalist) with whom we shared the former screening room, now an improvised dormitory. When the fighting in the neighborhood was heavy, we all trooped down to the cellar and slept on a Persian carpet brought downstairs from the reception room.

A dark figure, lost in prayer, sat in one corner of the cellar: Jozsef Cardinal Mindszenty, Hungary's prince primate, liberated by Freedom Fighters only three days before from the prison where he was serving a life sentence. A mournful and forbidding figure, the cardinal summoned my mother and sister and me one evening and offered Mass for us in the improvised chapel that had been set up for him in the ambassador's corner office (which Mindszenty would occupy for the next fifteen years). "Through you," the cardinal said, spreading his hands on our heads, as we kneeled in front of him, "I bless every Hungarian woman and child."

Cardinal Mindszenty was accompanied by Monsignor Egon Turchanyi. In stark contrast to the forbidding prelate he served, the monsignor was a smiling, playful priest. He sat on the carpet with my sister and me, and diverted us from the sound of gunfire outside, teaching us to build a house out of toothpicks.

Despite the strictly observed curfew, my father kept leaving the legation to follow the Russian advance through the city. "It was a curious war," he recalled, "tanks on one side, small groups of freedom fighters, students and young workers, soldiers and policemen, fighting with small arms or occasionally a machine gun or an antitank gun, on the other. . . . A tank can do nothing but destroy, and that was what the Soviet tanks did."

By November 10, the heavy fighting was over. Our journalist companions in the American legation formed a convoy that left from Freedom Square for Vienna. "It was a depressing moment," my father remembered, "when we shook hands with our colleagues. . . . What could they say to [those] who stayed behind with no protective passports? . . . It appeared most unlikely that we would see each other again."

We had nowhere to go but back home. As we drove through the city we peered out the window of our car in silence. We passed blocks of apartment buildings without windows and with entire walls blown off. There were crater-size holes in the streets and overturned buses and burned-out trams littering the boulevards. Our own house had been hit by mortar fire from Soviet artillery on the hilltop.

Still, we were back with our gang of kids and—with schools still closed—we took advantage of the heavy snowfall to test our new sled in the field behind our house. We rushed out of the house to see Soviet jet fighters scream and swoop overhead, before we were shepherded down to our cellar. Everyone in the house commented on the absence of the Kalmar family, and there was speculation that the AVO had its own bomb shelters. We received packages marked, mysteriously, "From the Danish People," which contained powdered milk, some sort of pressed meat, and packages of Winston cigarettes, which our elders snatched excitedly from our hands.

As sad as the landscape were our parents' faces. It was as if a light had been switched off. Unsmiling resignation replaced the animation of the last weeks. The realization that the country had spent its blood and courage for *this* was overwhelming. For them, it was back to the misery of the post–world war days, but now without hope. Soon Radio Budapest was back broadcasting in its old fake, cheery tone. People weren't individuals anymore, just Comrade this and Comrade that. The Revolution was now called a Counterrevolution. Freedom Fighters were called Gangsters, Capitalists, Imperialists, and Fascists. The Big Lie returned.

My sister and I queued for hours in the bitter cold outside food shops littered with rubble and very little food. If President Eisenhower and Secretary of State Dulles felt neither remorse nor shame, other Americans did. John MacCormac wrote Simon Bourgin, on November 26, 1956, "For the rest of my life I shall never be able to think of [the Revolution] without a lump in my throat. Half the time I had tears in my eyes," the *New York Times* correspondent wrote. "I doubt if ever newspapermen have covered a story which so tore at their emotions. It was terrible to see it fail and know that you were a part of the West that had failed them."*

By the end of November, the Russians had crushed the last armed resistance, though not without a bloody struggle. Seven hundred Soviet soldiers were killed fighting the Hungarians. But Hungary, with a population of under ten million, was a grieving nation: 2,500 people, mostly civilians, were dead, 20,000 wounded. Another 200,000 had fled across the suddenly open frontier to Austria. For my parents, following the exodus of the Western press (only Russell Jones of UP

---

* Private papers of Simon Bourgin.

and Ronald Farquhar of Reuters stayed on), there was a new story to report: Civil disobedience following armed resistance.

On November 23, one month after the outbreak of the Revolution, an eerie silence dropped over the city. Buses, trams, and cars stopped in their tracks, workers laid down their tools, waiters stopped serving, cooks stopped cooking, shopkeepers shut their cash registers. The whole city observed a one-hour "silent strike." The remarkable part of this was that there was no public announcement—newspapers and radio were by then back under Communist control. The protest was organized entirely by people passing it through word of mouth. I sensed that in the midst of the melancholy, my parents were proud of their country—perhaps for the first time in their lives. In her journal, my mother recorded, "When we sat down for our first dinner [following our return from the U.S. legation] Kati asked, 'Mama, have you ever been free, except in these few days?'"

From Budapest's battered streets, subdued now by giant tanks, and under the watchful eyes of Russian troops, the story shifted to factories and workers' councils. "Some of your parents' most courageous acts," Tom Rogers recalled in 2008, "took place in the last phase of the Revolution, after the fighting. Janos Kadar [the Soviet puppet who betrayed the Revolution and then held power for the next three decades] was clamping down on the workers, rounding up their leaders. Your parents continued to meet with them. Your parents were elitists—especially your father, who was very conscious of class differences. The way he dressed, his pride at his upbringing. But during this final phase of the Revolution, I observed his respect and admiration for the most unsophisticated, uneducated workers."

Reuters's Ronald Farquhar also remembered "hunting," as he called it, with my parents in the postrevolutionary days, toward the end of 1956. "It was in all our interests to stay close together, and share everything we learned," Farquhar, a Scot whom I recall for his flaming red hair and freckles, said in 2008. "Russ [Jones of UP], your parents, and I, with your parents doing most of the sharing," he continued, warming to his half-a-century-old memories of my mother and father. "I was terribly impressed by both of them. Your father was very cool, never showed fear or anger, this man with a pipe, who just didn't get upset. He was a man you would trust with your life. And after what they'd been through—to shelter an AVO man! And your mother was very funny, made very sharp observations about the Russians. For me, it was a big story. For your parents, it was about their country."

At a meeting of the Greater Budapest Workers' Council, in early December, the union's young president, Sandor Racz, turned to my mother. "We might need you tomorrow," Racz said. "But come alone." In answer to the puzzled looks of her three male colleagues, Racz added, "You're a woman. They might prevent men from entering the plant." "They" were the AVO who were guarding the Beloyannis Factory, a huge precision instruments plant in Budapest's XII District. "I had a car," Farquhar remembered, "a little Skoda. I drove your mother to the plant. A cordon of militia surrounded the factory. I told your mother, 'You won't make it. At best they'll just turn you back.' But she went ahead, while I waited for her in the car around the corner."

Stopped by an officer, my mother showed her press card. Seemingly puzzled, he signaled for her to go ahead. "See if they let you in," he said with a shrug. Inside the factory gate, the workers were waiting for her. Racz told her that someone had tipped off the authorities about their secret plan for a general strike. "They raided our headquarters this morning," Racz told her, "and arrested everyone there. They cut all our phone lines. You are our only means to get the word out that the strike is on for Tuesday and Wednesday. The world should know. If foreign radio repeats it, all Hungarian workers will know what to do."

My mother rushed out the gate and into Farquhar's waiting Skoda. "I got it!" she said, beaming. "We drove off to the Duna Hotel," Farquhar recalled, "so she could get her story out to UP." But there was a complete news blackout on the city. There were no open phone lines anywhere. With a major story in their hands—and thousands of Hungarian workers awaiting instructions regarding the planned strike—my parents huddled with their Reuters colleague in his hotel room. "Suddenly my phone rang," Farquhar remembered, "it was the Reuters London office calling. I was very embarrassed. I mean, it was your mother's story, but I had the phone line. Your parents said, 'Go! We have to get the story out!' So I did, with your mother translating the call for the strike into English. Then, when I finished, I asked Reuters to transfer the call to your mother's office in London. She started to dictate 'A general strike was called today . . .' and just like that the line went dead. Somebody must have got wind of it. But by then Western radio was already reporting back to Hungary about the strike order. The strike was on."

My parents' steps were again dogged by the agents of the newly restored and empowered police state. My mother's role in getting the news of the strike out was more incriminating than anything she had ever done before. Sometime around Christmas, in the middle of dinner, our phone rang. My father picked up the phone. "I recognized [the voice]," my father recalled, "of a worker whom I had met almost nightly in November, in the smoke filled, shabby premises of the Greater Budapest Workers' Council. 'You know who I am, don't you,' he began. 'We understand that they plan to arrest you tonight. I would advise you and your wife not to stay in your apartment,' the man said and hung up."

I remember my father returning to the dinner table and very quietly and calmly telling us to get our coats. My mother needed no explanation. "The hole," she said. He nodded and so, single file, we crept quietly out the door, but not to the street. We moved quickly to the back of the house, separated from the Rogerses' residence by a chain link fence, covered with shrubbery. Sometime earlier, an American diplomat (no one can quite recall anymore whether it was Don Downs or Tom Rogers) had taken wire cutters to that fence and made a hole large enough for human passage. Although the shrubbery was thickly overgrown, we nevertheless found the hole, squeezed through one at a time, and emerged on American diplomatic territory on the other side.

"I remember you bursting in on us that evening," Arabella Meadows-Rogers recalled. "There was a fire in the fireplace, Daddy was reading the newspapers, we were playing on the floor, and you were the first in. You looked around, and then you burst out in tears. Until that moment, I had no real sense of what you were going through." The predawn pounding of our city by Russian guns, the close call of our flight to American sanctuary, just one bridge ahead of the tanks, the nights my sister and I were alone while our parents "hunted" for stories of the Revolution's aftermath. All of this barely a few months after our parents' freeing, when, briefly, we thought our "normal" lives could resume. For weeks, I had held my fears in check, because that was expected of me. In that warm room, with a blazing fire and a scene of normal domesticity, I felt safe enough to behave like a child—and to cry.

We stayed with the Rogerses for about a week. They were loving, warm, and informal and my sister and I reverted to being normal little girls on a sleepover. But we knew we had to go home, that this was yet another temporary asylum. When my parents judged that the first wave of arrests had passed, we moved back to our apartment. "I was there one day in December," Ronald Farquhar recalled, "and your mother was reading a newspaper and suddenly she started crying. It was an article about how the Iron Curtain had been rebuilt, the mines, the guard dogs, the watchtowers, all restored after 200,000 Hungarians had escaped. 'You see,' your mother said to your father, 'we missed our chance again. We'll never get out now.' Your father got up and walked over to her and said, 'I promise you.' He told her, 'We will get out.'"

Now, for the first time since he was freed from prison, my father focused on us, and not on the "story of his life." "They were literally contemplating going back to jail," Tom Rogers remembered. "Your father weighed things and the prospect of Hungary slowly heading toward democracy and freedom did not appear to be very strong. He had to think about you. You would have faced an even grimmer life than before. That was the overriding factor in his decision." At the same time, Ambassador Edward Wailes and his wife, Cornelia, whom we had gotten to know during our stay at the American legation, announced their readiness to adopt my sister and me if our parents were rearrested. The Waileses, wealthy and childless, approached my parents for their approval. "But Sarah and I protested," Tom Rogers said. "We already have four daughters, we told the Waileses, so we wouldn't even notice! We told them, two little girls would turn your lives upside down. An argument ensued, and ultimately we won. Once that was decided, Wailes drew up the document, in the form of an agreement which your parents signed."

The following week, the AP Vienna bureau chief, Richard Kasischke, called on the Hungarian Foreign Ministry to preemptively protest my parents' impending arrest. Kasischke also informed the ministry that the AP wanted to transfer my father to its Vienna bureau. The AVO files reveal that on December 21, 1956, my father contacted Colonel Arpad Jambor, his minder, and requested that he come to our apartment. (My father's meetings at the Café New York had ceased with the outbreak of the Revolution.) Aware that ultimately our fate would be decided by the real power in Hungary, which took its directions directly from Moscow, my father asked for Jambor's help in securing passports for the four of us. Jambor noted that the AP wanted to transfer my father to its Vienna bureau and that "Marton will be a big success . . . in the West." Furthermore, Jambor related, "Marton says he will always regard Hungary as his home . . . and hopes to return here in the future." In closing, the colonel noted, "The Martons will assume important American news bureaus in Vienna. Moreover, Marton could be useful in the future, on a half social, half patriotic basis."

My father was skillfully playing a very poor hand. This time, he put his family ahead of his profession and his own pride. He had nearly lost his wife, his children, and everything else that meant anything to him the last time. A humbler man now, he was willing to bargain with the devil himself to preserve his family. This time, he persuaded his enemies that letting us go was in their interest. He would always be "a good Hungarian" (his definition of that was of course different from theirs). They had ample evidence to support his claim that he would be nothing but trouble if he stayed—even as their prisoner. Jambor, too, had his own plans for the future. "In the event that he shirks from [being a good Hungarian]," the secret police colonel noted, "we can always rely on [the name is blacked out] to put pressure on him." I have been unable to figure out who the reference is to.

Leaving no doubt as to who was in charge, Colonel Jambor sent the following message to the minister of the interior: "I informed Marton that he will receive his passport within one week. I gave a similar reply to Comrade Szarka, of the Ministry of Foreign Affairs, who requested our decision in this matter." Jambor, I realize now, was actually helping us, a silent tribute to Papa.

Within days we had our passports. We packed for a journey we knew would be final without a trace of regret. The Marton family's nearly one hundred years in Budapest had come to this: we could hardly wait to leave. I remember jumping up and down with wild abandon on the rolled-up Persian carpets, our grandparents' treasured legacy, that we were leaving behind. It felt as if our lives were just about to begin. My sister and I were each allowed one suitcase with the clothes and toys of our choice. An entire "sentimental" suitcase was filled with photo albums and family memorabilia. The Rogerses took some larger pieces of furniture, old armchairs, paintings, and bric-a-brac, which traveled with them through several continents until finally being returned to us in Washington.

The AVO files reveal no quid pro quo for our passports. Except one. It was a bitter cold, overcast January day and we were busy packing for an early start the next morning. The telephone rang. If my father's pulse quickened at the sound of Colonel Jambor's voice on the line, he did not show it. "We know you are leaving tomorrow," the AVO officer said, "would you do a last favor for your country? Take Cardinal Mindszenty out with you and we will roll out the red carpet at the border." Is this a trap? my father wondered. "I understand your suspicion," Jambor read his silence. "But you should understand me. Mindszenty at the American legation is a nuisance for us and for the Americans. If he gets out he will be on the front pages of your newspapers for how long? For three days perhaps. Then he will disappear behind the thick walls of a monastery somewhere in Rome and the world will soon forget him."

"Too great a risk," Ambassador Wailes said, when my father called to relay the offer.★ Wailes said he would not even inform the cardinal of the proposal. So, for fifteen years, until the Vatican and the Kremlin worked out a deal granting him safe passage west, the cardinal lived in the ambassador's office.

On January 24, 1957, Ambassador Wailes sent a confidential memorandum to the State Department entitled "The Case of the Andrew Martons, Associated Press and United Press Correspondents," which gives a remarkably detailed evaluation of the American view of my parents.

Dr. and Mrs. Marton . . . left Hungary legally with their two children on January 17 for Vienna to which they had both been transferred by their agencies. This departure ended a relationship with this Legation which extended over many years.

It began during the immediate post war years when the Martons first assumed their positions as journalists and was maintained throughout except for the period when both Martons were under arrest. As accredited correspondents for American news agencies, some relationship was to be expected, although for a number of years virtually any contact with Ameri-

---

★ Tom Rogers to author.

cans was generally thought to be dangerous. . . . From approximately 1949–1950 until the arrest of Dr. Marton they came regularly to the Legation once a week for discussions with Legation officers . . . [even as] all correspondents except the Martons ceased coming due . . . to the arrest of one or more [correspondents]. The attitude of the Martons has been strongly anti-Communist. . . . There was always some suspicion held by Legation officers, particularly before their arrest in 1955, that the Martons were acting, perhaps against their will, as agents of the secret police. No proof of such activity has ever come to light. Whatever may have been the case . . . they provided a great deal of valuable information to the Legation. More information of value regarding Hungary was received from the Martons than from any other local contact.

Dr. Marton was arrested in February 1955, and Mrs. Marton in June of the same year. They were both released (with many others) under the influence of the atmosphere of the Soviet 20th Party Congress and possibly the desire of Hungary to improve relations to a certain extent with the U.S. . . . A large part of the material filed by Western news agencies from Hungary [during the Revolution] came from them either directly or through other journalists who received considerable assistance from them . . . they were also of considerable value to this Legation in this period. . . . The fact that they did not leave illegally during October, November and early December when it was relatively easy was explained by them as concern over the fate of their small children on such a journey and reluctance to leave the country during the greatest "news story," as well as some uncertainty as to the future of the country. At about the time that illegal exit became more difficult, however, they were both transferred to Vienna by their agencies and decided to apply for legal passports, and if these were turned down, to consider an illegal exit.

As to why the Hungarian regime should see fit to issue passports to two people who have been so obviously opposed to it in every way as the Martons have, the Legation speculates that . . . to permit them to continue to operate in Hungary had the strong disadvantage of providing the Western press a great deal of accurate information. To arrest them would irritate the

West and the United States unnecessarily (the favorable passport decision was given at a time when substantial aid from the U.S. had not been ruled out). To refuse the passport and have them leave illegally would have served the regime no useful purpose. Furthermore, they could hardly write more against the regime outside the country than they had already done from within.

A close reading of this memorandum shows how carefully Wailes (and Tom Rogers, who drafted it for him) dealt with the climate of suspicion that existed in Washington in the 1950s about anyone living in a Communist country. Wailes sought to allay any concerns regarding this rather unusual case. It was 1957, Joseph McCarthy, though already censured by the Senate, was still alive, and the paranoid J. Edgar Hoover was, at the height of his powers, Director of the FBI.

None of that, however, did I understand as we crossed the barren, snow-blanketed countryside, driving through deathly still villages on that winter day en route to the Austrian border. There were virtually no private cars on the road. We passed military trucks carrying Russian troops toward Budapest. Four hours after leaving our apartment on Csaba Utca in Tom Rogers's paneled Ford station wagon, we reached the barrier. A Hungarian soldier wearing a Soviet-style greatcoat, with a red star pinned to his fur cap, leaned in and asked for our passports. Minutes later, the barrier we had spent my entire life trying to cross was lifted and the soldier waved us through. I was too young and too self-absorbed to wonder what it felt like for my parents to leave forever the country of their birth, and which, despite what they had endured under the Fascists and the Communists, they still loved.

As soon as we cleared the no-man's-land on the Austrian side, Tom Rogers pulled off the road and produced a bottle of brandy and three small glasses. The adults drank in silence while my sister and I tried to contain our excitement. From his overcoat pocket, Tom then produced a typed document: the adoption papers my mother and father had signed, making the Rogerses our parents. With great flourish, my mother ripped it up. This, I understood.

Dusk was falling when we returned to the bleak, snow-covered road that led to Vienna.

Chapter 17

AMERICA

Papa is back as foreign correspondent—filing first
from Vienna, then, ultimately, from Washington, D.C.,
where he covered the State Department for the
Associated Press.

I WILL ALWAYS REMEMBER Vienna as the first place where I ever
felt safe. Like exhausted swimmers who had made it safely ashore, my
parents began to relax the clenched tightness on their faces. The four
of us basked in the city's *gemütlichkeit*: its sparkling lights, shops, the
aroma of coffee and pastries floating over the Kärtnerstrasse, and, after
Budapest's empty shelves and dinginess, its *plenty*. With its cobblestones
and grimy Habsburg-era palaces, it was a friendlier, richer version of

Budapest. My father, though no longer covering "the biggest story of his life," savored having real colleagues, not informers masquerading as such. Fräulein Angela Riese, the middle-aged AP bureau manager, treated him with the deference due a Cold War hero and the blushing embarrassment of an adolescent. My father thrived in the cosmopolitan atmosphere of the city that had first enraptured him as a boy.

With the excitement of kids off to summer camp, my sister and I jumped on the yellow school bus that picked us up near our boardinghouse, the Hotel Atlanta, each morning. In no time at all we joined the other kids in endless rounds of "A Hundred Bottles of Beer on the Wall" on the way to the Vienna International School. We loved the chicken soup at the Rathauskeller, and raced up and down the first escalator we had ever seen in a shopping center on Mariahilferstrasse (also the first shopping center we had ever seen). Without a dangerous outside world forcing us to be nice to each other, my sister and I reverted to normal siblings, taking swipes at each other when our parents weren't looking.

Mama, however, was not happy. Secure at last, she could afford to indulge her anxieties. Soviet troops had only recently withdrawn from Austria and she felt Hungary's proximity like a cold wind at her back. She seemed more fretful than in Budapest. When we received word in February that my parents would be awarded one of journalism's highest accolades, the George Polk Award (the first couple ever so honored), she saw an opportunity. We would go to New York to receive the prizes—and never return! She was finished with the Old World.

The AP had other plans. They had never had a non-American covering America. They much preferred keeping my father in Europe. But my parents' case was helped by the publicity their arrest and trial had generated. Their coverage of the Revolution had made their bylines—especially my father's—familiar to Americans. A number of congressmen and senators were eager to have them testify at hearings about the Revolution. Still, general manager Frank Starzel continued to balk, writing to AP board president Robert McLean on

January 25, 1957, that it would be "inexpedient and imprudent for us to consider having Marton come to the United States at this time." Starzel's letter is cold-blooded in the extreme: "I asked [Washington bureau chief William] Beale to put a damper on one Congressman's proposal that he would move to get U.S. citizenship for Marton. Marton represents a potential problem and must be handled carefully. He, and particularly Mrs. Marton, would like very much to come to the United States; I am convinced that we would have great difficulty returning them to Europe if they were brought here at this stage. Later on, after they have settled down in Vienna, we can consider it on a promotional basis. . . . I will reserve a decision until much later this year. . . . The congressional Committees don't need Marton for factual evidence and the several Representatives aren't interested in him for this purpose. They recognize that Marton would be a fine vehicle for obtaining personal publicity for themselves."

But this time my father put his family ahead of his profession. On March 19, 1957, Ambassador Llewellyn "Tommy" Thompson cabled the State Department from Vienna: "Marton has now informed Embassy he and family desire to proceed to the U.S. with intention to remain there, regardless of AP's wishes. He is completely willing to cooperate with Senate Sub Committee."

"AMERICA," THAT magical word, had been infused with special properties. It promised great things, which were hard to imagine, but you knew they would change your life. Now they would be ours. As we prepared to leave Vienna for Munich, where we would catch a refugee plane to New York, my father had an unexpected visitor: Keirn Brown, the chief of security at the embassy. They had traced the leaks in the Budapest legation that had caused Papa so much difficulty. The traitor, Brown told Papa, was Richard Glaspell. "Until then," my father recalled, "I never thought that somebody working at an American mission overseas could have betrayed to the Communists what

211

was said in confidence in the Legation." My father never publicly disclosed Glaspell's name, but from time to time I would hear my parents mention him, more in sadness and astonishment than anger. How could anyone betray the greatest nation on earth?

My sister and I did not sleep on the plane from Munich. We "helped" the stewardesses serve our fellow refugees. By the time we touched down near Camp Kilmer, New Jersey, we were exhausted and wildly excited, and ready for America. Before leaving the plane we stashed away a lot of unused plastic cutlery for future use. We had much to learn about the throwaway culture—and everything else.

My first sighting of the Promised Land was not pretty: an Army camp of plain wooden barracks, set up for World War II POWs, transformed into a sort of minor, landlocked Ellis Island to process the flood of Hungarian refugees. But I barely had a chance to look around. It seemed we were getting special treatment. Pulled out of the long line of weary and disoriented fellow passengers, we were escorted to the head of the queue. I recall U.S. Marines looking up from their desks and smiling at the little refugee children. *I had never before seen anyone in a uniform smiling.* Then they stamped a sheaf of documents, bam, bam, bam, one after the other. Welcome to America! When they noticed that it was my birthday, silver dollars were produced. (Which I briefly fondled, before my mother took possession of them and kept them for me in a little purse in her drawer until my sixteenth birthday, whereupon I spent them. Another regret.)

Then, something unforgettable. New York City police escorts, with sirens blaring and the help of motorcycle sidecars, sped us up the New Jersey Turnpike, to the great city across the river. I craned my neck to finally see what America was all about. Brown marshland on either side of an asphalt ribbon. Where were the people? I saw only cars. Hungarian and even Austrian roads always had a human presence, bicyclists, pedestrians, women lugging baskets, students bent over by backpacks. Here, I saw no people whatsoever. But this cannot be the real America, I told myself. Just then, we vanished into a tunnel and, after what seemed like a very long time, emerged on the other side: Manhattan! But nothing pretty here, either: tall, ugly buildings, more cars where people should have been, and noise, the roar of engines, the screech of tires, and impatient blasts of horns. It seemed as if the whole city were rushing to some place known as the Hotel Roosevelt. We made it just in time to some big luncheon. Loud applause greeted our little family when our arrival was announced from the podium. Cameras popped in our faces, flashes blinded our sleepy eyes. Welcome (again) to America! An award to Mama and Papa! What was going on?

That night, from the thirty-fourth floor of our West 57th Street Henry Hudson Hotel room, the four of us ordered steak sandwiches. When a waiter pushing a groaning trolley with giant slabs of what looked to us like entire sides of beef arrived, we knew we had entered the land of plenty. (Keeping them in the windowsill, we lived on those sandwiches for days.) My sister and I would not let our parents sleep on this first night. We dragged our father down to the hotel swimming pool. When he asked the lady in charge for just two towels for his girls, as he had no plans to swim himself, to my proper father's absolute astonishment, she shot back, "Wassa matter, ya chicken, or somethin'?" That little exchange became one of my father's favorite welcome-to-America anecdotes.

On April 4, 1957, *The New York Times* reported our arrival: "2 Hungarians Get Polk News Prize—Husband-and-Wife Team of Reporters Honored Here for Revolt Coverage." "Within three hours after their arrival in this country," the *Times* wrote, "a husband and wife team of Hungarian correspondents received a special George Polk Memorial Award yesterday for 'distinguished achievements in journalism.' Endre Marton, former Associated Press resident correspondent in Hungary who sent out the first eyewitness account of the revolution there last November, accepted the award at a luncheon in the Roosevelt Hotel. He shared it with his wife, Ilona, who worked for the United Press in Hungary. Both were imprisoned by Communists. In receiving the plaque, Mr. Marton said, 'Don't forget my unhappy country. Keep the story of Hungary alive.'" So my father kept his word to his former secret police minder. He was still a good Hungarian. A patriot. But not quite in the way the AVO had hoped.

On May 6, at the eighteenth annual Overseas Press Club Awards dinner, in the Grand Ballroom of the fabled Waldorf-Astoria hotel, Papa received another award. That night, he shared the podium with a young senator from Massachusetts named John F. Kennedy, who called for a new American policy toward the "captive nations" of Europe: "The so-called satellite nations constitute the Achilles' heel of the Soviet Empire," JFK told the media gathering. "We have had enough of anguish and despair and empty promises. . . . It is time to act," he proclaimed, six months after the failed Hungarian Revolution. My father was presented the Overseas Press Club's first President's Award, for his "faithful adherence to the highest journalistic code under most unusual harassment and political pressure."

It seemed like every time we stepped out of our hotel, there was a photographer to capture our first reactions to New York traffic (scary), American supermarkets (scary and cold), department stores (we wanted everything, and sometimes burst into tears when our mother told clerks we were "just looking"; we still wore mostly hand-me-downs during that first year). We were the picture-postcard refugee family: the heroic parents (my mother pregnant), the little girls learning English by memorizing TV commercials ("Brusha, brusha, brusha—Use the New Ipana!" being my favorite). Magazine stories were written about our ordeal at the hands of the "Commies." A story in *Better Homes and Gardens* entitled "The Christmas When the Good World Came to Two Lonely Children" chronicled our Christmas without our parents when "a strange little procession was on its way to a shabby old house outside Budapest. . . . In the lead was the United States Minister to Hungary, alone in a black limousine . . . bringing gifts to the little Martons." The Christmas feature went on to relate the story of how my sister and I were abandoned by the friend who had promised to take care of us after our mother's arrest. "We were told by many who watched them during the later months how bravely they behaved," my mother was quoted. "Once Juli broke down, another time Kati, but one of them always found words to encourage the sobbing sister."

The article concluded with this cheery message: "The family is together. The Martons cherish their new country and their new freedom. All have a quiet pride in the fact that the new baby will be born an American citizen—the first in the family. They look forward to the day when their own naturalization will be completed."

I am reading this quaint, Cold War–era article—and others like it—for the first time in 2008. In those days (even if my English had been up to the task) I was far more interested in the American girl I was determined to become. I did not look back or ponder what was lost in the past year—nor the pain of the one before. With nothing but our four suitcases and my father's wire service salary, it was understood that each of us had our work cut out. My mother had suddenly announced that she was pregnant. This was astonishing news. She seemed to me too old (she was forty-five) and, given our precarious existence as refugees, the timing struck me as odd. But Andrew Thomas Marton (the Thomas was in honor of Tom Rogers) arrived on December 16, 1957, and, if anything, strengthened our already strong family bonds. It is a role he continues to play to this day.

Our parents did not need to tell us that this journey was about *us*. Europe was their continent—even if their own country had betrayed them. Our future was here. Four generations before me a rabbi's son—my great-grandfather, Maurice Mandl, born in the revolutionary year 1848—had traveled on a rickety train from Bohemia to Budapest—for *his* children's future. Now, our parents had crossed the ocean for ours. The rest was up to us. First, my sister and I had to learn English, and then achieve a deeper transformation: from refugees to "normal" American kids.

My father traveled the country giving speeches about the Revolution. In 1957, Hungary had captured America's heart. Safely reelected for a second term, President Eisenhower dubbed Budapest "the new and shining symbol of man's yearning to be free." *Time* picked "the Hungarian Freedom Fighter" as its "Man of the Year." That fall, my misty-eyed suburban Washington third grade teacher introduced me to the class as "Katie, our Hungarian refugee." I was mortified.

In sworn testimony behind the closed doors of the Senate Internal Security Subcommittee in May, my father advised against sending any American foreign aid to the newly repressive postrevolt Hungary. "I think you should aid Poland," he told the senators, "because Poland is gray and with aid you can prevent Poland from turning black again. But Hungary is black. As black as it can be." When asked if he planned to stay in the United States, Papa replied: "I hope to become a citizen. My family and I. We are happy in this country." Hungarian agents, according to the AVO files, paid a Senate stenographer $20 for a copy of his secret testimony. The memo notes, "she [the stenographer] is available for future assignments."

THE AP assigned Papa to the State Department (Mama's triumph, as her refusal to return to Vienna forced the AP's hand), and we moved to Washington and settled in the suburbs. My sister and I pitched ourselves headlong into becoming regular American girls. What my limited English vocabulary prevented me from expressing, I tried to convey by smiling constantly. (When, a couple of years later, I asked a friend why she had voted for me—a non–English speaker—for captain of the safety patrol, the first of many offices I sought and won, she answered, "Because of your smile." My winning platform.)

There was nothing about suburban life we didn't love: bowling, roller skating, Mass at Our Lady of Lourdes on East West Highway (though with the priests' sermons laced with bake sale announcements, I soon lost interest; I missed the cold stones and clandestine feeling of our dark church on Csaba Utca). By the 1960s, we felt like all-American girls. Only during summer breaks did I revert to my dreamy ways and bookishness, spending weeks on the living room couch with Henry James, Leo Tolstoy, Sinclair Lewis, and (to please my father) Rudyard Kipling. I read *Crime and Punishment* in one August weekend, barely moving from that couch. But I also made sure I mastered the steps to the Locomotion the summer it was the hot dance. I was avid for it all—and fast!

With a mortgage, a houseful of new furniture bought on the "easy monthly payment plan," a new son, and three enthusiastic female consumers to support, each night Papa jotted down every nickel we spent on milk at lunch, and Cokes at Hot Shoppes on Wisconsin Avenue. Yet, when he returned from a fall trip to New York covering the opening of the United Nations General Assembly, my father presented my sister and me with full fencing regalia. These extravagant items were probably the very last things on our wish list (fancy bikes or a stereo set would have been nearer the top), but he was determined to make fencers out of us, presumably hoping to restore a family tradition, since he had been a fencer himself and a part of the triple gold medal–winning 1936 Hungarian Olympic fencing team, as a juror (and had refused to salute Hitler during the opening ceremony in Berlin). I can still picture my father in our basement recreation room prodding us to advance, "quickly and quietly, like little mice," on each other, thrusting and parrying with deft, light movements we could not imitate. But ordinary American kids didn't fence, and we wanted to be ordinary American kids, not Old World relics.

Our parents seemed far too European for us to want to show them off, except once a year when my father was invited to speak to the Leland Junior High School assembly about the state of the world as seen by the AP's senior diplomatic correspondent. That other world of his was a mystery to me. All I knew of it was that each morning, wearing one of his beautifully tailored dark suits, his silvery hair brushed sleekly back, his pipe already lit, my father got in his car to drive to the place he called "State." He spoke of secretaries of state with a sort of reverence, even John Foster Dulles, who had encouraged, and then turned his back on, the Revolution. A photograph of Dulles at one of his press conferences, with my father bent over his notebook in the front row, inscribed, "To Endre Marton, whose able reporting of the Hungarian freedom revolt provided a solid basis for free world judgments of that important event, Signed, John Foster Dulles," always hung above Papa's desk.

In 1963, my father's fellow diplomatic correspondent, CBS correspondent Marvin Kalb, had just returned from covering Moscow. "Your father played a very special role for the rest of us journalists," Kalb recalled in 2008. "We covered the Cold War. But he had *lived* it. He was an authentic source. He was very generous with his time and became a real mentor to a number of us. I never pressed him about his time in jail. If he was marked by it, he hid it well. For me, he was an elegant, gallant man from whom I could learn. I felt it was a kind of privilege when he came into the CBS booth. The way he looked, the dignity about him—you did not easily approach him. But once you accepted that fact—the natural distance he imposed—he was warm and friendly. He didn't ask too many questions at news conferences. You had the feeling that he had his own sources and didn't need to. He represented a whole era of diplomatic reporting. He was a splendid man."

Another reporter who attributes his choice of a career in journalism partly to my father's coverage of the Hungarian Revolution is Strobe Talbott, now president of the Brookings Institution. In the 1970s, as *Time* magazine's diplomatic correspondent, Talbott was my father's much younger colleague in the State Department. "Andre," as my father was now known, "Endre" being too hard to pronounce, "would slow down as he passed my cubicle on his way out, catch my eye, arch his eyebrow slightly, with a smile playing on his lip. The message was clear, 'How is it going? Anything I can do to help?' wordless, usually, so that I didn't need to do anything more than smile or wink back, or I could say, 'Could you give me a hand with this one?' in which case his answer was always yes. And the hand was expert. I sought him out quite often, usually in person but sometimes on the phone. He was always, *always* available and helpful and deft at not making me feel too much the greenhorn." Strobe, a respected foreign correspondent, *Time* Washington bureau chief, and *Time* columnist until he became U.S. Ambassador at Large in 1993, told me in 1995 that his inspirational moment on the way to a career in journalism was Papa's final telegram from Budapest as the Russians moved in.

None of that interested me in the early 1960s. We were too busy to look back, thrilled by the ordinary rituals of the American middle class—the image of a suburban family.

Chapter 18

"FLOWER"

Mama and Papa in their late seventies.

I HAD ORIGINALLY INTENDED to end this memoir at this point, from which it becomes an ordinary American story. Or so I thought. For in our sprint to embrace our new lives, Juli and I were oblivious to invisible and dangerous currents, which only surfaced late in my research. These only appeared when I obtained the B Dossier on my parents. "B" stands for *Beszervezes,* a word for which there is no precise English translation, as we have no such tradition of "recruiting in" the unwilling for espionage. So this story does not end when we reached America. The B Dossier begins in 1962, five years after we arrived in the Promised Land.

Some people had observed my father's growing reputation and his frequent byline, with unfriendly intentions. In May 1962, the month Jerry Stacy, the cutest boy in Leland Junior High School, informed me that he wanted to "play the field," the Hungarian Foreign Intelligence Section began surveillance of my parents. One of their secret agents, code-named "Virag" ("Flower"), was assigned to befriend my parents, "with a view to recruiting them." Other agents began "outside surveillance" of the Martons.

According to the files, agents, like so many termites, swarmed all over my parents that year. (I am trying to imagine trench-coated agents skulking around peaceful, boring Bethesda, Maryland, without calling attention to themselves. Did they follow my father on his weekly trips to the Safeway supermarket in the Bradley Shopping Center, as well as his ritual stop at Bradley Drugs, and, if I were along, a quick stop at the Freshly Baked Donut Shop, which rewarded my steady patronage with my first-ever summer job, dipping donuts into powdered sugar? I wonder if any agent ever bought a donut from me during the summer of 1963, when I worked there?)

"Flower" was well placed for this assignment. As foreign correspondent of the official Hungarian news service, MTI, he had a press pass to the State Department and routinely stopped by the diplomatic correspondents' room. "Flower" introduced himself to Papa, recently elected president of the State Department Correspondents' Association. They addressed each other in Hungarian. As he was helpful to Marvin Kalb and Strobe Talbott and so many others, my father was equally so to the new colleague from Budapest.

On May 21, 1962, the Hungarian Ministry of the Interior requested the Washington embassy's Intelligence Section to begin "recruiting or at least opening channels of communication with [Marton's] wife, with recruitment in mind." "Flower" was instructed to maintain his relationship with my father, to avoid anything that might arouse suspicion, but to draft a detailed memorandum regarding my parents' "character, their vulnerabilities, their passions, their positive qualities. What is their relationship to each other, as well as toward their children? What is their financial situation? What are their plans, the circumstances of their social lives, and who are their friends? What is Dr. and Mrs. Marton's view of the current situation in Hungary? To what extent have they adapted to life in America? Agents are requested to find out the location of their home, their places of work, and to begin the usual external surveillance. *Which of the two Martons is better suited for recruitment?*" "Flower" was told to collect intelligence and pass it to the half-dozen intelligence agents posing as diplomats at the embassy, who then transmitted it to the home office.

And so, once again, the watchers resumed their work. Did Papa suspect that his Hungarian "colleague," a frequent presence in the State Department, was an agent spying on him, hoping to recruit him? Marvin Kalb believes he must have. "We were always on guard with Soviet Bloc 'reporters.' You just assumed that they had to report to the authorities to keep their jobs. Until persuaded otherwise—that the individual was actually a journalist—I would have been very wary. And of course your father doubly so."

In Washington, where the watchers were themselves watched by Hoover's FBI, my parents were safer than they had ever been in their own country. What they could not have guessed was that agents in both Washington and Budapest were scheming to lure my parents back to Hungary. Reading the hundreds of cables and memos that flew back and forth between the two cities, I am repelled at the sheer vileness of the effort, after all they had already put my parents through. At the height of the Cold War—the year of the Cuban Missile Crisis—the Hungarians initiated this new recruiting effort when we already felt safe in America. What gave them the idea that my parents, whom they could not bend to their cause when they had them in custody, would now, in Washington, relent?

The AVO files make the explanation clear. What "secrets" could my father reveal to "Flower"? Papa and Mama were no more privy to state secrets in Washington than they had been in Budapest. But that was not the point of this enormous effort. The goal was to find something compromising about the target—and then blackmail him or her into service. If you looked long and hard enough, steamed open enough letters, listened to enough phone taps, you could find *something*—on any human soul. Once you found that little something, the machinery clicked into place. The files reveal that the AVO thought they would need only two hours to turn either my mother or father—once they had located that precious *something*. And this was "Flower"'s assignment.

Such utterly wasted human effort. The sheer uselessness of it! The hundreds of man-hours agents in two capitals devoted to assessing the best way to intercept my mother on her daily drive to Robert E. Peary High School in Rockville, Maryland, while others calculated our monthly expenditures to see if money might be the lure. (I recall how hard my mother worked to become the ranking high school French teacher in Montgomery County, Maryland, staying up late most nights, correcting her students' essays on Camus's *L'Etranger* and Saint-Exupéry's *Le Petit Prince,* while her fellow countrymen, who did not even bother to learn English for their new "diplomatic" assignment, worked equally hard at their base task. And this, only six years after a revolution that was fueled by rage against these very people, who knew how loathed they were.)

And all these dark plots were hatched in such an unlikely place. Housed in an elegant Georgian mansion on Fifteenth Street, with its circular driveway and trimmed hedges, from the outside the Hungarian embassy resembled most other medium-size foreign missions in Washington. In fact, this was not a real diplomatic mission, but a nest of die-hard Cold War spies, tasked with preventing détente or any sort of "normalization" from getting off the ground. These "diplomats" lived in a hermetically sealed Socialist subculture in

Washington. They did not mix with Western diplomats or Americans, knowing that if they were tempted, their driver, housekeeper, or even spouse would immediately report that fact to Budapest, and a few days later the suspect diplomat would be recalled, with no prospect of ever leaving Hungary again. They were on the front line of a never-ending struggle with America—although their real enemy was the Hungarian people themselves, whose valiant but unsuccessful Revolution had left them in a state of permanent alienation from their Communist masters.

During this period—primarily from 1962 until 1967—there were hundreds of hours of intelligence chatter, in the most convoluted secret police–style prose, between Washington and Budapest, speculating on which of the two Martons would make a more promising agent. The fact that Mama had begun broadcasting for the Voice of America made her an even more appealing target than she had been as a simple high school French teacher.

"Flower" found an opening in the summer of 1962. Planning a summer vacation in Budapest, he offered to take a gift package to my Aunt Magda. My parents hastily assembled a parcel of cosmetics and used clothes. By August, "Flower" was back in Washington, and on August 10 he filed his report. "Marton called to thank me for delivering the package and said his wife would like to personally thank me [with dinner]. I accepted the invitation, my first opportunity to really talk to Mrs. Marton. The dinner was very pleasant. Two facts emerged from the dinner which I have already noted: 1. The Martons are not yet American citizens, which has caused Mrs. Marton some hardships regarding her teaching job. Marton explained that Senator Jacob Javits wanted to speed up their citizenship papers but the AP vetoed this as an unacceptable 'favor.' I also perceived a deep nostalgia on their part for Hungary. They know they cannot return and they have built a decent life here, but they are still very drawn to the Hungarian lifestyle."

The following month "Flower" added an intriguing nugget: "The Martons are dissatisfied with their financial situation." On October 2,

1962, General Jozsef Kira of the Ministry of the Interior sent a memo to the Washington embassy: "In the Matter of 'Izorche' [my father's code name] and his wife," Kira wrote, "[Marton] was given only one task [by the AVO] and that was to take Mindszenty out of the country with him. The Americans, however, would not agree to this." In a revealing passage, Kira accurately describes Papa as a "patriotic Hungarian who blames us [the Communists] for the fact that he was forced to leave Hungary. Comrade Jambor [my father's AVO case officer] regards Marton as an honest and upright man who does not chase women, who, if ever he should get involved with another woman, and break with his family, would do so only if he fell deeply and romantically in love. . . . His wife is without deep political convictions. She likes an adventurous life, to have fun, drink a little, and has been involved with other men." On the margin next to this, someone scribbled, "This is good—but we need names!"

Near the end of 1962, the Hungarian embassy formulated a plan of action regarding my parents: "Flower" was to "deepen his connection" and exploit my father's "homesickness" for Hungary. The agent should spend more time with the Marton family, get to know them and let Marton know that he could easily get a visa to travel to Hungary. "If [Marton] and his wife should agree to this trip, we will establish contact with them and determine their availability for recruitment. We have asked the other [Socialist] comrades for help in this regard. Signed, Szanto."

A year later, on August 1, 1963, General Kira of the Ministry of the Interior sent the following directive to his Washington agents: "Open Marton's recruitment file." (So far they had only been *talking* about it.) Based on "Flower"'s information, Kira recommended, on February 3, 1964—they moved very slowly!—that in the event of my parents' travel to Hungary, "if their recruitment is unsuccessful, they be taken into custody and interrogated."

However wary Papa was of his "colleague," I think he would have been astonished to learn that his most innocent-seeming conversations with "Flower" were turned into fodder for the AVO. Here is "Flower"'s assessment of my father in a secret cable dated September 12, 1964:

> *Marton has excellent connections at the State Department. He knows everyone and everyone knows him. At a recent reception [Secretary of State Dean] Rusk approached Marton and addressed him in a very intimate tone. . . . Marton can call anyone at the department and his call is immediately returned. My personal opinion of Marton is that he is many-sided and subtle, with quick reflexes. He never lets on what he is really thinking, never gives himself away with the slightest facial expression. . . . As to the prospects for getting higher-quality information from him, I am very doubtful because not only is he very shrewd, he is also extremely careful and seems to know precisely how much he can share. Marton's greatest utility for us would be that through him we can get our own information out to anybody in the State Department, including the secretary of state.*

Throughout 1965, "Flower" and his masters in Washington and in Budapest schemed to get my father to Hungary, the only way they could see to arrange for the two undisturbed hours they said they needed to "persuade" him to come over to their side. Many plans were floated as to what sort of story would bring my father to Hungary.

They had not given up on my mother, either. On March 10, 1965, the AVO intelligence chief in Washington told Budapest, "We have plans to proceed with Mrs. Marton's recruitment this year. . . . But we still have problems finding the right place and time, which requires a minimum of two hours to accomplish. We need still more data on her daily routine, her customary route, does she drive alone or in the company of her husband or anyone else? Does she ever teach in the evening? How far is her house from her school? How frequently and for how long does her husband leave Washington? Her children's plans? Is anyone else staying in their house? We plan on inviting Mrs. Marton to the April 4 [Hungary's Freedom Day] celebration so the comrades can familiarize themselves with her appearance and can engage her in conversation." This memo had a photograph of my mother attached to the original.

There is no record of whether my mother accepted this invitation to the Hungarian embassy, which strongly suggests she did not. But on December 10, 1965, my father walked unannounced into the Hungarian embassy, crossed the elegant marble foyer, and took the elevator to the third floor consular office, where Papa, the former prisoner of the AVO, requested a visa to Hungary. I can only imagine the tremors this unexpected visit shot through the building. What to do? The reason my father gave for his urgent visa request was his wish to accompany President Lyndon Johnson's special envoy, Averell Harriman, on his trip to Budapest as part of a worldwide diplomatic peace effort on Vietnam. Hungarian foreign minister Janos Peter had hinted at opening a separate channel to North Vietnam, which Harriman wanted to explore in Budapest. (The channel proved to be a sham invented by Peter.)

The Hungarian embassy—more practiced at scheming than making decisions—urgently requested advice from Foreign Minister Peter. How should we handle this unexpected event?

As the AP's diplomatic correspondent Papa's request to accompany a high-profile American negotiator made sense. But the risks were also very high—far higher than he realized. When I read the files, my reaction is akin to watching a film that I know will have a happy ending and still gasping in horror when the hero makes a sudden, dangerous move. Don't do it! I want to shout at my father. But in the end, Harriman himself saved the day by calling off his stop in Budapest before excited agents could mobilize for my father's arrival.

And so it continued, the mindless chatter between the two capitals as to which Marton would make a better agent, and how to lure them to a place where it would be safe to try to recruit them.

One day in June 1967, a shy, unobtrusive thirty-three-year-old embassy third secretary named Erno Bernat, a Moscow-trained spy under diplomatic cover, disappeared without warning from the Hungarian embassy. In a scene from a John le Carré thriller, the spy, his wife, three sons, and his mother-in-law all vanished from their modest red-brick Takoma Park, Maryland, home. Bernat, practiced in the art of making people disappear, now performed the same trick for his own family. The FBI or the CIA arranged a safe house and new identities for the whole family. From that moment, the Bernats disappeared without a trace. Bernat's disappearance and apparent defection were, in those Cold War days, a big story for a short time. Then, with no details forthcoming, he dropped from sight, presumably into a witness protection program. I was unable to find him; if he is alive today he would be seventy-nine. What is important is that Bernat was in charge of the effort to recruit my parents. He had also been running agent "Flower." Presumably, Bernat told all he knew to the FBI and the CIA, but I will never have the chance to ask if it was disgust with his wasted life or just the human desire to give his three children a different future that drove him. Whatever his motive, I am grateful to Bernat. His defection blew the cover off the AVO's final attempt to "recruit" my parents. The FBI was now aware of the entire operation.

Six weeks later, Bernat's own chief of mission, a forty-five-year-old career diplomat named Janos Radvanyi, placed an urgent call to Secretary of State Dean Rusk. Radvanyi, the acting ambassador, requested political asylum. He was not part of the embassy's spying operation, but it was a high-level defection, which got far more public attention than Bernat's. Radvanyi never needed a witness protection program; today he is a professor at Mississippi State University. "The whole place was a nest of spies," he told me in the fall of 2008. "I could bear it at the beginning, because I worked as a professional diplomat, and kept out of their way. But then I couldn't stand it anymore. 'Flower,'" he told me, using the agent's real name, "was a very skilled, hardworking agent. He once boasted to me that the AVO rewarded him with a full set of Herend china in recognition for his work. He was that good."

Radvanyi also told me that Rusk had called Papa to ask his advice about granting the Hungarian diplomat asylum. "Presumably your father, who knew me well, approved the idea." Radvanyi, the highest-ranking Soviet Bloc defector during the Cold War, was tried in absentia by a Budapest court and sentenced to death for treason. With the collapse of the Soviet Empire in 1989, his sentence was annulled.

A month after Radvanyi's defection, on July 14, 1967, General Kira of the Ministry of the Interior notified his colleagues in Washington that the Marton case had been "blown" by the two defectors. That same year my sister, Julia, studying in France, planned to visit Hungary, the first member of our family to do so since our departure. Agent "Flower" passed this information along to his masters, but they were no longer interested. The Marton file was officially closed.

Thus ended twenty years of intense surveillance of our family, ten years after our arrival. Our lives—whether we knew it or not—were free at last of strings to the Communist hacks still in power in Budapest.

Chapter 19

TO BUDAPEST
AND BACK

On my first trip back to Hungary since our escape, in the spring of 1979, as an ABC news correspondent, already expecting my daughter, Elizabeth.

I AM BACK IN Budapest for my final research trip. As always, I inhale the familiar smells, which haven't changed: the aroma of coal and oil wafting from the Danube barges, the nutlike smell of the great chestnut trees, and the whiff of coffee that hangs in the air. My relationship to this city is akin to an old and hopeless love; a sense that between Budapest and me there is no future, only past. Old fears are mixed with an inexplicable longing for that brief and interrupted childhood. I have come this time to reconnect with old friends. And to meet "Flower."

As I sit in the gleaming atrium of a French-owned hotel facing the Danube, waiting for "Flower," I have no idea what to expect. He has consented to this meeting, oblivious to its real purpose. I have contacted him because he is a now retired but still very well known journalist who was my father's colleague. I am writing my parents' biography and interested in his memories of them. It is the truth but not the real reason I need to see him. An ambiguous explanation for an ambiguous situation. In fact, I want to see the man who tried to turn my parents into spies while presenting himself as a friend.

A very old man emerges from the revolving door. He is carefully dressed in a faded suit, with wide 1970s style lapels, a handsome silk tie, a shirt collar that is now too big for him. He walks with a shuffle and leans on a burly young man for support. His driver. I cannot see his eyes behind enormous, thick glasses, crafted, I suspect, when he was a larger man. His balding head has scabs from too much sun. My father had a similar skin condition at the end of his life. My father walked with the same shuffle and, until the end, dressed as carefully for special occasions. As I reach for "Flower"'s gnarled, spotted hand, I am fast losing courage. He reminds me too much of my father. I suddenly feel like a predator, stalking too small a prey.

I have brought pictures of my parents, I tell him, as we sit down. From the period you knew them, to refresh your memory. I produce photographs from the 1960s and 1970s of a tanned, youthful, handsome couple and their daughters. I expect him to say, as others have, How handsome your father was! How pretty your mother! What adorable children, you and your sister! (The files reveal that he had been to our house in Bethesda in the 1960s. He had told the AVO that the children's English was good, but their Hungarian even better.) But "Flower" says not a word and barely looks at the photographs.

"Flower"'s coldness hardens me as well. I begin my interview as if it were just another among the thousands I have done in my writing career. When did you first meet them? "Well, of course I knew about them here, in Budapest, in the 1950s," he says. "But we weren't allowed to speak to your parents. They were working for the Americans." Who forbade you from talking to them? I want to ask, but refrain. Many people, Hungarians included, talked to my parents. What kind of an order is that, to prohibit a journalist from speaking to a colleague? I am merely thinking all this. Then "Flower" relates with some pride that the man who made all Hungarians tremble, Matyas Rakosi, once called him and asked him to become editor of a certain newspaper, "Because you are the best," Rakosi told him, and "Flower" accepted the position. Then he tells a joke from those days, a familiar one, about one neighbor telling another, "I have some good news! What is it? Three men in leather coats knocked on my door last night. That's good news? Well, yes. It wasn't me they came for. They only wanted me to show them which was Janos Szabo's apartment." I find this joke a peculiar choice under the circumstances. But "Flower" does not yet know what those circumstances are.

"I really met your father for the first time in Washington, in the State Department," he continues. "I was of course delighted to be the colleague of such a distinguished man. But," "Flower" pauses here, "your father was very careful with me. He really did not want to get too close. For all he knew," he says with an ironic smile, "I might have been a spy!"

I feel a strong urge to blurt out, "But you were!" I resist, barely.

"You know," "Flower" continues, "he was always very helpful to me. Always ready to introduce me to people, to give me background information on stories. He was a good colleague."

Now I see my opening. "Then how could you inform on him?" I ask, my tone apologetic. "I don't want to upset you," I quickly add. But there is not a trace of any emotion on his face. "You see," I forge ahead, "I have read the files. I know that you were reporting on my parents to the AVO."

He removes those gigantic glasses. He has large bluish pockets under his small eyes, which are piercing. "I never informed on them!"

"I am sorry," I begin, and I really am. He is an old man and he reminds me of my father. "Would you like to see these files?" I am rolling the dice here, as I do not have the files with me. I had not expected a flat-out denial. I had expected remorse, an attempt to elicit sympathy, followed by an explanation of how he was forced to perform such base work. "Well, that's just the way things were then," I thought he would say. "I hated having to do it, but had no choice." I did not expect *this*. A denial without a shade of regret. I rise. "I will get them. It will only take a few minutes."

"Yes, yes," "Flower" says, confident and defiant. "Let me see them."

I race to the elevator, sprint to my room, and scoop up the purple file marked "Flower" that is on my bed. I am calculating that even if he wanted to flee, I am faster. File in hand, I hurry back to our table with the Danube view, to find him unsmiling, but utterly calm. I am reminded of a scene in Aleksandr Solzhenitsyn's *The First Circle,* where Stalin, the master butcher, is scornfully ruminating about Tito, a naïve, small-time grocer. I feel like Tito to "Flower"'s Stalin. A man who has not merely *survived* Horthy, Hitler, Eichmann (for "Flower" is Jewish), but Stalin, Rakosi, Kadar, and now the New Hungary, a member of the European Union and NATO. "Flower" has *thrived* under every succeeding regime. This man is not about to cower at the sight of my purple file. Still, he must have assumed he had dodged history's final bullet, and had eased into retirement an eminent and honored figure, a distinguished career as foreign correspondent in half a dozen countries behind him, a son with an important position as a representative of his country.

I show him the documents, none of which reveals his real name, only his code name. He does not bother denying my accusation a second time. "I never put anything in writing," he says. "They wanted me to submit written reports. But I refused. Yes, I would go by the embassy, once a week. Maybe twice. We'd play cards—bridge and canasta—with the fellows. Those guys"—he shakes his bald head—

"they never got out. They knew nothing! They didn't speak English. Imagine: they didn't know the difference between Goldwater and Humphrey! I was their lifeblood," he says with pride. "So they would ask, '——————, what's new?' And I would give them the political gossip that I picked up around town."

"But you wrote this, it says so right here," I reply. "And it says that the meeting was in a safe house. So, not in the embassy."

"You know," he says moving smoothly to his next explanation, "they didn't send correspondents overseas without an agreement from us that we would report to the local embassy. There were twelve of us overseas and we all had to sign a document saying we would cooperate. That the embassy was our real boss."

"What if you didn't sign?" I ask.

"Then I would not have been sent abroad. You know," he interrupts himself, "those sixteen years abroad were my happiest. And four of them were in the U.S. I interviewed Hubert Humphrey, Jack Lemmon—"

I cut short this review of his career. "But they were trying to recruit my parents as agents. And you were helping them! My parents were in danger."

"Not for one minute did it occur to me that I posed a danger to them!" he says with sudden heat. "What did I report that was dangerous for your parents?" This question is irrelevant; "Flower" was well aware the secret police could turn the smallest shard of information into a weapon. Financial worries, too strong an attachment to his wife and children, a delay in their naturalization, my mother's love of an "adventurous" life—all of them "Flower"-relayed nuggets, and he never questioned to what end they were being used. And for what in return? "Flower" was not in a life-or-death situation. Accepting the AVO's conditions for overseas assignment was a good career move. In his mind he was just a small cog in a giant machine. But that machine was the essential engine of the Terror State.

I am emotionally drained from confronting "Flower" with what

I had believed would be shattering news. But I am more shattered than he is. The old man seems energized and eager to battle on. "They never asked my permission to use this information against your parents!" he protests. "I would have alerted your father, had I known there was real danger. They used *me*. They saw an opportunity through me to get close to your father. But I never had any instructions from them." I recall the very precise list of items he was instructed to cover in his meetings with my parents: their financial situation, their relationship to each other and to their children, etc., etc. His protestations of innocence are followed by outrage. "That they could do this to your father! A man who was tortured in his own country!" He shakes his head. He is appalled by *them*. He had nothing to do with *their* work.

The fact that he is so unrepentant makes it easier for me. I had dreaded confronting a more sympathetic man. I would have been pained to disturb the peaceful old age of a more compassionate figure. "I did not *think of myself* as an agent," he says finally, no longer able to deny the obvious fact, but clinging to his own version of it.

I've had enough. I have no interest in exposing him in his own country—full of others who made similar calculations. Blame the system, I was told early on. Not the people it turned into cogs. That would have been my parents' view of "Flower": insignificant. Why bother?

BUT I still have others to see. The next afternoon, I observe an elderly man sitting in the hotel lobby, a stranger, but not quite. He is beautifully dressed in a soft gray flannel suit, blue-checked shirt, red silk tie, a crisp trench coat over his shoulder. His profile has a familiar line. Lajos? I ask. Yes, he smiles and rises to greet me. He is hours early for our appointment. He is still very tall and straight, and I am suddenly overwhelmed by memories of my mother, and this handsome man, and my sister and me, at the lowest point in our lives. He has come from his home in Munich to see me. I have dozens of questions to ask him, but I am too moved to ask anything. Instead, I take his arm. It seems the most natural thing to do, as we walk out into the rainy city where we last saw each other half a century ago. I feel no distance between myself and this man, who by rights should be a stranger to me. What remains of the eager-to-please, mischievous little girl in the American woman seated next to him in the taxi?

A mysterious bond binds us—a sudden proximity to my mother. It seems perfectly natural when he reaches for my hand and I cover his with both mine. Emotional intimacy transferred from one generation to the next. At the comfortably shabby Hungarian restaurant where the menu has not changed since my parents brought me there, the headwaiter recognizes him. "Daughter?" he asks, with a nod toward me. "Sadly, no," Lajos answers. He has no daughters. Married rather late in life, he is the father of a son. "Did you know?" he asks, when we are seated. He does not have to elaborate: about him and my mother. "Well, I guessed," I answer. "Later on, when I was older, I figured it out." Later on, there was no Lajos in our lives, though I knew he, too, had fled Hungary in the Revolution's aftermath. He had vanished completely. From that abrupt break I gathered there had been an intense prior connection. "You were such a good friend to us," I say. "When we had so few good friends."

"Your mother was one of the great loves of my life," he says in a matter-of-fact tone. "She broke my heart." How could my mother break the heart of this handsome, tender, romantic man? "When we met again, after she came out of prison, I remember her exact words. She said that it had been great fun, but just one of those things. You know, from the song." I am struck by the deliberate coldness of this, the hurtfulness, and I am slightly ashamed of my mother. But of course prison had changed her and strengthened the bond between my parents. Maybe the only way my mother could break with Lajos was this seemingly cold way.

"I was picked up by the FBI," he tells me, "when I arrived to

New York. They wanted to know if I had worked for the Hungarian Communist Party. Somehow they knew the AVO had questioned me about your mother. That was on my record. But your mother testified to the FBI about my good character, and they let me go. That was the last time I saw her." Twice Lajos had gotten in trouble because of my mother. And yet he has generous memories of her. From his jacket pocket he produces a photograph of Mama. She is laughing, she looks relaxed, no doubt amused by something she just said. For just a moment she looks like a woman in the company of a handsome man who adores her—not the anxious, terrified wife whose husband has disappeared. "She had a very amusing, original way of looking at things," he says, momentarily lost in a memory. "She told me she was being followed, that she was under constant surveillance. Well, then, I said, they have some interesting material." And so, all these years later, do I. While doing everything possible to help her husband, and simultaneously looking after two distraught children, she had someone who made her happy.

In each other's company Lajos and I both feel my mother's presence. We part as friends, each grateful to have the other back.

MY "BIG SISTER" Cunci, now Dr. Maria Natali, has come from her home in Rome for our meeting. At the Café Central, my pulse quickens, as if in anticipation of seeing an old love. She walks in: slim in a black suit with stylish short blond hair, effortlessly cosmopolitan. I jump up from my booth to hug her. I am taller and larger than the woman in whose soft curves I snuggled as a little girl who missed her mother. I search for a familiar feature in her nicely lined, sunweathered face. The eyes are familiar. "You were my little sister!" she exclaims, surprised as I am by our present incarnations. "And you were my protector," I reply. Our conversation glides right back to those days: the cold, the hunger, the sadness, our mutual need for affection and warmth. "Do you remember I dreamed of having an egg all to myself!" she recalls. We talk of her estrangement from her tyran-nical father, my longing for mine. "But you never complained," she repeats several times. She, like Lajos, escaped during the Revolution. Her family stayed behind and was punished for her "defection." Her younger sister, Andrea, was kept from university and from good jobs because of the black mark of Cunci's escape.

When we finish with our memories we turn to less safe territory. Maria, no longer Cunci now, rants about America, the corrupt empire in its twilight, paralyzed by its salacious destruction of one president (Clinton), followed by another (Bush) who took a wrecking ball to the world. Her anger and my refusal to engage, even though I share some of her views, open a gap between us. "Cunci," I say, wanting to return to that other, safer place. She's back. She smiles. We kiss and promise to meet again.

I FINALLY get permission to visit my parents' prison, the Fo Utca, now a maximum security prison for Hungary's worst criminals. A plaque on the wall of the massive red-brick structure is a reminder of one of the many criminal acts committed inside: "On June 15, 1958, Imre Nagy and his comrades were condemned to death in a secret trial in this building." My mother often said that from her cell she could hear the laughter and cries of children playing. There it was: a playground less than a block away, from where the cries of children not her own might easily have drifted to my mother's cell.

The prison warden, Brigadier General Csaba Boglyasovszky, is waiting for me outside. He is a large man in a black leather coat. Despite his size there is nothing intimidating about him. The warden leads me through the first of six steel doors that click shut behind us. He is friendly and chatty and has done an Internet search on both my parents and me. I am focused on trying to imagine what it was like for my parents: the sound of the steel door dropping like a guillotine, fol-lowed by a series of smaller doors, slamming one after the other, until, with the final door closed, the iron bolt slides into place and you are alone in your cell—utterly helpless. AVO guards with revolvers stuck in their belts and rifles over their shoulders no longer stand at every turn in the labyrinth of those corridors, but the building is as secure and as remorseless as ever.

We climb several flights of brightly lit stairs (I had always imagined prisons to be dark places, but of course the prisoner's every twitch must be seen). We pass hard-looking men, heads shaved, manacled and angry, being led to their cells. "At least these prisoners know what they are here for," the warden comments, in reference to my parents. With his broad frame and long arms, the brigadier general makes a safe space for me. We reach his office, painted a sunny yellow, with soft armchairs and a reproduction of a famous Hungarian nineteenth-century landscape above his desk. Stalin and Dzerzhinsky once glared down from these walls.

"Cappuccino?" the warden asks. He tells me the history of this prison, the scene of so many inglorious chapters in the country's life since 1919. "There are no political prisoners left here," he tells me with quiet pride. "Not since 1989." Sipping my cappuccino, I ask if this might be the room where my father was nearly blinded by the single light shone directly in his face, the interrogation room where Captain Babics shouted obscenities at him and where another agent warned my mother not to behave like a whore on the street? Very likely, it was this room, or another like it, just differently decorated, the brigadier general tells me. The interrogators liked their rooms comfortable.

Cappuccino consumed, we climb the stairs to another floor, the one where my father spent eighteen months. A guard unlocks a cell with a small, high window covered by bars and a grille on the back wall. A Dolce & Gabbana cologne ad of a well-tanned man in tight underwear is taped inside the steel door. I ask to be left in the cell. At first the guard shakes his head. It is illegal to lock up the innocent in today's Hungary! The warden repeats the request, this time as an order, which the guard follows. "Bye, bye!" the warden says with a bright smile as they withdraw. Of course there is no comparison between my parents' incarceration and my short, voluntary stay. Still, it is a terrifying sound: a bolt you have no control over, sliding into place—and then, no contact with anyone else.

For a split second I feel the rising temperature of an old fear. I am absolutely without resources or protection in this sealed vault. It is a terrible feeling. What if the warden was only pretending to be friendly? What if "Flower"—whom I have just unmasked—still has some power? Still, I know I am imagining things. I will be free in a few minutes, while for my parents there was no knowing how long they would stay.

The gentle warden returns in ten minutes. "Had enough?" he asks with a smile. I nod. I extend my hand. "Thank you," I say, and start for the door. The warden laughs. "You think it's that easy to leave here?" he asks. "I have to take you out." And so we pass through the steel doors, one after the other, this large, friendly man signaling the guards to release bolts and latches and raise the final barrier to the courtyard.

Outside, I breathe deeply the familiar, damp air of the Danube. I extend a hand to the warden. He holds mine for a beat. "Do you ever get over such a thing?" he asks. "You," he repeats. I am moved that a man who presides over hundreds of hardened criminals is concerned about me. Standing in the shadow of this place, he sees through the polished American to the child whose parents were once inmates of his prison. "I don't know," I answer.

WITH MY daughter, Elizabeth, in tow, we head off for my old neighborhood, Csaba Utca. En route, we stop off at the Varosmajor Catholic Church, at the foot of the steep hill. A wedding is underway, so we stand in the back, next to the elaborately carved wooden confessional. Here, nothing has changed. The same wooden apostles flank the altar before which I knelt on so many Sundays. Suddenly, the chilly nave is bathed in the sound of Handel's "Hallelujah Chorus." I turn away so my daughter does not see my tears.

Across the street from the church, in front of the new John Bull Pub, we pass a girl with dreadlocks in camouflage pants who would look at home in Williamsburg, Brooklyn. But as we climb the steep hill toward my old house, we pass men with gnarled hands who lean hard on canes, and short, stout women, who are not part of the New Hungary. We stand for a while at the intersection of Csaba Utca and Roskovics Utca, where I learned to ride a bicycle and from where my parents were snatched by the secret police. There are no children on bikes, nor in the garden where our noisy gang played ipiapacs, the Hungarian version of hide and seek.

Our old house is freshly painted in bright yellow but has a somnolent feel. It is no longer a place where children call out to each other from one apartment to the next. Lizzie and I peer into our old apartment. It is dark, partly shuttered by what looks like the same wooden venetian blinds that Madame once raised with maximum clatter over my head. An old lady in a housecoat, holding a mop, steps out on the balcony where I used to sit on my grandfather's knee and practice our first English words. Attycake, pattycake, baker's man.

"Now I know why lilac is your favorite flower," Lizzie comments, spotting the lilac bush that still grows outside our nursery window. But the fence between this house and the one next door (still an American diplomatic residence) is a flimsy thing, no more barbed wire at the top. The hole we squeezed through the night my parents were going to be arrested is long gone.

Our final glimpses of Hungary come on the way to the airport. Our taxi passes a long motorcycle gang. They are wearing black leather and Wehrmacht-style helmets. The cyclist at the front of the long line brandishes a huge banner, a version of the old Arrow Cross tricolor. Though modified in the details, the flag's message is clear. We are used to seeing long lines of bikers stream through our vacation town of Telluride, Colorado, middle-aged men and their biker "girls" reliving their Jerry Garcia fantasies. But this gang is not out for a good time. Their faces grim, their heads under the helmets shaved, these are sullen, angry people, carrying the debris of Hungary's worst moments, when the Arrow Cross teamed up with Adolf Eichmann to hunt down Jews. Passersby avert their eyes, pretend they don't notice the long black line snaking through the city. Again, I feel a twinge from history. What if they had no police escort? What if they drew up next to our taxi, asked to see our papers? How long would I remain this cool and composed? But we are at the airport. Heading home to America.

Chapter 20

ANOTHER SURPRISE

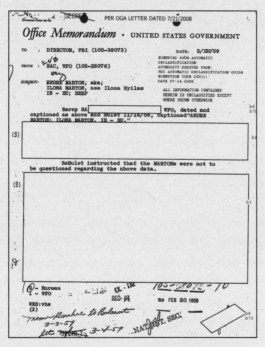

Still redacted page from the FBI file on my parents, which
I obtained through the Freedom of Information Act.

I AM BACK IN New York after my final research trip to Budapest.
A package is waiting for me on the front hall table. The return address
snaps me out of jet lag: Federal Bureau of Investigation, Department
of Justice, Washington, D.C. Specialists had informed me that it might

take many years to get the documents I requested under the Freedom of Information Act. But here they are: the Marton File, 215 pages of heavily redacted material, sixty-five pages still withheld for reasons of national security. Before I even unpack my Budapest suitcase, I dive into the file.

The first document, an internal FBI memorandum, is dated May 10, 1955, and shows that Cold War paranoia ran as deep in Washington as in Budapest. Papa's arrest is noted, but is followed by this astonishingly stupid statement: "Marton's coverage of [the show trials of Laszlo Rajk and Cardinal Mindszenty] would indicate that Marton was in the good graces of the Hungarian government at the time of the trials [as] coverage of these trials by representatives of the Western press was extremely limited." At this point, my father had been an inmate of the Fo Utca prison for three months and my mother was spending her last month of freedom looking for a place for her children. For the FBI that seems beside the point. Papa was a suspicious figure. How else to explain his coverage of the show trials? He was in the Communists' "good graces."

The next document in the file is dated May 27, 1957, two years later. J. Edgar Hoover requests information from the State Department's Office of Security regarding the alleged leak in the Budapest legation, as reported by Papa to security people at the American embassy in Vienna. Hoover notes that the intelligence breach had been reported to the Army's Intelligence Division (the sole allusion in the file to U.S. Army Chief Warrant Officer Richard J. Glaspell's role) but wants more information himself.

The files reveal something more dramatic. From 1957 until 1959, my parents were, in the FBI's jargon, "of investigative interest as foreign nationals who may have cooperated with the Hungarian Communist Government and furnished information to that government." Apparently, several people (whose names have been redacted) alerted the FBI to the possibility that Mama and Papa were AVO agents, "based on the fact that the Martons were allowed to live well in Hun-

gary despite their affiliations and western orientation." Also suspicious
was "the Martons' release from a lengthy jail sentence, and their ability
to leave the country without objection from the Hungarian officials."

So the same qualities that had aroused the AVO, "their affiliations
and western orientation," while living in a Communist state, now
made my parents untrustworthy in J. Edgar Hoover's Washington. As
I had already guessed, neither the AVO nor the FBI trusted them. In
the era of Kim Philby and James Jesus Angleton—the first a notorious British double agent for the Soviets, the second the crazed, paranoid chief of CIA counterintelligence—my parents fit the category
of people who would have made valuable assets for either camp. So
while I thought my parents were welcomed as Cold War heroes, and
they were by many, in Washington they were shadowed by the FBI.
Once again, their freedom was conditional.

On December 11, 1958, FBI agents interviewed Papa, "under secure conditions," and found him "completely cooperative and agreed
to notify the Washington Field Office if contacted in the future by
representatives of the Hungarian Government." So my parents were
cleared in the first round. But they were not quite free, not in the
world of J. Edgar Hoover.

Four years later, on May 1, 1962, an FBI internal memo "disclosed
no participation in subversive activities [by the Martons]. Since their
arrival in this country, the Martons have cooperated with numerous
United States Government agencies in furnishing information con-
cerning conditions and individuals in communist Hungary."

Even though the FBI had cleared Papa of suspicion of being a
Communist agent himself, he was obviously under pressure to give
the FBI information on his activities and contacts. Between 1958
and 1962, Papa was, according to the FBI file, "in periodic contact
with the Washington Field Office." This relationship with the FBI is a
surprise to me. Of course these contacts, unlike the forced meetings
with the AVO officer at the Café New York in Budapest, were based
on Papa's belief that he was supporting *his* side in the Cold War. But

even in Washington, my parents were not quite like everybody else. And again, all of this was going on right under my nose.

In 1962, around the time the AVO reopened my parents' file for recruitment purposes, the FBI also showed renewed interest in the Martons. This is surely not coincidental, since "Flower" was being closely watched by the FBI and they must have observed his interaction with Papa. Agents shadowed this "journalist," whom they describe as having no "diplomatic status, but for all practical purposes operates out of the Hungarian Legation in Washington, D.C., and the Hungarian UN Mission in New York."

On May 23, 1962, an FBI agent named Folet interviewed Papa "under secure conditions at which time he advised that he sees ["Flower"] daily in the Press section of the State Department where both have space. The contacts are of a very casual nature and he has no other association. ["Flower"] stopped by Marton's house one Sunday afternoon with his family and hinted at possible additional get-together which Marton ignored. ["Flower"] is leaving his car at Marton's residence while absent in Hungary on vacation." I have no memory of a strange car in our driveway during that summer. But I marvel at how my seemingly mild Papa kept agents of two hostile powers at bay.

When, in the summer of 1967, Erno Bernat, "Flower"'s control officer, defected, he was, of course, taken into FBI custody. Bernat exposed the Hungarian legation's spying operation, including the attempt to recruit my parents. Now again the FBI came looking for my parents. "Interviews of Martons are now our most logical next step," an agent (whose name has been redacted) wrote to FBI senior official William C. Sullivan on May 7, 1968. That interview, he said, would "determine whether Martons represent any security risk and whether they have any potential for exploitation by the Bureau."

Like the AVO, the FBI also preferred interviewing targets—even married couples—one at a time. Thus a "discreet background investigation" of Mama was authorized on August 8, 1967. "Subject [Papa] would then be interviewed as shortly thereafter as possible," an internal memo dated April 23, 1968, explains, "and their stories will be compared."

My parents made a good impression on their interrogators. "Ilona and Endre Marton," wrote the interviewing agent on July 30, 1968, to Director Hoover, "were very friendly, evidenced no nervousness or apprehension, and appeared to be truthful in their statements. Both individuals are extremely well educated, occupy positions requiring considerable intellectual ability, and it appears inconceivable that they could have been approached for recruitment [by the AVO] without being aware of same. Marton stated that during the time he has been in the U.S. . . . he has been alert to the possibility that someone from Hungary would attempt to persuade him to do something for his native land. He has kept this in the back of his mind during all his contacts with people from Hungary as well as other Eastern European countries. He stated that he considers himself a reasonably intelligent man and to the best of his knowledge no one has ever made any attempt to obtain information or utilize him for any foreign country. He stated that he . . . would report immediately if any approach were made to him to solicit information or recruit him to work for any foreign Government.

"In view of information set out herein," the July 30, 1968, secret internal memorandum to J. Edgar Hoover concludes, "it does not appear that Mr. and Mrs. Marton represent a threat to security at this time. The informant potential of Mrs. Marton appears to be negative and Mr. Marton's potential appears to be related to that of a source of information. He will continue to be contacted in this regard as the occasion warrants."

It is the final document in my parents' FBI file. From that time on, my parents lived the lives of an ordinary suburban couple. Mama and Papa had survived the Cold War. They were finally home, in America.

EPILOGUE

My favorite picture of my father—taken at the State Department, where he was a diplomatic correspondent. Reporter's pad in his lap, he awaits Secretary of State Henry Kissinger.

I WOULD NOT HAVE written this book if my parents were still alive. They loved history, but not their own. Barely looking back, they plunged into America. Not for them the émigré world of nostalgic gatherings around steaming pots of chicken paprika and old memories. Whatever anger or resentment they felt while living in one of Europe's murderous regions during the blood-soaked twentieth century they channeled into building new lives in America. If they looked back, it was to a long-vanished and semifanciful culture of refinement, tolerance, and worldliness that had only existed briefly in their gleaming city on the Danube. They were unhappy at my discovery of our Jewish roots. They withheld from us many extraordinary facts about their lives, even though we would have craved such information, and would have only admired Mama and Papa more if we had known. But I see that my parents earned the right to forget. Yet discovering what they lived through in such detail makes their ultimate triumph that much sweeter, my understanding and admiration of them so much greater. How many men and women spent their days setting traps for them—and yet failed.

Their reluctance to talk about the past used to frustrate me when I was avid for our history. Our roots in America were shallow. I needed stories about my grandparents and great-grandparents. Every child does. "Do I look like my grandmother?" I would ask my mother. The tears that would fill her eyes were her reply. So many other questions went unanswered. "I left my emotions at the barrier," my father used to say of our crossing the Austro-Hungarian border, so many years ago. Marton, "Flower" reported, "never lets on what he is really thinking, never gives himself away with the slightest facial expression." All those sublimated feelings made it hard for an emotionally needy child to get close to a parent, and to the past. But they enabled my parents to survive. No doubt I, too, would be different had my parents nursed wounds and regrets throughout their lives. During their lifetimes, and especially after my book on Raoul Wallenberg, I had tensions with my parents over their withholding of information from us. But now that so much more of their story has come my way, thanks to the AVO, shaded in ambiguity, rarely black and white, I wish I could tell them that I understand their choice.

They signed on with the Americans not only out of conviction. They also wanted to enjoy life after the war. As a result, they unintentionally endangered their children's lives as well as their own.

After he was released from prison, my father met with a secret police agent at the Café New York, and then sought his help in obtaining our passports. My mother had to meet with an AVO officer at a safe house above a movie theater. They invited "Flower" to our home in Washington, to thank him for delivering a package to Aunt Magda. These were the small fees they paid for the infinitely larger prize of freedom. I wonder now how I would have survived under a system based on degrading people. What accommodations would I have been willing to make?

They loved America with all the passion of the dispossessed. The banal rituals of suburban life were precious to my mother and father: the weekly shopping trips to the cornucopia of the world's largest and coldest supermarkets, their Saturday tennis games, and the hours spent raking the leaves of our suburban front yard supplanted memories of afternoons loitering at the cafés along the Andrassy Boulevard. My mother became a world-class cook and my father gave up trying to teach his children to fence, focusing instead on making skiers out of his four grandchildren, a task in which he succeeded. In these rituals, they found their joy.

I used to wonder how they could stand a suburban life of metronomic predictability. I see now that boredom and predictability were rare jewels for people for whom the twentieth century lacked both. "Once before," my father wrote to Major Arpad Kretschmer, from the depths of the Fo Utca in 1955, "ten years ago, we lost pretty much everything we owned and I have absolutely no hope that in my lifetime I can start to rebuild again." In America, they recovered from the two great twentieth-century experiments on humans, and built new lives.

No one played a bigger role in my life than my father, who was so sparing with praise. I think I even chose my life partners with him in mind. In 1977, when I was hired as an ABC News foreign correspondent, Papa told me to observe and learn from Peter Jennings. "Now there is a man who has all the important qualities: intelligence, a sense of the world, great good looks—a man, Kati, who has it all."

So, I recall thinking at the time, that is the sort of man he would like as his son-in-law. Until the end of his life, though we had divorced, he considered Peter, the father of his grandchildren, as a son-in-law. And vice versa. After I married Richard Holbrooke, then an assistant secretary of state, Richard and Papa would sit for hours reminiscing about ambassadors and deputy secretaries and undersecretaries who had served with distinction, and about the most revered figures in my father's pantheon: the secretaries of state whom he had covered and admired, John Foster Dulles, Dean Rusk, and Henry Kissinger. Had he been more fortunate in time and place of birth, my father would have made an excellent diplomat.

Most deaths bring both grief and relief. With my parents' deaths the taboo on the past was lifted. As I mentioned earlier, Papa never opened that first AVO file. It sat untouched on his desk in its plain manila cover with the AVO Archives stamp on it. After he died, I opened it. I began reading the file early one evening and did not stop until early morning. I wept, for I had not known the depth of their humiliation. I had always thought of prison as a relatively brief incarceration in my parents' lives (just under two years in my father's case, under a year in my mother's). Now I know they were their country's prisoners until we reached America, and even, a bit, afterward. They were watched, stalked, and treated as Enemies of the People by both Fascists and Communists—and not fully trusted by the Americans.

At times during my research I felt as if I had joined the army of watchers. But my motives were different from the AVO's. And though I wrote for my own reasons, and for my children, this is not my story. A large segment of humanity lived, at a certain time, in a certain place, this way. It is important that we know this, before we move on, before it is forgotten.

I began the bureaucratic process of retrieving the rest of their files, never imagining there would be so much. As papers began to arrive, I realized the risk I had taken. What if the files revealed some terrible deceit? The loss would have been mine. In the end, the opposite was the case. Reading and rereading these pages has made me feel closer to both my parents.

I wrote at the beginning of this journey that children never really know their parents. Both parties conspire to make that so. Now, in large measure thanks to the AVO, I feel as if I do know them. My parents are no longer the demigods of my youth. They are vastly more interesting, shrewder, and more complicated than I ever realized. And much more *human*. At Lake Balaton, my father drinks beer and shares intimacies with a woman not my mother. He falls romantically in love with a cool English beauty. My mother finds solace in the admiration of a much younger man. Prison brings them very low—to the brink of suicide in my father's case—but it brings them back together.

Of course they would have found this book too intimate. They would not have liked to be laid this bare. To write, as the great Turkish writer Orhan Pamuk has said, is to make someone angry. It is a risky business. At the end, my father would have said, "Well, it's your book. You're the author." He almost never intruded in my life, which is why I so valued his opinions. He was a devoted father, but he was not easy to please. Thanks to the files, I know that his children were my father's greatest weakness, the only soft spot agents on two continents could identify. "I am certain," reported his cell mate/informer Dr. Leo Benko, "that if his wife and, even more, his children, were placed in harm's way, there is not a secret he would not disclose to save them." AVO Colonel Arpad Jambor reached the same conclusion. "Flower" in Washington confirmed it. For this knowledge I am grateful to them all.

Could any child ask for a greater proof of love than this: "Yesterday," my father wrote to Major Kretschmer on September 2, 1955, "was the first day of September, and fortunately I was not interrogated, because all I could think about was that it was the first day of school and I don't know a thing about [my children]."

During his final year, after my mother's death, Papa lived with us. Each time I returned from Budapest, he would ask, "What's new in Pest?", his cloudy old man's eyes briefly alert. It wasn't the people and certainly not the politics he was interested in, but *his* Budapest. Tell me, he would ask, what's happened to the Gresham Palace? A Four Seasons Hotel! My God, he would shake his head, no doubt recalling when he and my mother had found shelter from rampaging Arrow Cross vigilantes in 1944 in what is now one of Europe's grandest hotels. And the Café New York? An Italian chain owns it now! And the Opera? Are there voices as sublime as Mihaly Szekely's bass-baritone? And then, we would rewind the film, to those long-ago days when the great opera star (no one sang *Don Giovanni*'s Leporello like Szekely! he would say) visited my sister and me, the year we had no parents. A wonderful man, we would agree, for the umpteenth time. My parents never dwelt on those friends who failed to visit.

"No city," he would assert, after each such conversation, "is as blessed by geography—not even Paris. The way the river cuts right through its heart."

He had little joy in life without my mother. I knew he was just not interested in living anymore when he stopped lighting up his pipe. We used to watch old movies together in the evening. A week or so before he passed away, we watched *Cyrano de Bergerac,* the old black-and-white classic, with José Ferrer as the gallant wit with the long nose. When the hero ends his weekly report of court doings to his beloved Roxanne, my father recited the familiar lines from memory, "And on Saturday, the twenty-sixth, an hour after sundown, Monsieur de Bergerac died of murder done upon him . . ." Then my father smiled and said, "You know, those lines are really more beautiful in Hungarian."

He passed away at home the day after his ninety-fifth birthday. Among the last things he said to me was, "Your mother was a very good partner."

JET LAG woke me early on this spring morning. A familiar New York City siren wails in the distance. After my final glimpse of Budapest, the long black line of the motorcycle gang brandishing that banner of

EPILOGUE

exclusion, that siren sounds benign—almost reassuring. As I write this,
I look up at my favorite photograph of my father, in its silver frame
in our living room overlooking Central Park. He is sitting on a couch
outside the secretary of state's office, his reporter's pad is on his lap, he
is looking away from the photographer's intrusive lens. Wearing his
armor of dignity, my father is a somewhat detached figure, composed
and alert. I wish he could hear me say, Thank you.

ACKNOWLEDGMENTS

THIS IS A book of memory, based on my own recollection of events, some of them historic, most of them personal. Memory is of course imperfect. Many of my earliest recollections, going back more than fifty years, were, however, kept vivid by my parents' and sister's retelling of them over the years. In writing *Enemies of the People*, I have also drawn on my parents' own memoirs, my father's prison memoir, *The Forbidden Sky*, published by Little, Brown, in 1971, and my mother's unpublished and untitled journal, which she entrusted to my keeping a few years before her death in 2004. Under the laws of post-Communist Hungary, I am entitled to my family's files, kept by the AVO—the dreaded Hungarian secret police—in its Budapest archives (the so-called Allambiztonsagi Szolgalatok Torteneti Leveltara). I thank Dr. Katalin Kutrucz, the head of those archives, for helping me navigate through them, one of the thicker files in their collection. Those files, key parts of which I read and translated from the Hungarian, were my primary source for the precise details of the Terror State's twenty years of near total surveillance of our family and my parents' prison torment. Throughout the narrative, I indicate where I am drawing on the AVO files.

Since our family's narrative is also part of the much larger Cold War chess game, I needed Washington's diplomatic records as well. To trace the role played by the State Department under Secretary of State John Foster Dulles in my parents' arrest and trial, I drew on diplomatic files from 1948 to 1957, stored in the National Archives, in College Park, Maryland. Sam Sherraden of the New America Foundation helped me search those files and discovered a trove of materials. At the State Department, Ambassador John Negroponte and Margaret Grafeld were helpful in locating still other classified department files on my parents' case. In searching for the classified documents regarding my parents' case, I was fortunate to have the counsel of Tom Blanton, head of the National Security Archives at George Washington University. Valerie Komor guided me with expert hands through the Associated Press Archives, which also revealed their secrets.

To round out my own memories of those years, I also relied on surviving actors in and experts on the Cold War, both Hungarians and Americans. They provided invaluable human witness to this memoir and I am grateful to them all, but perhaps to none more than J. Thomas Rogers, the Foreign Service officer who was my parents' closest friend in Budapest, who drove us across the Austro-Hungarian frontier to freedom and who filled in details my memory could not.

Others without whom I could not have written this work are:

Tamas Lorinczy
Laszlo Jakab Orsos
Laszlo and Judit Rajk
Arabella Meadows Rogers
Donald Downs
Geza Katona
Istvan Deak
Attilla Szakolczai
Ferenc Partos
Ernest Nagy

Helen Nagy

Marika Hallosy

Magda Pless

Lajos Csery

Janos Radvanyi

Simon Bourgin

Maryanne Szegedy Maszak

Richard O'Regan

Ronald Farquhar

Peter Kokas

Balint Kokas

Békes Csaba

Sandor Liptay-Wagner

Dr. Maria Hellei Natali

Andrea Hellei

Conchita Glaspell

Elizabeth Jennings

Christopher Jennings

Andrew Marton

Julia Marton Lefèvre

Nicolas Marton Lefèvre

Mathieu Marton Lefèvre

Brigadier General Csaba Boglyasovszky

Katalin Bogyai

Christopher Hill

Strobe Talbott

Walter Isaacson

My friends the writers Steve Coll and Larissa MacFarquhar, were among my first readers, and gave generously of their time and made valuable suggestions for improving the manuscript. I am indebted to them both for their gift of friendship and moral support throughout the project. My book has benefited from Eliza Griswold's close reading and her natural gift for language. Daniel Mendelsohn, Frank Rich, Dexter Filkins, Richard Bernstein, Ben Skinner, and George Packer also played their invaluable part with suggestions for making the book better. My son, Christopher Jennings, helped groom the manuscript in its final stages. My assistant, Loryn Hatch, was resourceful and un-flappable throughout this project. Roger Labrie and Gypsy da Silva at Simon & Schuster once again worked their magic. I thank them all.

This book would not have been written without the early sup-port and sustained cheerleading of my brilliant editor and devoted friend, Alice Mayhew. Alice and Amanda Urban, my agent for six of my seven books, are the essential pillars of my writing life. Alice and Binky are also the most stalwart friends anyone could ever wish for.

Richard Holbrooke lived this book—the most painful and per-sonal I have written—and shared my every wrenching discovery along the way. I cannot ever fully thank him for the role he plays as my interlocutor, my spur, my primary source of courage and confi-dence. It is impossible for me to thank Richard or my children, Eliza-beth Jennings and Christopher Jennings, enough for their love, their boundless enthusiasm, and their patience during this project and in all else. Elizabeth accompanied me to Budapest on my final research trip and shared the final, dramatic discoveries with me. I only regret that their grandparents, the twin heroes of this tale, did not live to see its publication. As forward-looking as they were, I think Mama and Papa would have approved of this glance back into the twentieth century's heart of darkness.

INDEX

Page numbers in italics refer to pictures.

Abbott, George M., 38, 40, 46–47, 157
Ady Cinema (Budapest), 179, 180
African Americans, 48
Ajtonyi, Attila ("Andrassi"), 47–48, 65, 69, 70, 115, 116, 123, 130
Allied Control Commission, 17
American Broadcasting Company (ABC), 231, 253
American legation (Budapest), 15, 38, 40, 46–48, 51, 51–58, 116, 131, 154
  accusations against Martons of spying for, 68–72, 117–18, 128–30, 139
  arrests of employees of, 122–23, 181
  AVO surveillance of, 54–55, 96
  Fourth of July celebrations of, 67, 76
  leaks in, 70–72, 82, 158, 211–12
  and Martons' arrests, 91, 108–9, 111–13, 121–22
  Martons' departure from Hungary arranged by, 204–207
  and Martons' release from prison, 175, 178, 185
  Mindszenty sheltered at, 195–96, 204
  during 1956 revolution, 194–96, 198, 202
  official accusations against, 26–27
  reports to AVO on, 156–58, 179
  travel restrictions on, 55, 168
  weekly press conferences of, 46–47, 61, 126
  see also names of specific diplomats

"Andrassi," see Ajtonyi, Attila
Angleton, James Jesus, 247
Anschluss, 11
Anti-Semitism, 10, 15, 16, 34
Army, U.S., 70, 97, 212
  Intelligence Division, 246
Arrow Cross, 14, 15, 37, 90, 105, 138, 191, 242, 256
  anti-Communism of, 26–27
  Jews rounded up by, 11, 243
Associated Press (AP), 25, 57, 95, 100, 107, 142, 154, 156, 169, 181, 193, 194, 210–11, 225, 228
  American legation and, 163
  Christmas greetings from General Manager of, 72
  De Luce as Budapest correspondent for, 21–22, 24
  Endre becomes accredited correspondent for, 22
  and Endre's conviction and sentence, 167–68
  Endre's release covered by, 182, 183
  financial support from, 175
  Ilona and, after Endre's arrest, 107–11
  inquiries to Hungarian Foreign Ministry by, 112, 113
  Martons' arrest reported by, 122–23
  and Martons' escape plans, 66
  phoning in stories to, 32, 43
  show trials coverage for, 22–23

Associated Press (AP) (*cont.*)
　　State Department coverage for, *209,*
　　　216, 217
　　Vienna bureau of, 63, 178, 202, 204,
　　　210
　　World Peace Council coverage for, 27
Astaire, Fred, 11
Auschwitz concentration camp, 13, 21, 104,
　　162
Australia, 32, 33, 75, 77, 120, 185
Austria, 138, 197, 206
　　Hitler's takeover of, 11
Austro-Hungarian Empire, 8
Avner, Gershon, 157
AVO, *see* Hungarian Secret Police

Babics, Captain Zoltan, 82–83, 92–96, 98,
　　101, 135–40, 155, 240
Bacsi, Andras, 149
Balazsi, Captain Bela, 93–95, 139
Balogh, Mihaly ("Ferenc Krassoi"), 97–98
Bambi (movie), 56
Barna, Mrs., 147–48
Barnes, Spencer, 91, 131, 167
Beale, William, 211
Beloyannis Factory (Budapest), 199
Benko, Leo, 133–34, 139, 141, 255
Berlin Olympics (1936), 217
Bernat, Erno, 228–29, 248
Better Homes and Gardens, 214
Bika Hotel (Debrecen), 80
Boglyasovszky, General Csaba, 239–41
Bosnia, 8
Bourgin, Simon, 18, 175–76, 197
Boy Scouts, 18
Britain, 15, 18, 21, 32
　　Soviet double agent in, 247
　　in Suez War, 192
British legation (Budapest), 15, 33, 38, 47,
　　56, 74, 113–14
　　see also names of specific diplomats
Brody, Sandor, 104
Brookings Institution, 218
Brown, Keirn, 211, 212
Brundage, Avery, 113
Budai, Andras, 26
Budapest Opera, 150–51, 256
Budapest Police Department, 106

Budapest University, 112
Buddenbrooks (Mann), 9
Bulletin of Atomic Scientists, 166
Bush, George W., 239

Café Central (Budapest), 238
Café Gerbaud (Budapest), 40–41, 62, 105,
　　130–31
Café New York (Budapest), 16, 180, 183,
　　202, 247, 253, 256
Calvinist University (Debrecen), 104
Camus, Albert, 224
Catholics, 33–34
Central Intelligence Agency (CIA), 3, 19,
　　21, 53, 57, 91, 122, 157, 229, 247
Churchill, Winston, 37
Clinton, Bill, 239
Cloister and the Hearth, The (Reade), 152
Cold War, 2, 4, 14, 26, 52, 72, 112, 138, 156,
　　210, 215, 223, 224, 249
　　claustrophobic atmosphere of Budapest
　　　during, 55
　　Communist prisons during, 127
　　FBI paranoia during, 246, 247
　　journalists covering, 218
　　Soviet Bloc defectors during, 229, 230
　　training of diplomatic personnel
　　　during, 71
Columbia Broadcasting System (CBS),
　　218
Communists, 2, 3, 10, 12, 15, 58, 126, 127,
　　142, 160, 171, 211, 213, 230, 254
　　control of news by, 138, 198
　　FBI paranoia about, 206, 246, 247
　　"important," 36
　　jargon of, 26
　　moderate, 67
　　newspapers banned by, 25
　　policy toward foreign reporters of, 169
　　prisons of, 135
　　propaganda of, 27, 66, 82
　　religious orders disbanded by, 34
　　secret police of, *see* Hungarian Secret
　　　Police
　　trial procedures of, 162
　　see also Hungarian Communist Party;
　　　Soviet Union, Communist Party of
Cooper, Gary, 11

Crime and Punishment (Dostoyevsky), 217
Crosse, Mathew, 99
Csery, Lajos, 76–77, 110–11, 115, 164, 236–39
Cuban Missile Crisis, 223
Cyrano de Bergerac (movie), 256
Czechoslovakia, 63

Daily Telegraph (newspaper), 20
Darkness at Noon (Koestler), 22–23
Davis Cup soccer matches, 110
De Luce, Daniel, 21–22, 24
Dickens, Charles, 36, 152
Disney, Walt, 56
Donaldson, Allyn C., 171
Don Giovanni (Mozart), 256
Downs, Don, 38, 53–54, 90–91, 100, 119–21, 177, 200
Dowson, Ernest, 75
Dulles, John Foster, 46, 48, 108–9, 168, 170, 175, 192, 197, 217–18, 254
Duna Hotel (Budapest), 42, 194, 199
Dzerzhinsky, Felix, 92, 240

Ecuador, 186
Education, Hungarian Ministry of, 20
Eichmann, Adolf, 10, 12, 13, 16, 18, 104, 138, 234, 243
Eisenhower, Dwight D., 39, 129, 192, 197, 215–16
Elizabeth I, Queen of England, 56, 113
Engels, Friedrich, 37
Erasmus, Desiderius, 152
Etranger, L' (Camus), 224
European Union, 2, 234

Farquhar, Ronald, 190, 198–201
Fascists, 2, 10, 11, 206, 254
    anti-Communists denounced as, 20
Faust (Gounod), 151
Federal Bureau of Investigation (FBI), 206, 223, 229, 237–38, 245–49
Feher, Captain Zsigmond, 105–6
Ferrer, José, 256
Fields, Harry C., 71, 87
Fields, Louise, 87
Finger, Max, 57, 157
First Circle, The (Solzhenitsyn), 234

"Flower" (AVO agent), 222–27, 229, 230, 232–36, 241, 248, 252, 253, 255
Folet (FBI agent), 248
Foreign Intelligence Section, Hungarian, 222
Foreign Ministry, Hungarian, 28, 40, 47, 108, 167, 202
    Associated Press inquiries to, 112, 113
    during Revolution, 187, 188, 190, 192, 193, 197, 199, 202–4
    State Department censure of, 169, 170
Foreign Service, U.S., 52, 71–72, 177
Four Seasons Hotel (Budapest), 138
Fo Utca prison (Budapest), 89–102, 163, 174, 182, 192, 239–41
    incarceration and interrogations of Martons in, 92–102, 125–30, 132–36, 143, 246, 253
France, 44, 192
Franz Joseph, Emperor, 8
Freedom Fighters, *187,* 189–90, 195, 197, 216
Freedom of Information Act, 46, 245, 246
Freidin, Seymour, 167
Fulop, Sandor, 93

"Gaspar" (informer), *see* Guillemet, Gabrielle
Gellert Hotel (Budapest), 111, 194
Geneva summit (1954), 128, 129, 167
George Polk Memorial Award, 210, 213
German-Hungarian Friendship Treaty, 29
Germany, 10–17, 19, 20, 29, 137, 171
Gero, Erno, 114, 176, 181
Gero, Major Tamas, 117–18, 125–28, 139, 149, 159–60, 162, 174, 177–78, 183
Gestapo, 2, 14
Glaspell, Claudia, 70, 186
Glaspell, Conchita, 70–71
Glaspell, Gregory, 70, 186
Glaspell, Mimi, 70, 158, 186
Glaspell, Richard J., 70–72, 82, 97, 158, 186, 211–12, 246
Goldwater, Barry, 235
Grass, Günter, 2
Greater Budapest Workers' Council, 199–200

Gresham Palace (Budapest), 138, 256
Guillemet, Gabrielle (Madame), 44–45, 48,
      64, 73, 116, 176, 242
   reports to AVO by, 5, 45, 70, 74, 81–82,
      110, 114, 115
   and Ilona's arrest, 120
   during search of Martons' apartment,
      86, 88
Gulag, 12, 127
Gundel's restaurant (Budapest), 16, 37

Habsburgs, 79, 209
Hallosy, Bela, 14, 25–26, 115, 137, 148
Hallosy, Melinda (Marika), 24–26, 114
Handel, George Frideric, 242
Hankey, Lady, 52
Hankey, Lord Robin, 157
Harriman, Averell, 228
Hellei family, 145, 146–49, 166, 173–74,
      239
Heller, Ilonka, 105, 120–21, 131, 142
Heller, Laszlo, 121, 131, 142
Helsinki Olympics (1952), 30
Henry Hudson Hotel (New York), 213
Hiroshima, atomic bombing of, 165
Hitler, Adolf, 10, 11, 13, 18, 27, 29, 217, 234
Holbrooke, Richard, 254
Holocaust, 14
Hoover, J. Edgar, 206, 223, 246, 247, 249
Horthy, Admiral Nicholas, 9, 11, 26, 82, 190,
      234
Hotel Atlanta (Vienna), 210
Hotel Bristol (Budapest), 54
Hotel Roosevelt (New York), 213
Humphrey, Hubert, 235
Hungarian Communist Party, 26, 18, 20, 22,
      29, 38, 65, 67, 181, 183, 238
Hungarian legation (Washington, D.C.),
      168, 222, 224, 226–28, 248
Hungarian Revolution (1956), 2, 12, 36,
      162n, 187, 187–207, 210, 213–15,
      217–18, 225
   aftermath of, 198–207, 237, 239
   crushed by Soviet troops, 192–98, 219
   outbreak of, 185
Hungarian Secret Police (AVO), 10, 21, 28,
      32, 39, 77, 120, 141, 149, 150, 155,
      180, 214, 240, 252

American legation and, 52, 57, 63, 82, 83
archives of, 1–8, 12, 14–15, 254–55
arrests of Martons by, 7, 87–92, 105–9,
      111, 116–23, 125, 131, 132, 139, 141,
      151, 159, 176
attempted recruitment of Martons in
      America by, 6, 224, 226–29, 232–33,
      235
bank accounts frozen by, 142
blackmail attempts of, 71
CIA and, 19–20
code names used by, 5, 33, 45, 166
conditions for Martons' release by,
      178–79, 185, 253
"confession" extracted by, 136–40
Csery questioned by, 238
evidence obtained by, 70–72, 133
headquarters of, 37
incarceration and interrogations of
      Martons by, 7, 89, 92–102, 125–30,
      132–36, 133, 143
informants of, 5, 23–25, 30, 44–45,
      65, 74, 81–82, 93, 96–98, 110–11,
      114–16, 130, 133–34, 140, 216
internment camp run by, 58
language of records of, 131–32
letters to, 154–57
and Martons' FBI file, 246–49
officer of, as Martons' neighbor, 36, 177
photographs kept by, 1, 12, 26
possessions seized, 12, 142
during Revolution, 187
searches of Martons' apartment by, 76,
      86, 88, 120
Sovietization and, 17–18
surveillance by, 7, 17, 41–42, 54, 61,
      78–79, 86–87, 114, 133, 158
translations of newspaper stories and
      reports for, 23, 141
trials by, 161–64
wiretaps by, 68

Interior Ministry, Hungarian, 90, 94, 129,
      167, 181, 189, 230
   Counterintelligence Section, 91
   Ilona's attempts to obtain information
      on Endre from, 107, 108, 114
   Washington embassy and, 222, 226, 230

International News Service, 61
International Olympic Committee, 113
Israel, 192
Italy, 138
Ivancov, Colonel, 96

Jambor, Colonel Arpad, 185, 202–4, 255
James, Henry, 217
Janissaries, 142
Javits, Jacob, 225
Jazz, 54
Jennings, Elizabeth, 180, 231, 241–42
Jennings, Peter, 253–54
Jews, 9, 16, 20, 28, 158, 171, 234, 252
    American, 157
    assimilated, 9
    during World War II, 10–15, 21, 138,
      243
    see also Anti-Semitism
Jonas, Bela, 161, 162
Johnson, Lyndon, 228
Jones, Russell, 197–99
Judenkommando, 104
Justice Ministry, Hungarian, 174

Kabos, Endre, 78n
Kabos, Mrs. Endre, 78
Kadar, Janos, 198, 234
Kalb, Marvin, 218, 222, 223
Kalmar, Zsuzsi, 36, 39, 118–19, 177
Kalmar family, 36, 193, 196
Kapotsy, Bela, 83
Kasischke, Richard, 202
Katona, Geza, 53, 57, 91, 157
Kefauver, Estes, 167
Kelly, Grace, 88
Kennedy, John F., 214
KGB, 2, 17, 92, 147
Khrushchev, Nikita, 130, 174, 176
Kipling, Rudyard, 36, 152, 217
Kira, General Jozsef, 226, 230
Kis Ujsag (newspaper), 20
Kissinger, Henry, 251, 254
Koestler, Arthur, 22–23
Kokas, Balint and Peter, 35, 130
Korry, Edward, 28
Kossuth, Louis, 79
Kovacs, Major Rezso, 180

Kretschmer, Major Arpad, 131, 140, 142–43,
    153, 164, 181–82, 192, 253, 255
Kundera, Milan, 2
Kutrucz, Katalin, 1–3, 5–6, 185–86

Labouchère, George, 113
Lafoon, Sidney, 31, 58–59, 96, 100
Langreuter, Miss, 137
Leland Junior High School (Bethesda,
    Maryland), 217, 222
Lemmon, Jack, 235
Lenin, V. I., 37, 92, 162
Lewis, Sinclair, 36, 217
Life magazine, 88
Lloyd, Rupert, 48
Luce, Clare Boothe, 53

MacCormac, John, 167, 178, 181, 183, 190,
    197
Magic Flute, The (Mozart), 151
Makarenko, Anton, 147
Mandl, Maurice, 215
Mann, Thomas, 9, 36
Marines, U.S., 69, 212
Marton, Andrew Thomas (brother), 12, 215
Marton, Endre (father)
    and American legation, 43–44, 46–49,
      52, 56–59, 61, 68–72
    as AP Budapest correspondent, 21–25,
      28–30, 32, 43, 72, 122, 175, 191,
      198–200
    arrest of, 3, 7, 26, 32, 71, 73, 87–92,
      103, 105–12, 114, 122–23, 132
    arrival in America of, 211–15
    in automobile accident, 64–65
    attempted recruitment as Communist
      agent of, 6, 26, 221–30, 232–33, 235
    AVO files on, 3–8, 32, 45, 66, 77, 82,
      185–86, 189
    awards given to, 2, 3, 213, 214
    birth of, 8
    birth of son of, 215
    British and American journalists and,
      18–19, 24, 28
    CIA and, 20
    confession of, 98, 100, 116, 138–40
    Csaba Utca apartment of, 35, 36, 74,
      176

Marton, Endre (father) (*cont.*)
  death of, 4, 254, 256
  defiance of Communists by, 3–5,
    15–18, 40
  departure from Hungary of, 200–207
  early life of, 8–11
  emigration of parents of, 33, 74
  escape plans of, 62–66
  evidence against, 118, 23
  false accusations against, 61–62
  family life of, 31–33
  FBI file on, 245–49
  incarceration of, 92–93, 95–99, 127,
    130, 133–36 140–42, 151–61,
    165–66, 177–78, 255
  interrogations of, 7, 82–83, 92–97, 131,
    135–38, 140
  Jewish origins of, 8–10, 12–13, 21, 252
  jobs lost by, 14, 20
  letters written in prison by, 98–101,
    133–35
  during liberalization period, 67–68
  literary heroes of, 11
  marriage of, 10, 14–15
  during 1956 Revolution, 187–92
  old age of, *221,* 255–56
  personal history hidden by, 2, 12, 13,
    21, 251–52
  personality of, 9–10, 41
  physical appearance of, 9, 33, 40, 182–84
  press coverage of case of, *117,* 122–23,
    166–70, 182, 183
  release from prison of, *173,* 180–86
  romance of Peggy Simpson and, 74–77,
    104, 164, 255
  during Russian invasion, 192–99, 219
  search of apartment of, 85–86, 88
  Senate testimony of, 216
  sentencing of, 3, 162–64
  social life of, 25, 40–41
  sons-in-law and, 253–54
  at State Department, *209,* 216–19, 223,
    233, *251*
  suburban American life of, 217, 253
  surveillance of, 6, 7, 17, 41–42, 44–46,
    61, 72, 78–79, 106
  travels of, 7, 16, 18, 20
  trial of, 143, 154, 157, 159, 161–62

  in Vienna, *209,* 209–10
  during World War II, 10–12, 14–15, 21,
    137–38
Marton, Mr. and Mrs. Erno (grandparents),
    31, 32, 36, 47, 58, 62, 146, 242
  emigration to Australia of, 32–33,
    74–75, 80–81, 120, 185
Marton, Feri (uncle), 32, 185
Marton, Ilona (mother)
  and American legation, 43–44, 46–49,
    51, 52, 56–59
  arrest of, 3, 7, 32, 73, *103,* 114–16,
    118–23, 125–27, 131, 134
  arrival in America of, 211–15
  at celebration of anniversary of "Lib-
    eration" by Red Army, 79–80
  at diplomatic reception, *51*
  attempted recruitment as Communist
    agent of, 6, 26, 221–30, 232–33, 235
  in automobile accident, 64–65
  AVO files on, 5–8, 32, 45, 66, 77,
    178–79, 185–86
  birth of son of, 215
  British and American journalists and,
    18–19, 24, 28
  confession of, 128
  Csaba Utca apartment of, 35, 36, 74,
    175
  death of, 4, 254, 255
  defiance of Communists by, 3–5,
    15–16, 18, 40
  departure from Hungary of, 200–207
  early life of, 8, 104
  and Endre's arrest, 87–88, *103,* 103–16
  Endre's letter from prison to, 99–101,
    133–35
  and Endre's release from prison,
    182–85
  and Endre's romance with Peggy Simp-
    son, 74–77
  escape plans of, 62–66
  evidence against, 118, 123
  false accusations against, 61–62
  family life of, 31–33
  FBI file on, 245–49
  incarceration of, 127–30, 132, 140–41,
    151–52, 159–61, 165, 166
  interrogation of, 7, 117–18

Jewish origins of, 10, 13, 21, 252
jobs lost by, 14, 20
during liberalization period, 67–68
marriage of, 10, 14–15, 104
during 1956 revolution, 187–91
in old age, *221*
personal history hidden by, 2, 12, 13,
    21, 104–5, 251–52
physical appearance of, 33, 49, 113
press coverage of case of, *117,* 122–23,
    166–70
release from prison of, *173,* 174–79
during Russian invasion, 192–991
search of apartment of, 85–86, 88
sentencing of, 3, 162–64
social life of, 25, 40–41
suburban American life of, 217, 253
surveillance of, 6, 7, 17, *61,* 44–46,
    106–7, 116
travels, *7,* 16, 18
trial of, 143, 161–62
unpublished memoir of, 21–22, 62, 101
as UP correspondent, 22–24, 30, 32,
    43, 122, 175, 198–200
in Vienna, 209, 210
during World War II, 10–12, 14–15,
    104–5, 138
Marton, Julia (sister), 1, 3, 4, 94
adoption offers for, 170–72, 202
arrival in America of, 211–15
childhood photographs of, 12, *85*
departure from Hungary of, 200–207
and escape plans, 62–64
family history kept from, 2
after father's arrest, *103,* 103–5, 110,
    113–15
French governess of, 44–45, 48, 81
happy years of childhood of, 25, 31–41,
    56–57, 62, 80–81
and mother's arrest, 119–23
during 1956 Revolution, 187–90
during parents' incarceration, 128–30,
    133, 141–42, 145–52, 160–61, 163,
    165, 166
and parents' release from prison, *173,*
    174–77, 182, 183
during Russian invasion, 192–97
during search of apartment of, 85–86

secret police file mentions of, 5, 41–42
suburban American life of, 12, 216–17,
    221
during summer of father's romance,
    76–77, 79
in Vienna, 209–10
Marton, Kati
as ABC news correspondent, *231*
adoption offers for, 170–72, 202
arrival in America of, 211–15
award presented by Hungarian govern-
    ment to, 5
childhood photographs of, *1, 6,* 12, 26,
    31, 85
departure from Hungary of, 200–207
and escape plans, 62–64
family history kept from, 2, 12–13
after father's arrest, *103,* 103–5, 110,
    113–15
FBI file on parents obtained by, 245–46
French governess of, 44–45, 48, 81
happy years of childhood of, 25, 31–41,
    56–57, 62, 80–81
Jewish roots discovered by, 12–14,
    252
Lafoon and, 58, 59
marriages of, 253–54
and mother's arrest, 119–23
during 1956 Revolution, 187–91
during parents' incarceration, 123–25,
    128–30, 133, 141–42, 145–52,
    160–61, 163, 165, 166
and parents' release from prison, *173,*
    173–78, 182–84
on research trips to Budapest, 1–6,
    179–80, 185–86, 231–43, 245,
    255–56
during Russian invasion, 192–98
school experiences in Hungary of,
    37–39, 79
during search of apartment of, 85–86
secret police file mentions of, 5, 6,
    41–42
suburban American life of, 12, 216–17,
    221, 222
during summer of father's romance,
    76–77, 79
in Vienna, 209–10

Marx, Karl, 37
Maugham, Somerset, 156
McCargar, James, 19–20
McCargar, Monique, 20
McCarthy, Joseph, 58, 206
McKisson, R. M., 171
McLean, Robert, 210–11
Meadows-Rogers, Arabella, 150, 177, 201
Mindszenty, Jozsef Cardinal, 24, 38, 112,
    167, 195–96, 204, 226, 246
Mississippi State University, 229
Moulin Rouge nightclub (Budapest), 54
MTI (Hungarian state news service), 122,
    222
Murphy, Robert, 195
Mussolini, Benito, 29

Nadasdy, Ann, 177
Nagasaki, atomic bombing of, 165
Nagy, Ernest, 48–49, 52, 54, 57, 58, 71–72,
    179
Nagy, Helen Stephens, 49, 54
Nagy, Imre, 67, 68, 79, 80, 188–89, 192–93,
    239
Natali, Maria ("Cunci"), 146, 147, 149,
    173–74, 238–39
National Geographic, 88
National Police, Hungarian, 106–7
Nazis, 6, 15, 25, 29, 90, 138, 171, 185
    Hungarian resistance to, 14, 21, 137
    internment camps of, 58
    Jews murdered by, 13–14, 104–5
Neumann, Anna and Adolf, 12–13, 21,
    104–5, 162
New York Post, The, 167
New York Times, The, 3, 122, 167–70, 178,
    181, 183, 190, 197, 213
New Zealand, 21
NKVD, 17, 92
North Atlantic Treaty Organization
    (NATO), 234
Nuclear weapons, 165–66

Olympic Games, 30, 78n, 113, 217
O'Regan, Richard, 27–28, 63, 65–66, 107,
    109, 142
O'Sheel, Patrick, 98
Ottoman Empire, 8, 142n

Our Lady of Lourdes Church (Bethesda,
    Maryland), 216
Overseas Press Club President's Award,
    214

Pamuk, Orhan, 255
Parliament, Hungarian, 79–80, 110, 123
"People's Teachers," 37
Peter, Janos, 228
Peterson, Oscar, 54
Petit Prince, Le (Saint-Exupéry), 224
Petrovics, Lieutenant Gyula, 120
Philby, Kim, 247
Piros, Laszlo, 107
Pista, Pesti, 41
Plenk, Henry R., 170–72
Pless, Laszlo ("Laci"), 40, 131, 151
Pless, Magda, 40, 120–21, 130, 131, 145,
    149, 174, 225, 253
Poland, 216
Politburo, Hungarian, 54
Porgy and Bess (Gershwin), 168
Pravda, 126
Priegle, Mrs., 73, 74, 82, 86, 175, 177, 183
Pulitzer Prize, 21

Rachmaninoff, Sergei, 97
Racz, Sandor, 199
Radio Budapest, 197
Radio Free Europe, 122, 175–76
Radvanyi, Janos, 229–30
Rajk, Laszlo, 23, 38, 246
Rajk, Laszlo, Jr., 23n
Rakosi, Matyas, 39, 45, 51, 55, 65, 79, 92,
    114, 162, 167, 175
    American reporter threatened by, 22
    AVO controlled by, 129
    Berlin visit of, 29
    fall and resurgence of, 54, 67–68, 72,
        77, 80–81, 130
    final removal from power of, 176, 183
    "Flower" and, 233, 234
    and Helsinki Olympics, 30
    personality cult of, 37, 38
    purges carried out by, 163
    rise to power of, 20
    during Soviet occupation of Hungary,
        17

treasonable offenses under, 161
Ravndal, Christian, 38, 49, 51–52, 57, 90,
    96, 109, 118, 163, 186
   AVO surveillance of Endre with, 69
   background of, 52
   celebrations hosted by, 67, 81
   climate of trust created by, 71–72
   Endre's profile for AVO of, 158
   first interview of Rogers with, 52–53
   Lafoon and, 58
   and Martons' incarceration, 98,
     100–101, 112–14, 163, 168–69, 175,
     182
   and posting of African-American dip-
     lomat to Hungary, 48
   visits Juli and Kati at Hellei home,
     149–50
Raymond, Jack, 167
Red Army, 16, 17, 19, 79
Reuters news service, 23, 122, 190, 198,
   299
Riese, Angela, 210
Robert E. Peary High School (Rockville,
   Maryland), 224
Rogers, Arabella, see Meadows-Rogers,
   Arabella
Rogers, Elinor, 150
Rogers, Jordan Thomas ("Tom"), 38, 52, 77,
   96, 150, 175–77, 179, 200–201
   arrival in Hungary of, 53
   during Hungarian Revolution, 190,
     198
   first interview with Ravndal of, 52–53
   Hungarian budget provided by Endre
     to, 69–71, 100
   Lafoon and, 58
   and Marton family's departure from
     Hungary, 201–203, 206–7
Rogers, Louisa, 177
Rogers, Sarah, 53, 150, 177, 190, 201–3,
   208
Rosenberg, Julius and Ethel, 130
Rusk, Dean, 229–30, 254

Saint-Exupéry, Antoine de, 224
St. Mark's Hospital (Salt Lake City), 170
Salvatore, Josephine, 54–55
Senate, U.S., 206

Internal Security Subcommittee, 211,
   216
Shakespeare, William, 9
Sherer, Albert ("Bud"), 62, 63
Sherer, Carroll, 62–63
Show trials, 22–24, 246
Sik, Endre, 109, 114
Sima, Andras ("Bandi"), 189
Simpson, Gerald, 38, 74, 76, 157
Simpson, Peggy, 38, 74–77, 104, 111, 164
Simpson, Toni, 74
Snow White (movie), 56
Social Democrats, 29, 61
Socialism
   diplomatic subculture of, in Washing-
     ton, 224–26
   indoctrination of children in values of,
     37, 147
   With a Human Face, 68
Solzhenitsyn, Aleksandr, 234
Soviet Union, 15–16, 22, 57, 112, 126, 139,
   155, 214, 247
   Austria and, 210
   collapse of, 230
   Communist Party of, 38, 130, 174,
     205
   de-Stalinization in, 130, 174–76
   Gulag of, 12, 127
   and Hungarian Revolution, 186, 188,
     190–201, 206, 219
   indoctrination of children by, 37
   postwar occupation of Hungary by,
     16–18, 20, 32, 134
   reporters in Washington from, 223
   in World War II, 16, 23, 79
Sport Hotel (Tihany), 75, 78
Stacy, Jerry, 222
Stalin, Joseph, 23n, 69, 72, 77, 130, 234
   death of, 65–67, 73, 97
   displays of portraits and photographs of,
     36, 37, 92, 162, 240
   Khrushchev's speech on crimes of, 174,
     176
   secret services of, 17
   siege mentality of, 91
Stalinism, 38, 52, 57, 80, 130, 163, 189
Starzel, Frank J., 63–66, 72, 109–10, 142,
   168, 210–11

State Department, U.S., 54, 59, 122, 170, 227
    Endre as foreign correspondent at, 209, 216–19, 223, 233, *251*
    and Martons' arrests, 109, 112–13, 168–69
    and Marton family's departure from Hungary, 204–6, 211
    during McCarthy era, 58
    and 1956 revolution, 194
    Office of Security of, 246
    Ravndal at, 52, 53
    report on Hungarian budget to, 69, 71
State Department Correspondents Association, 222
Stevenson, Adlai, 192
Suez Canal War, 192
Sullivan, William C., 248
Sviridov, General Vladimir, 16–17
Szabo, Janos, 233
Szall, Jozsef, 141
Szarka (Foreign Ministry officer), 203
Szatmary, Jeno, 61–62, 65, 68, 107
Szekely, Mihaly, 150–51, 174, 256
Szekely, Piroska, 150–51
Szilard, Leo, 166

Talbott, Strobe, 218–19, 222
TASS, 155
Teleki, Count Pal, 11
Thompson, Llewellyn ("Tommy"), 211
"Tibor" (informer), 158–61
Time magazine, 18, 175, 216, 218, 219
Tito, Josip Broz, 23*n,* 38, 137, 234
Tolstoy, Leo, 217
Tryon, Ruth, 39
Turchanyi, Monsignor Egon, 196
Turcsan, Jozsef, 107

United Nations, 122, 128
    General Assembly, 217
    Hungarian Mission to, 248
    Security Council, 192
United Press (UP), 3, 25, 57, 104, 108, 111, 116, 122, 167–70, 194, 204, 213
    Endre's release announced to, 182
    Ilona hired by, 22
    Ilona rehired after release from prison by, 175, 178
    phoning in of stories to, 32, *43*
    after Soviet invasion, 197–99
    Vienna correspondent of, 28
United States Information Service, 27
Uruguay, 52

Varosmajor Catholic Church (Budapest), 34, 241–42
Vienna International School, 210
Vietnam War, 228
"Virag" (AVO agent), *see* "Flower"
Voice of America, 27, 161, 225

Wailes, Cornelia, 202
Wailes, Edward T., 192, 194–95, 202, 204–6
Waldorf-Astoria Hotel (New York), 214
Wallenberg, Raoul, 12, 252
Wehrmacht, 16
World Peace Council, 27, 28, 66
World War I, 9
World War II, 10–16, 29, 74, 180, 191, 212
    bombing of Budapest during, 16, 19, 37–38, 194
    Glaspell's service in, 70
    Hungarian Jews in, 10–14
    resistance movement in, 14, 21, 137

Yeats, W. B., 107
Yugoslavia, 11, 23*n,* 127, 137

Zold, Ferenc, 9

ABOUT THE AUTHOR

Kati Marton is the author of six books, including the *New York Times* bestseller *Hidden Power: Presidential Marriages That Shaped Our History* and *The Great Escape: Nine Jews Who Fled Hitler and Changed the World* as well as *Wallenberg, The Polk Conspiracy,* and *A Death in Jerusalem.* An award-winning former NPR and ABC News correspondent and the mother of a son and daughter, Marton lives in New York with her husband, Richard Holbrooke.